Unclaimed, But Loud:

The Memoir of a Shy and Retiring Boy Who Was Neither

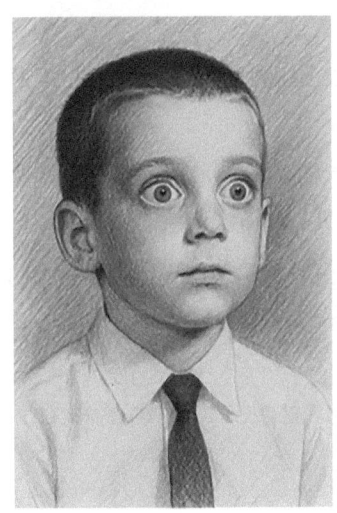

By

Keith Howard

KDP ISBN: 979-8-9988718-0-1

Cover design by D R Coté

Interior design by D R Coté

Printed in the United States of America

Some names and identifying details have been changed to protect the privacy of individuals.
This is a work of memory, not investigative journalism. Emotional truth takes precedence.

Follow the author at: https://keithhoward610044.substack.com

LITTLE
FANNY
PRESS

Dedication

In 1959, more than 450,000 kids lived in foster care or orphanages. The average kid was in those places for two to five years.

I got plucked from foster care in 1959. A good family. A warm bed. Food. Clothes. Love.

All luck. Nothing I did but be born white and healthy.

And slightly cuter than average.

This book is dedicated to the kids of 1959 and today--the kids who drifted into the system and got grabbed by a rip tide that wouldn't let them leave.

You *deserve what luck/chance/randomness gave me.*

When we meet, let me at least buy you the biggest piece of pie in the joint.

Epigraphs

I don't know which way; the ball just bounces
I don't know, maybe the cards just fall
Or maybe there's some ancient chain of causes and effects
Got one man walking proud while another man falls.

   --Tonio K

We are here and it is now. Further than that, all human knowledge
is moonshine.

   --H.L. Mencken

Darling, it's a hard life if you're lucky.
Ah, but it's a short life if you're not.

   --Tonio K

We are all just artists of the past,
layering fragments into something we can live with.

   --Ancient Wisdom I Just Made Up

Prologue

Schrödinger's Cowboy Hat

Contents

Volume I

Baby Boy Newell and How He Grew (1958–1976)

Part I: How I Became Keith Howard

Volume III

Keith Howard and How He Grew Up (2007–Present)

Author's Note

This is a true story--except for the parts that aren't. I wasn't keeping notes. I didn't know I'd be writing a memoir--I was just trying to survive the plot.

I've done my best to piece it together with care. But memory isn't a filing cabinet. It's a collage inside a fire-damaged haunted house. Some rooms are locked. Some have mirrors that lie. And some I only dared reenter when I finally worked up the nerve to jiggle the doorknob.

The people in this book are real. So are the ghosts. I changed a few names, blurred a few faces, and sanded down some sharp corners--mostly out of kindness. Occasionally for legal reasons. And once or twice just so I could stand to look myself in the mirror.

You're holding a bargain: a three-volume memoir in one volume. A clearance sale on bad decisions. A full box set of regrets and redemption, bundled for your convenience.

Volume I is about what a perfectly normal childhood can do to an adopted kid who was weird right from the womb. That's me. No sweeping life lessons. No tidy revelations. Just a boy in a time and a place, doing his best to stay upright.

Also, it's very funny. In places. When it's not tragic.

Volume II was the easiest to write. And the hardest to live through a second time.

Volume III is about how--thanks to a bunch of people in a bunch of church basements--I turned that Volume II into a cautionary tale instead of a suicide note. It takes the scenic route. I always do.

I wrote this for the kids who didn't fit. The loud ones. The too-quiet ones. The ones who were smarter than their decisions. The ones who saw it coming and still ran straight into the fire.

If you're reading this, thank you. That already means more than I expected. And more than I ever thought I deserved.

--Keith

NB:

Who can believe in coincidence? And who can live without such faith.

Unclaimed, But Loud's three parts happen to divide so Volume I covers my initial 18 years, Part II the next 30 years, and Volume III the past 18 years. If you add them together, you get 66--my current age.

It wasn't on purpose. But it feels like it means something. Sort of like life.

PART I

Baby Boy Newell and How He Grew

Prologue

Schrödinger's Cowboy Hat

If memory is a diary, mine was doodled in the margins by a sentimental dadaist with a flair for chaos. It rearranges events, erases others altogether, and spotlights moments I barely noticed the first time. Trusting memory is like asking a toddler to guard your wallet: endearing, but rarely wise.

And yet, we trust it anyway. We hang its imperfect collages on the walls of our minds and call them truth. Worse, we argue over them, as if debating which of us has the coolest imaginary friend. Spoiler alert: they're both made up.

Take my childhood cowboy hat. My mother loved to recount how, at age five, I refused to take it off for Christmas dinner. She'd paint the scene in vivid detail: me, all swagger, tipping the brim to shovel in mashed potatoes while my grandmother pleaded for grace. I carried that memory with pride, imagining myself a pint-sized *Gunsmoke* star.

Then one day, flipping through an old photo album, I

waited for the proof--the picture of me in my cowboy glory. But there was nothing. Not at dinner, not under the tree, not even in the house. The hat had vanished, as if memory itself had conjured it from nothing.

And yet, I still remember it. That hat--one I never actually wore--feels like part of me. Memory, I've come to realize, isn't about accuracy. It's about meaning.

A mosaic is deliberate--carefully arranged tiles forming a single image, a story the artist intends. A collage is chaos: smudged edges, torn pieces, scattered meaning. It lets the viewer decide what to see.

Some memories are neat little tiles: birthdays, school photos, newspaper clippings. Others are just rips and scraps--no source, no context, but somehow they stick. Memory is a collage, not a mosaic. It grabs at scattered moments, smudges the edges, and layers them haphazardly. It does not provide clarity, but rather a sense of something--a mood, a truth, a version of the past we accept, even if the pieces don't quite fit. If memory can conjure a cowboy hat, what else does it revise? What do we erase or embellish to make sense of the past?

The summer I turned thirteen, I began building my Personal Statement to the World--on posterboard, with glue sticks and scissors. My bedroom wall featured an oversized posterboard collage, a chaotic mix of football players, Bob Dylan's halo of curls, my own school pictures, and magazine cutouts. It was nearly perfect--except for one glaring white space at the top.

That void nagged at me until I found it.

That cowboy hat, real or not, was how I imagined myself at five: bold, a little defiant, a miniature outlaw tipping his brim to no one. Now 13, another image--a magazine clipping of George McGovern--took its place, pinned at the top of my bedroom collage. McGovern looked wise, kind, and determined: the kind of man who'd return library books on time.

In my mind, he was the opposite of Nixon, the anti-scoundrel. If a cowboy hat had once made me feel like a hero, McGovern's portrait made me feel like I was part of something bigger, something good. And if I could just arrange the world the right way--like the images on my wall--it would all make sense. That fall, I went door-to-door campaigning for him, certain my efforts would tip the scales. McGovern was too *good* to lose.

Nixon won in a historic landslide, of course, but on my wall, McGovern triumphed. In my memory, he's become a patron saint of lost causes, a steady presence watching over me with quiet dignity as I pursued my own.

I sometimes wonder what became of that McGovern clipping--if it was lost when my wall was dismantled, or if, for a while, it lingered in a forgotten drawer, a relic of my thirteen-year-old certainty that the world could be rearranged if you just picked the right pieces.

For years, my memories of my maternal grandfather formed a portrait I never questioned: six feet of silence, a stern gaze, the smell of pipe tobacco and autumn leaves. He taught at the university, had a building named after him, hunted in fall, fished in summer, and tolerated small talk the way a trout tolerates bait--warily, if at all. When I was four, he took me on the first and only fishing trip we'd ever share.

I remember asking him a stream of questions--about the fish, the worms, the lake. He answered with monosyllables at first, then silence. I filled the quiet with chatter until he turned to me, eyes unreadable, then looked away.

When we got home, he said to my mother, "He's not cut out to be a fisherman." Then he drove away.

That moment has stayed with me, vivid and unchanging, as proof of my inadequacy. I carried it like a diagnosis.

But recently, I've begun to wonder: was his silence disapproval, or was it simply his way? Did he mean those words as an indictment, or as a simple truth? And if it was the latter, why have I carried them like a wound all these years?

As a child, I knew only one interpretation. As an adult, I wonder if I've been holding onto the wrong one.

A mosaic would provide a clear image, a single truth. A collage, however, is full of gaps, contradictions, and reassembled scraps of time. The collage isn't the man. It's just my attempt to make sense of him--and, by extension, myself.

So here we are, you and I, about to embark on a journey through these collages of mine. I can't promise you accuracy; memory's job isn't to record but to reinterpret. What I can promise is honesty--as far as I remember it.

This is a story of searching: for identity in the face of adoption, for certainty in the blur of childhood, for belonging in places I never quite fit. It is about what we choose to carry, what we leave behind, and how memory rearranges it all over time.

These stories are as real as the cowboy hat I never wore--and as true as the lies that keep us warm. In the end, we are all just artists of the past, layering fragments into something we can live with. Something warm enough to carry forward.

Something to keep the cold at bay.

Chapter One

Not Peanut Butter

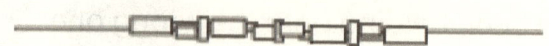

Families are weird. Mine was cosmic-level weird: casseroles, fate, and adoption--not necessarily in that order. Becoming Keith Howard wasn't mainly about getting a name. It's about being claimed. It's about belonging--or at least trying to--and how sometimes, the best parents are the ones who weren't obligated to be.

I was born Baby Boy Newell. That's what it says on my original birth certificate, stamped and filed like a lost baggage claim. It wasn't a name--it was a placeholder. A human draft copy. A grocery store label that basically said, "**not peanut butter.**"

At the time, my biological mother, Sally Piper, was drifting through a life full of bad choices, bad men, and unresolved ambition. She had at least four pregnancies, three of which resulted in lost children--either to adoption or stillbirth. I was one of them.

But unlike my older half-brother, Richard, who stayed behind, I got out.

That was my great stroke of luck. The coin flip that saved my life.

But the thing about fate is, no one tells you who's flipping the coin, what kind of coin it is, or whether it even has two sides.

Sally was born in 1932, the daughter of a corporate lawyer for a massive milk company. In her high school yearbook photo, she looks out with the soft arrogance of a girl who believes the future belongs to her--dark hair neatly parted, collar crisp, lips smirking.

And for a little while, maybe it did.

She went to an elite private girls' school and spoke with the kind of sharp, clipped enunciation that made sure you knew she had been properly educated.

But by the time she was pregnant with me, whatever money, family support, or stability she once had was long gone.

She was living in a two-room apartment above a hardware store in New Hampshire. Thin walls, weak heat, a cracked linoleum floor that always felt cold. The smell of sawdust and machine oil from the store below seeped through the floorboards. Her one window rattled in the wind, iced over in winter, stuck open in summer. The radio on the counter fuzzed in and out, the dial always drifting from the station, tinny voices vanishing into static.

A social worker visited her in 1958 and summed up Sally in one brutal sentence:

"Less common sense than her five-year-old son."

She was 26. Richard was the five-year-old. I was growing inside her. Sally had a husband on paper--Robert Newell, my legal but not biological father--but he wasn't in the picture. My bio-dad, according to the records, was just some unnamed guy in Florida who sold magazines.

Maybe he knocked on the wrong door.

Whatever happened, it led to me. And a while later, it led to my adoption.

My friend Joseph was born into a world much like mine would have been. He was the son of a woman who made bad choices but couldn't let go. A woman immortalized in *Peyton Place*--Grace Metalious's scandalous novel that stripped away the polite fiction of small-town respectability. Grace was Joseph's aunt. His mom's sister.

The thing about *Peyton Place* is, people assume it was fiction. But Joseph's mother was real. And she was in the book.

Her drinking, her scandals, her mistakes--they weren't just family secrets. They were *literature*.

Joseph hated Peyton Place for that reason. He hated that his mother's failures were the stuff of paperback gossip, that strangers could buy her shame for fifty cents at Woolworth's.

The state took him from her when he was four or five, deciding life with his mother wasn't just colorful, but dangerous. Joseph was sent to an orphanage in Manchester, raised by staff who were paid too little to care much. He was shuffled from place to place until, at 17, he joined the Army.

That didn't last either.

In his fifties, Joseph was sleeping down by the river,

drinking himself into oblivion most nights. He smelled of damp leaves and cigarette smoke. He laughed through broken teeth. His hands shook, but his wit was razor-sharp.

One day, he told me he kept photocopies of his VA card stashed in his jacket, his bag, his tent, sometimes even in his boot.

"If someone finds me on the street," he said, "they'll bury me in a veterans' cemetery."

I'd taken him out to lunch, wanted to make sure he had at least one meal that day. He had a few beers, but not as many as he would've liked. After his third, he wiped his mouth with the back of his hand and said,

"Funny, huh? We could've been brothers."

I didn't say anything.

We both knew he was right.

We were born into the same kind of chaos.

The only difference was, someone chose me. No one chose Joseph.

There's a moment in every adoption story where fate takes a hard left turn. One version of life disappears, another takes its place.

For me, that moment came when Sally decided I wouldn't stay with her. Instead, she relinquished me to the state. For six months, I was neither here nor there--just Baby Boy Newell, floating in bureaucratic limbo, waiting for a permanent name.

Then, in May 1959, the call came.

A couple in Durham, New Hampshire was looking to

adopt. Richard and Beverly Howard.

He was a dental technician, owned his own business. She worked for the university. College-educated. Responsible. Completely ordinary in the best way.

They weren't like Sally.

They weren't waiting for life to restore them to some lost grandeur.

They weren't clinging to a photograph of the past.

They had a stable home, a normal life, and--best of all-- room for me.

And just like that, the coin landed.

I became Keith Howard.

No longer just "Not Peanut Butter."

Sally Piper died young. Thirty-three years old. May 3, 1965. Coronary thrombosis.

That was the end of her story.

For years, I didn't know she was dead. I don't think my parents knew either. I grew up with this vague sense that somewhere, out there, my biological mother existed--living some kind of life in a parallel universe.

When I finally discovered she'd been gone for decades, I felt nothing.

No grief. No loss.

Just the mild surprise of discovering a milk carton in the fridge had expired a month ago.

I had spent years assuming she existed somewhere--maybe still making bad choices, maybe getting her life together. But I had never imagined her gone. I had never imagined there was nothing left of her but a line in an old death record.

I'd thought she was out there, existing in some dim corner of the world. Knowing she wasn't didn't change much--but it did close a door I'd never quite realized was open.

The only real difference between me and Joseph is that someone, somewhere, at some point, made a choice in my favor.

Maybe it's not luck at all.

Maybe it's just belonging.

This book isn't about DNA.

It's about who I belonged to.

And belonging is the only part that matters.

Genetics are just paperwork.

Even Baby Boy Newell could have told you that.

Chapter Two

A Bunny Looks to the Sky

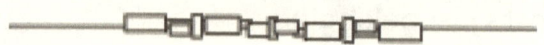

First memories are unreliable. They slip in and out of focus, half-formed and uncertain. But they're ours, and that makes them real. They catch us off guard, emerging in fragments: a beam of sunlight on a cat's eye, the smell of toast, the sound of laughter--or despair. Ask someone about theirs, and you can see it happen. Some ancient code buried deep in their mind starts to unlock, and they begin tracing shapes in the mist.

"What's your first memory?" I ask, often as a conversational icebreaker. It's a question that rarely fails to intrigue. People's answers are as unique as their fingerprints.

"I was three," someone might say. "My brother and I were playing in my grandmother's yard, and a butterfly landed on his nose."

Or: "I remember choking on a peanut butter sandwich. My dad saved me, but I never ate peanut butter again."

Or: "I was in the bathtub with a red-and-blue toy boat. I

remember feeling sad when the bubbles were gone."

So what does this have to do with my first memory? Everything.

My father and his twin, Roger, were what's known as mirror twins--two halves of the same whole, perfectly reflected. Dad was left-handed, Roger right-handed. Dad's hair whorled clockwise; Roger's swirled counterclockwise. Even their smiles curved opposite directions, so when Dad looked in the mirror, it was Roger's face looking back.

"Sometimes I can hear Roger thinking," Dad liked to say.

"Right now, he's thinking about Ted Williams' batting average in '46."

It was impossible to verify, but I didn't doubt him. Their bond felt like magic--unchanged by distance, unbroken by time. They weren't just twins. They were mirror twins, and Dad made sure everyone knew the difference.

In 1994, when they were 71, Roger died suddenly of a blood clot to the heart. Two weeks later, my father developed a clot behind his knee--the same kind, only it traveled south instead of north. Doctors amputated his leg to save his life. Roger had moved to Virginia after college, 45 years before. Mirror twins to the end.

"Mirror twins," I conclude when telling the story. "It's an amazing thing." By then, my listener usually looks both sympathetic and confused.

"But I thought we were talking about your first memory?"

"We are," I say. "That's just the background. Now we're ready for the main event."

My first memory takes me back to when I was three living in a small house in Durham on Faculty Road. It was a summer afternoon--the kind where the air smells like freshly cut grass and everything feels alive. I'd been sent outside with a big metal spoon and an assignment to dig holes at the edge of the garden, Mom's way of getting rid of me. She warned me not to get dirty, but that's like telling the sun not to shine. I dug diligently, lost in thoughts of bunnies--a recurring theme in my young mind--until the rhythmic clang of metal on metal pulled me back to reality. Dad paced the yard, measuring tape in hand. He drove a metal stake into the ground with a sledgehammer, counted his steps, and planted another. I watched him curiously, but digging was serious business, and I soon returned to my work.

Then came the crunch of tires on gravel. I turned, spoon in hand, as an unfamiliar car rolled to a stop. A woman stepped out, followed by three girls, the oldest maybe ten. They were followed by a man who looked exactly like Dad. My heart skipped. I'd heard vague mentions of Dad's twin, but at three, I didn't understand what that meant. Now, staring at two identical men, my world turned inside out.

Mom scooped me up, dusted me off, and carried me to the front yard where the grownups were mingling. My cousins were kind enough, but my eyes stayed fixed on Dad and his brother. They moved together like reflections in a mirror--perfectly synchronized, eerily identical. Even their voices were indistinguishable. It felt like the universe was playing a cruel trick.

Then The Big Joker in the Sky introduced a new shot of confusion. The conversation took, to me, a very dark turn. Everyone was talking about who looked like other family members.

My parents hadn't tried to protect me from the idea of genetics or the heritability of physical characteristics; it just hadn't come up much in my short life. I'd known I was adopted since before I could even know anything. When you're adopted, people don't talk about whom you resemble--you are sui generis, sprung from the head of, if not Zeus, a social services system. For me, the conversation that followed was like a color-blind person trying to follow a lecture on Mondrian. Each little girl gazed at Dad and declared she had inherited his cheekbone, his eyebrow or his elbow.

This type of talk had existed as long as families had, but I felt myself becoming more and more isolated, alone on an ice block drifting out to sea. As a desperate rescue plan, I looked at Cousin Elizabeth, the oldest one, and declared:

"I've got your nose!" I said, pinching it between my fingers. Elizabeth smiled.

"You just don't get it," she said, almost gently. "You're not really one of us."

The words hung in the air for a second, weightless and inevitable, like the pause before a glass shatters on the floor.

It may be she was trying to be kind. It may be she was softening the blow of my eternal otherness. It may be she didn't realize the harshness of her judgment.

Or maybe she did.

Maybe, even at ten, she understood something I hadn't yet realized: that love and belonging weren't always the same thing.

I wanted to say something--anything--to prove her wrong. To make her take it back. Instead, I just stood there, gripping my spoon like a lifeline, my pulse thudding in my ears. If I wasn't one of them, then what was I? What was I supposed to be?

Seeds took root that day--ones that would bloom bitterly.

Mom tried without success to wash the comment away.

"Of course you're one of us, Sweetie. Elizabeth's just talking about looks."

I had not yet studied philosophy, so Mom's words felt like a distinction without a difference. If I wasn't my *looks*, what was I? My voice was the only other attribute I could think of, other than smell, and neither of those mattered like looks did.

I looked away from Mom, smiled into Elizabeth's face and felt something completely new: alienation.

Things came to a head at the grill. I wanted a hamburger, and Dad always made mine. But now there were two Dads, standing shoulder to shoulder, each holding a plate. My head spun as I tried to figure out which one was real.

Then Elizabeth chimed in. "Aw, look! Keith doesn't know which one is his real dad! That's so cute."

The adults laughed, a warm sound that chilled me to the bone. Elizabeth's voice wasn't mean, exactly, but it carried the sharp edge of someone trying to sound clever at my expense. It was a big-kid riddle, and I just couldn't get it. My confusion deepened into panic.

The two men crouched down, smiling, and each extended a hand.

"Come here, buddy," one Dad-looking man said.

"No, no," another said. "Don't go there. Come here."

I froze. I flicked my gaze between them, searching for some tiny flaw, some tell that would reveal the impostor. But they were seamless copies--same eyes, same smile, even the same slight head tilt as they waited.

The problem wasn't just picking the wrong dad. The problem was that I might *not* pick the wrong dad. What if I walked to one of them, felt his hand close around mine, and suddenly the other one faded, erased like a mistake in the fabric of the universe? Or worse, what if *I* disappeared? I wasn't part of this family the way they were--Elizabeth had already pointed that out. Maybe I was a copy, too. A version of a boy placed here by mistake. Maybe I'd vanish, leaving no more proof of my existence than a misplaced spoon in the dirt.

My stomach lurched. I was a very little boy, and already, the universe was playing a cruel joke. For a moment, I understood the vast indifference of the universe. Here I was, a three-year-old, surrounded by people who loved me, yet utterly alone in my existential dread. I was a bunny caught in the open, paralyzed under a hawk's shadow. Tears welled up in my eyes.

Before I could collapse under the weight of my despair, Mom swooped in and carried me away. She gently placed me in my father's arms. The real one. (I assume.) I buried my face in his shoulder, overwhelmed but safe.

That moment, trivial as it might seem, has stayed with me. I didn't have the words for it then, but looking back, I know that moment was my first brush with something bigger than fear--something closer to despair. The kind that makes you realize how fragile certainty really is. But I also learned that if you're lucky, someone who loves you will step in before you get swallowed up by it. It was the first time I tasted emptiness--like wetting my pants while licking an aspirin tablet--the kind that forces you to face the absurdity of existence.

That's where my story begins.

Chapter Three

Existence, Essence, and Mooning a Classroom

Television taught me early that families work like ensemble casts, each member assigned a role nearly impossible to escape. For instance, there's the gruff but lovable grandfather, the aunt who used to be wild, the wise father and the cousin who appears in a Very Special three-episode arc, then is never heard from again. Contract dispute? Interpersonal problems? Nobody knows.

In the nuclear family, these roles become even more entrenched. Once the casting decisions are made, breaking free is nearly impossible. While literature illustrates the possibility of growth, development and change, television demonstrates the immutability of human nature. Lovable losers do not become romantic leads; if they're lucky, they become psychopathic killers, but that's only to avenge the hurt they've suffered as young lovable losers. At least, that's the theory.

I became Keith Howard at six months old, long after the neediest, messiest parts of my story had played out off-camera. My parents were thrilled with the newest cast member, a blank slate to be filled with director's notes. They saw potential. They brought me home from the social worker's office like they'd just won the lottery.

"Oh, Keith," my mom told me years later, "you were perfect."

For three years, I was their entire world. The only child. The chosen one. My essence was shaped by their adoration. I was "sweet Keith," "good Keith," the boy who belonged entirely to them. I liked those seasons. The ratings were good. The producers, though, wanted a different angle. A different angel.

And then came Jennifer, as if Sartre's maxim--existence precedes essence--didn't apply to her. The rest of us aren't born with an assigned purpose, role, or identity. Instead, we exist first, raw and undefined, and we create ourselves through our actions. Jennifer was all essence from her first scene onward.

You'd think as the oldest child, I'd have a better than even shot at choosing my own role. My parents had been thrilled to pick me up at the casting director's--er, social-worker's office--review my papers and bring me home. Having had three years as the star of the show, I assumed my leading role was guaranteed.

All it took was one cute baby to displace me. Jennifer was life: its joy, its whole purpose She was existence itself. All light brown curls and big blue eyes, with a laugh so sweet it could've melted glaciers. Jennifer's essence seemed to arrive fully formed. I'd have to struggle to exist. She radiated essence. From the moment she arrived, it was as if she already knew who she was: the perfect daughter. The princess. The upgrade. Suddenly, I wasn't my parents' only child anymore. I wasn't the center of their universe. My essence--my role, my place--wasn't guaranteed.

Jennifer giggled, and my dad called her his "little angel." She cried, and my mom cradled her like she was made of glass. She'd wrap her tiny hand around Dad's finger and tears would appear on his face. They whispered over her crib, their voices soft with wonder, and I watched from the doorway, invisible.

I could feel myself fading.

Heck, even I found her adorable.

Since life is a situation comedy, not an existentialist manifesto, I won't claim this as my moment of freedom--the point where I had to create my essence through my actions. But to me, it felt like survival. If I didn't act, if I didn't define myself, I'd disappear. I might even be written off the show.

My parents now had a chance to compare me to a newer model. I didn't bear up well in the examination. While I had been a chubby baby with a ready smile, Jennifer's slender lines as an infant seemed so much newer, more up to date, less a reminder of the 1950's when I was born and more a symbol of the new Kennedy '60's. If we'd been used cars instead of used infants, I would have had a standard three-on-the-tree and Jennifer would have been a push-button automatic. If we'd been music, I was Perry Como and she was The Beatles. My parents may have fallen in love to Como, but they knew the Beatles were the future.

At three years old, I was becoming obsolete.

I'd assumed Jennifer would lose some of her luster after a while, but she didn't. It was as if her diapers maintained that new car smell. Even when she turned one, she was as delightful and sweet as she'd been when they'd picked her up from the shop.

If anything, she was better.

Too young to retire, I had to remake myself, stage a comeback as a new man-child. I had to defy television conventions. By the time I was four, I'd begun my transition from sweet, chubby preschooler to smart-aleck midget. I was physically very small, so small that when I began kindergarten, my mother had to lift me onto the bus or bring out a step-stool for me. This lack of size meant I couldn't perform amazing feats of strength, and even in kindergarten I knew dazzling people with my smallness was no winner against a baby for God's sake.

I would one-up Jennifer in sweetness.

Jennifer brought my mom wildflowers--clover and daisies with damp stems that left a trail of water on the kitchen floor. Mom sniffed them like they were roses and hugged Jennifer close.

I stormed into the garden, yanked a rose off its stem, and rushed into the house. The thorns had dug into my palm, leaving tiny red dots of blood. A nice touch, I thought.

In the kitchen, I held out the bloody rose triumphantly.

"Look, Mom!"

Her smile vanished. "Keith, what did you do to my roses?"

Seeing the hurt on my face, she briefly transformed into the old Mom, the Mom of the first three seasons. She held me tight and stroked my hair. She kissed each of my wounds before administering Band-Aids. In silence, Jennifer brought over one of her daisies and handed it to me. Damn, she was cute. She was sweet. She seemed perfect.

I could never compete with that essence.

If I was going to stay on the show, I had to break the chain, transform into a new boy, become what I'd never dreamed possible: I would be wicked, capable of upsetting any situation for chaos' sake. Entropy would now be my boon buddy traveling companion.

By kindergarten, I'd embraced my philosophy: existence as disruption. Jennifer was peace and harmony; I would be chaos and rebellion.

Take Cathy Palmer, for instance. She sat beside me during story time, legs crossed under her plaid skirt, hands folded like a little nun. She smelled like grape juice and crayons, and her shoes were so shiny you could see your reflection. She always sat on the far side of her chair, as if she were afraid naughtiness was contagious.

One April day, Mrs. Granger was reading a story about the joys of sharing--something dull and saccharine. Cathy sat there, practically glowing with goodness. Too good. Too still. The scene required something.

I shifted in my seat. No one was looking at me. Not even Mrs. Granger. I could feel the edges of the moment closing in, like the show was about to cut to commercial--without me in the frame.

I had to do something.

So I stood up, pulled down my pants, and waited.

No response.

I pulled down my underpants.

Cathy's mouth dropped open. Her face flushed a deep, blotchy red. She started crying like she'd stared into a nest of cobras instead of a little boy flashing a frightened inch of rebellion.

It wasn't about Cathy. Not really. It was about Mrs. Granger gasping loud enough for the kids in the back row to hear. About the way the room went dead silent, then erupted in whisper and giggles.

"Keith!" Mrs. Granger's voice shook, like she wasn't sure if she should be furious or just confused. Cathy froze. And me? I stood there, pants around my ankles, and thought, This is it. They'll remember this.

For a moment, I existed completely.

I didn't care about the punishment, or the disappointed looks, or the long ride home with Mom in silence, her knuckles white on the steering wheel. What mattered was the way the room had stopped. The way everyone had turned to look at me.

Mrs. Granger called Mom to suggest I stay home from school for the rest of the year, which was almost over anyway. Ostensibly, this was to give me a chance to run off my energy and because I had already mastered the kindergarten "curriculum."

Mrs. Granger had had enough.

At home, Jennifer floated through life like some kind

of cherub, humming as she colored, tidying up crayons that weren't even hers. My parents called her "an angel," and she lived up to it.

Meanwhile, I was entropy personified.

The sapling was my masterpiece.

Dad and I worked together to dig a hole in the front yard. Under my supervision, Dad planted a red maple tree. We looked upon the work, and saw that it was good. Dad beamed like it was the start of some great family legacy.

"Should I ask mom to start cooking?" I asked.

"Cooking?" he said, mystified. "Cooking what?

"Pancakes and waffles," I said, imagining rivers of maple syrup flowing out of this four-foot-tall plant.

He chuckled a bucket of cold water onto my head.

"Oh, Keith. This tree won't be ready to tap for 30 or 40 years. And it'd take more than one tree to make even a quart of syrup."

He did some dad calculating to check his prediction, but all I heard was the shattering of a dream. Immediately I lost all interest in dendrology in general and this useless maple tree in particular.

The next morning, Jennifer brought Mom another handful of flowers--dandelions because of course--and Mom sniffed them, tears glistening in her eyes.

"Flowers for me? Such a thoughtful little girl," she said.

"Dandelions are just weeds," I scoffed. "They're not real flowers."

"Keith!," my mom said with uncharacteristic sharpness.

"That's not very nice."

"It's true!" I said.

"It may be true, but it's not kind," she said. "Dandelions aren't flowers, you're right, but Jennifer's gift makes them the best flowers ever!"

I wasn't just angry about the dandelions or Mom's sharpness. I was angry about everything--about Jennifer's perfect halo and the way it bent all the light her way. About losing top billing on The Howard Show. About the flowers that were just weeds. About yesterday's stupid tree.

The tree was supposed to be mine. Or at least mine and Dad's. Our gift to the family. And like everything else, it had already failed to live up to expectations--Dad's, Mom's, and especially mine

Fueled by the unfairness of it all, I stomped outside, seized the sapling, and yanked with all the force of my unspoken frustrations. After a brief tussle, the roots tore loose with a wet, sucking sound, and dirt sprayed everywhere--on my sneakers, my pants, the driveway. This was no mere tree anymore. It was my rebellion, my statement of purpose, my cri de coeur. My essence wasn't carved from choice--it was yanked from the earth, roots and all, in a messy protest against being cast aside. I dragged it into the house, leaving a trail of destruction behind me.

"Look, Mom!" I cried, holding it up like a trophy. "Way bigger and better than a stupid dandelion."

Mom's uncomprehending face searched mine, falling dirt clumps tapping out the breaths she took before saying anything.

She held her stare, face blank with disbelief. Then her gaze flicked to Dad, who had just walked in, holding a cup of coffee. He took one look at the tree in my hands, the gaping hole in the yard, the trail of destruction leading to his once-proud legacy, and quietly turned around, leaving the room.

I heard his footsteps stop in the hallway. Then, very softly, he muttered, "Oh, for Christ's sake."

Mom, still staring at me, took a slow, steady breath through her nose--the kind that made my stomach drop.

"What . . . were. . . you. . . thinking?"

I wasn't thinking. I was carving out a space for myself. And now, apparently, a new hole in the yard.

This wasn't just about the tree. It was about who I was--or who I wanted to be. I was acting. I was defining myself. The producers might even devote a whole show to this.

No one could forget this!

Jennifer's essence didn't stop at the walls of our house; it seeped into the world around her, leaving traces of sweetness in every place she went. At church, she knelt at the pew's edge with her tiny hands folded just right, her light brown curls bouncing like some kind of pint-sized saint. She even smelled holy, a mix of baby shampoo and the lavender sachets Mom tucked into our drawers.

I, on the other hand, squirmed in my stiff Sunday clothes, yanking at the high, scratchy collar of my button-up like it was trying to choke me. The red and blue clip-on bow tie around my neck pinched like a vise. I unfastened it and bent it back and forth until the metal clasp snapped, then flicked one of the broken halves at Jennifer's leg. It bounced off her white tights, but she ignored me, either deep in communion with God or dreaming up some new and unbearably kind act.

Our little community church wasn't particularly pious--sermons usually boiled down to "be a good neighbor" or "dig deeper into your pockets for the collection plate." But now and then, some ancient rhythm stirred, and we had communion.

When the silver tray came down our row, Jennifer lifted a single wafer and a tiny glass cup, her eyes darting to Mom for approval. I grabbed a whole handful, skipping the wine altogether. Finally, a snack break at church!

The minister droned at the front, mumbling something I was sure God Himself was struggling to follow. I tossed a wafer into my mouth and bit down. Immediately, my tongue recoiled.

"Those are disgusting!" I blurted, my voice slicing through the solemn quiet. "They taste like dirty air and dust! How do you guys eat these things?"

I spat the mushy crumbs into my hand, wiped it off on the pew.

Dad's hand shot out, his fingers clamping onto the side of my neck like a steel trap. He didn't shake me or yank me, just held on with a slow, burning pressure. His voice came low and tight, a whispered thunderstorm.

"We. Are. In. Church. You WILL NOT behave that way. Do you understand?"

That phrase--*do you understand*--was my father's version of a red-alert siren. The declaration of martial law.

I swallowed hard and nodded, my lower lip trembling. His grip loosened, but his hand stayed put, a reminder that the storm hadn't entirely passed. I mumbled a quiet "sorry," but the weight of my shame crushed me. A mere apology wasn't enough.

So I doubled down.

"I'm doomed!" I wailed, flinging my hands in the air like some Old Testament prophet. "We're ALL doomed! Completely doomed!"

Every head in the church swiveled, every pair of eyes locking onto me--the wicked little boy who dared speak of damnation *with the Lord's body still in his mouth.*

But I didn't care. For once, I wasn't invisible. I wasn't forgettable. I was the church's most *memorable* child, the one they'd whisper about for weeks. Maybe even forever.

Then, a small, warm hand settled on mine. Jennifer.

I recoiled, glaring at her. *How dare she comfort me!* The gall!

I turned to her, ready to shove her hand away--but then I caught something unexpected in her expression. A flicker of mischief. A knowing little smile. A silent amusement at Dad's fingers still resting on my neck.

And in that moment, I saw the truth: even cherubs knew how to play their halos.

If life were a sitcom, there'd be a redemption arc. A kindly uncle would appear, sit me down, and explain the error of my ways. But life isn't television. There was no redemption, no prewritten script. Just me, pulling at the threads of my own existence, trying to weave something that looked like a life.

And maybe that's the point. Jennifer's essence was given to her--prepackaged and perfect. Mine? I had to build it from scratch.

Even now, I'm still piecing it together. The chaos has quieted, but the drive to create--to be seen--remains. The voice inside me still whispers: Do something. Be seen. Write it down to prove it happened.

And so I do.

Chapter Four

A Hairshirt Turtleneck, Two Sizes Too Small

Growing up in a college town means being surrounded by self-appointed experts--people who can turn even a discussion of a yield sign instead of stop sign into a thesis-worthy debate. My childhood was a front-row seat to unsolicited lectures, whether from the forestry professor offering voluntary rose advice or the political scientist with a perfect record of being perfectly wrong.

My grandfather taught at the university, and my mother, having grown up as a faculty kid, was a kind of honorary academic. She was allowed to join conversations but would never be granted tenure in the inner sanctum. By the time I came along, our living room had become a revolving stage for the professoriate. On any given afternoon, three or four academics might gather, sipping tea or playing cards, their dialogue peppered with words longer than my arm. I had no idea this revolving door of intellects would shape not only my upbringing but also the weight I'd carry for years to come

From an early age, I was primed for this world--or so my mother liked to believe. Among the random artifacts that came with me at adoption--a mysterious bundle I imagined as akin to the papers and keys exchanged during a house closing--was a tentative projection of my future IQ, based on a test given to me at just four months old. The prediction was about as scientific as reading tea leaves or consulting chicken bones, but the report suggested I might be a genius in the making, much as a field of grapes holds the potential for champagne.

For my mother, that was enough. Like all mothers in Durham in the early '60s, Mom believed Dr. Spock an infallible saint. According to Spock's developmental chart, I had spoken early (and hadn't stopped since). I had a bottomless appetite for questions and an unshakable eagerness to share my opinions on everything under the sun. Surely, these were signs of brilliance.

My mother's circle of academic acquaintances was a zoo of characters, each parading their peculiar talents and blind spots. But none left as lasting an impression on my life as Ida Aquino--and she did it in less than an hour.

Ida was a clinical psychologist of some note--or at least that was the impression she cultivated. Her dissertation, as I vaguely recall, examined whether people could tell when they were being stared at. A gripping subject, no doubt, though I can't remember if her conclusion was yes, no, or "it depends." Like much in academia, these findings were less important than the framed diploma they led to. Ida's precise, slightly smug demeanor made her an easy target for my budding sense of humor, but to my mother, she was a beacon of professional insight.

Ida had a knack for blending scientific authority with an enthusiasm for unsolicited contributions, so when my mother floated the idea of having her four-year-old evaluated, Ida leapt at the chance. They set a date for my testing or, for Mom, my coronation as a truly gifted child.

"She's the best," my mother said of her when she left that afternoon. "The absolute best."

On a crisp fall morning, we walked to campus hand in hand, my mother smiling as I narrated the journey like a pint-sized philosopher. "Mommy, do leaves know when to fall, or do trees tell them? What if a leaf doesn't listen?" She nodded as if I'd unlocked the secrets of the universe, her expression a silent hymn: *Behold, my gifted child.*

Still, she wanted me well prepared for the ordeal ahead, putting me through my preschool paces.. She quizzed me on colors. She asked me to count to 10. She casually wondered about the differences between dogs and cats. A more suspicious child would have sensed her waging a preemptive attack against my questions. I just responded as an Aristotelian, following each question down a child's taxonomy of wonder.

"Dogs are soft and nice and like to hug," I said, thinking of Tammy, our cocker spaniel. "They have floppy ears and they like to eat things off the floor. They like to sleep.

"Cats are sharp and cranky," I declared. "Mostly, they don't like anyone, and nobody likes them."

"Ida has a cat," Mom interjected, her tone suddenly earnest. "Please, don't offend the cat people."

"I'll pretend they're okay," I vowed solemnly, leaving the

phrase "but indwelt by Satan" left unsaid.

By the time we reached Ida's office, I was primed for greatness--or, at least, to be a total pain in the neck.

In the hallway outside Ida's office, my mother straightened my collar and closed the top button on my shirt. "This is very important. Relax. Do your best. Don't worry. It's important." She was so nervous, I don't think she recognized the small box of thorny contradictions she'd just stuffed in my arms.

Ida's office was every inch the academic stereotype: a tiny, square room with New Yorker cartoons taped to the door and the faint aroma of Lysol and *unsolvable* problems in the air. A small, sculpture of someone--Freud? Jung? Dr. Seuss?--took up a quarter of the desktop.

Photographs of cats covered one wall. More accurately, pictures of a cat--Sir Whiskers. He had the kind of bland, gray fur that made him look less like a pet and more like a sentient couch cushion.

Ida's chair faced the wall, possibly to avoid direct eye contact with visitors, possibly to let Ida gather more data for her long-ago dissertation. Two chairs sat stiffly across from Ida's. It was a room that screamed, "Sit. Stay. Behave."

When she turned to face us, Ida pointed at the wall of cat.

"That's Sir Whiskers," she said, a genuine smile on her face. "Isn't he just the most adorable animal you've ever seen?"

That was the last sign of pleasure, of joy, of any emotion, really, I would see from her.

Ida's expression hovered between resignation and regret, as if I were labeled *fragile but annoying*. Even sitting in her office chair, Ida was tall and thin. Her horn-rimmed glasses perched like commas on a face stuck in permanent disapproval. Her smile was less "welcome" and more "let's get this over with, shall we . . ."

Her outfit could have been lifted from a beige-themed fashion catalog: cardigan, blouse, skirt, all in various shades of "neutral." She radiated practicality in the way only someone who owns several lint rollers can. Even her voice carried a faint monotone, like a dial tone with aspirations. At four I couldn't articulate it, but the air in that room made me feel both important and strangely invisible.

"Sit down," she said, gesturing to the child-sized chair she'd procured for this occasion. I climbed aboard as my mother kissed me goodbye and whispered, "Do your best, sweetheart." I was four years old; my "best" involved scribbling outside the lines and creatively interpreting truth.

As the door closed behind Mom, Ida fixed her gaze on me, clipboard in hand. "Let's begin," she said, as though embarking on a psychological moon landing. I felt her eyes on me. I stared right back. Let her wonder

At four, I lacked both tact and shame. Ida spoke to me like I was a museum exhibit: fascinating, fragile, and best admired from a safe emotional distance. I could tell she didn't have kids. Her tone with me was like an anthropologist who's just discovered a new tribal group. When she sat down across from me, I pictured her living alone with Sir Whiskers, occasionally muttering to him about the state of humanity while drinking weak tea.

The test started with a picture of a horse.

"What is this?" she asked in a tone that suggested I might have been hit on the head recently.

I considered telling her it was a llama, just to see what would happen, but decided to play along. "A horse," I said, my voice dripping with four-year-old smugness.

She gave the tiniest nod, her expression unchanged. It was as if I'd answered "two plus two" correctly, and now we were both obligated to pretend it mattered.

Next came a set of blocks that I was supposed to arrange in some pattern she deemed acceptable.

"Make this," she said, pointing to a card with a geometric shape on it. I thought it was a bit presumptuous of her to assume I cared about her little pattern, but again, I played along.

She asked me questions about numbers, colors, and whether I could remember the sequence of some nonsense words. I deliberately got one wrong just to see her reaction. She blinked, wrote something on her clipboard, and muttered, "Interesting." For a moment, I wondered if my little joke was going to break science.

The highlight of the whole ordeal came when she handed me a pencil and asked me to draw a person.

"Can it be anyone?" I asked. She hesitated, probably calculating whether I'd draw something inappropriate.

"Yes, anyone," she said finally. So I drew her--tall, stiff, and frowning--standing next to the imagined Sir Whiskers. Because my hands and eyes had already begun the lover's spat that continues to today, she may well have seen a goblin eating a caramel apple.

After 45 minutes or so, my mother, unbidden, reappeared, hopefulness backlighting her face with a thousand watts.

"Well . . .?" she said.

Ida looked semi-sharply at her--they were friends, after all--and said the results would be ready within a week or two. As we left the office, I pictured Ida and Mr. Whiskers hunched in matching chairs while reviewing my drawing. Neither could figure it out. If, a day later, I'd been handed the scrawl, I wouldn't have been able to tell the cat from the caramel apple either.

True to her word, Ida mailed my mother a full report 10 days later. The results made my mother's beaming face from last week look like a flashlight in the Sahara. She shone atomically, and quivered with joy.

"This is from Ida," she said, holding the envelope like a sacred object. Then she read the verdict aloud:

"The four-year-old subject exhibits a Full-Scale Intelligence Quotient (FSIQ) of 151, with a Verbal IQ (VIQ) of 157 and a Performance IQ (PIQ) of 146, as measured by standardized psychometric assessment. The FSIQ results place the subject more than three standard deviations above the mean of all test takers."

I wasn't sure what language this was, but it wasn't one I ever wanted to learn.

"Was that the lady with the cat and the funny-smelling room?" I asked.

"Do you know what it says?" She asked, ignoring my non-sequitur. "It says you're a genius. A genius!"

That day, I learned a word it took years to unlearn: genius. For my mother, it was a beacon of hope, proof her child was extraordinary. For me, it was a weight, an expectation I couldn't meet, not with my scrawled drawings or my careless homework. Genius wasn't kind, or patient, or even fair--it was just heavy. It followed me into classrooms, where teachers expected brilliance and got half-finished homework instead. It hovered over dinner conversations, where my mother dropped "151" like it was a prophecy. It showed up in places it didn't belong--on spelling tests, in science fairs, in the lingering disappointment in my mother's eyes when I couldn't remember where I put my shoes. Genius wasn't a gift--it was a shadow I couldn't outrun.

Mom made my IQ her religion. Like a rosary, she counted it in conversations with teachers, relatives, strangers at the grocery store. "One-fifty-one," she'd say, a holy number, proof that the universe, the adoption agency, God Himself had delivered a prodigy into her arms. But genius isn't a gift--it's a scar, burned into you so everyone knows what to expect--and where you'll fall short.

Crossword puzzles, for example. Both my parents loved them and found validation in doing the Times puzzle in ink. From the moment I could write and spell, Mom assumed I'd be great at them. But crosswords felt like homework for someone else's approval--tedious and not my thing. Like Ritz crackers: they were just better than meh.

Until she died, Mom would ask me,

"What's an 11-letter word for 'someone who writes down another's spoken words'?"

My standard reply?

"I have no idea."

Each time, I could see disappointment briefly cross my mother's face. When you can't deliver, when you're just a tired kid scribbling cats that look like caramel apples, the world doesn't blame the test. It blames you.

Genius--a word she clung to and I couldn't live up to--became my two-sizes-too-small hairshirt turtleneck: constantly itchy, impossible to take off, and something I could never make fit.

If I acted badly in class, it was because I was bored, not because I lacked discipline.

If I didn't do my class- or homework, it was because the teacher didn't know how to challenge me, not because I was lazy.

If I asked my sixth-grade teacher where she bought perfume that smelled "like a plastic trash can in the sun on an August afternoon," it was because she didn't know how to work with a genius, not because I was rude and ill mannered.

Throughout the rest of my public-school career, the story was the same: on standardized tests, which required little more than native ability and a knack for reading the minds of the people who created such tests, I looked like a genius.

On classwork and homework, which required focus and effort, I looked slipshod and careless.

My mother favored the former as a description of me.

My teachers favored the latter.

Even as a kid, I leaned toward my teachers' position.

I've outgrown the IQ tests, the labels, and even Ida's clinical gaze. But hand me a pencil today, and my cats still look like caramel apples--a reminder that intelligence, like life, is more than just numbers on a page.

Chapter Five

Hook, Line, and Disappointment

Memory is supposed to be our personal archive, the trusted documentary footage of our lives. But really it's more like an old VHS tape that gets blurrier every time we play it--and, to make things worse, someone's been splicing new scenes into the reel so that the new, edited version looks just as crisp and authentic as the original. Every time we remember something, our brain tweaks the details, smooths over inconsistencies, adds a little color correction, and then saves the new version over the old one, making us none the wiser.

The result? We have no idea how much of what we "remember" is real and how much is a carefully curated lie we've been telling ourselves for years.

Consider a brief anecdote from my childhood. My family was visiting my dad's college roommate in Westport, Connecticut, a town known for its wealth and exclusivity. During our visit, the neighbors hosted a garden party, and among the invited guests were Paul Newman and his wife, Joanne

Woodward. My mother, a devoted Paul Newman fan, couldn't resist sneaking upstairs to peek out the window, hoping for a glimpse of the star.

That's the factual version.

But over time, my memory has turned this moment into a full-scale production, with Mom as a Lucille Ball-type character. In this version, she's perched on a chair, opera glasses pressed to her face, scanning the crowd with the intensity of a World War II pilot searching for an enemy lair. At first, she sees no sign of him--because he hasn't arrived. Then, after twenty minutes of relentless surveillance, she notices something: a faint glow emanating from the neighbor's kitchen. It grows steadily brighter, swelling into a supernova, until finally, the entire garden party is illuminated.

And then--there he is. The Handsomest Man in the World strides into the yard, exuding effortless charm. His piercing gaze sweeps the party, searching for someone. Finally, he looks up, directly at the bedroom window next door. Seeing my mother, he offers a two-finger salute and a slow, knowing wink.

And that's when she disappears.

She has passed out from joy and toppled off her perch.

I know that's not what happened. You know that's not what happened. My brain is certain that's what happened-- and has seamlessly installed it into my memory. If memory were honest, it would come with a disclaimer: "All events have been dramatized for effect." But it doesn't. It sells fiction as fact, blending imagination and reality so seamlessly that we forget there was ever a difference. At least dreams have the decency to be absurd.

Dreams don't bother with this deception. They're crazy from the start. If I wake up from a dream where I'm playing chess with George Orwell while an elephant officiates, I don't spend the rest of the day wondering if it really happened. But memory? Memory plays dirty. It has all the confidence of a lying politician--it doesn't just deceive you, it makes you believe you were *always* deceived.

And the scariest part is, the memories we revisit the most are the least reliable. Every time we pull them off the shelf, they get a little blurrier, a little more manipulated, until they're just well-rehearsed myths that feel truer than the truth.

So what's the difference between memory and dream? Not much—except that memory tricks us into thinking it's real. It's just a dream we've watched too many times to question, a VHS tape re-edited in secret. And by the time we notice? Too late. It's already the truth.

Some memories fade. Others grow into myths. And some, like my fishing trip with Gramper, sit in a strange in-between place—too detailed to be forgotten, too unreliable to be trusted. That fishing trip, for example—at this rate, give me ten more years, and I'll swear there was a thunderstorm, my grandfather was Hemingway, and I pulled a kraken from the depths with my bare hands.

That fishing trip with my grandfather was the last time I did anything at all with him, except avoid his gaze, composed as it was of anger and disgust.

I was four, a kid who looked even younger, the human version of a coat button--small, round-faced, and easily lost in the shuffle. My limbs seemed like afterthoughts, my hands and feet out of proportion, like a drawing a child would make of a person. My hair was an unremarkable shade of brown, perpetually tousled by wind, sleep, and whatever mischief I had been up to that day. My eyes were dark and darting, quick to take in everything, as if by sheer observation I could make up for my lack of size.

Gramper, by contrast, was a man built for command, over six feet tall with the lean, sinewy frame of a man who spent his life moving--walking, chopping wood, casting lines, always doing something purposeful.

His face was cut from stone, all hard angles, with deep-set eyes that seemed more accustomed to looking past people than at them. His hair, still thick in his sixties, was iron-gray, combed back neatly, not a strand out of place. His nose was prominent, as if it had been designed to lead rather than follow, and his lips were perpetually pursed, as though he were forever holding in words he deemed unworthy of being spoken. He had the hands of a craftsman, rough-skinned and calloused, fingers long and precise in their movements, capable of tying impossibly small knots on fishing lines without hesitation.

Looking at his tiny grandson, he may have resented a universe where his daughter, his little girl, my mom, was unable to have biological children. Maybe he resented having to live through her four miscarriages before she and Dad decided to adopt. Hard to say. Maybe my parents never shared with him the talk we had regularly.

"We are so glad to have you as our son, Keith. God has brought us together because we couldn't make a baby on our own, so he matched you with us. And it's a perfect match."

Or, maybe he just resented that he had to spend the day with me.

Oh, yes, Gramper's name. In New England, people throw the letter R in where it doesn't belong and ignore it where it does. Hence, 'Grampa' became 'Gramper.'

My grandfather's idea of love was leaving you alone. It's hard to picture him liking any kid, really. Any kid except, maybe, my mom. He started his career as a headmaster in Colebrook and Weare, back when schoolmasters could practically run their own private dictatorships, which I assume he enjoyed. But eventually, he got sick of the whining and chatter and moved on to a professorship at the state university, where he could let his mind wander, dodge faculty meetings, whatever it took to avoid "bickering."

As I said, Gramper didn't seem to like children. I always knew he didn't like me. Fishing may have started it.

To Gramper, hunting and fishing were sacraments to his real religion--silent solitude. I was Gramper's oldest grandchild, son of his beloved daughter. Although he never said it, even as a little boy I felt something unspoken between us--something stiff and unresolved. I feared he blamed me for my mother's serial miscarriages that led to my adoption. I wondered if he saw me as an intruder in his daughter's life, a substitute where there should have been a child with her nose, her smile.

Maybe that was nonsense, the overactive mind of a kid who saw ghosts in empty doorways. But I couldn't shake the feeling that, in his eyes, I had arrived at my mother's expense. Ante hoc ergo propter hoc isn't even a proper logical fallacy, but I still felt he suspected my involvement in his daughter's inability to bear children. In my mind, he identified me as a pretty slick operator, a midget Machiavelli. But I digress.

My memory of the day is hazy and inexact, but my mother filled in the details so many times that they became mine, too. Maybe I don't remember the fishing trip so much as I remember *her* remembering it. Maybe she was remembering *me* as I was supposed to be, the way a mother smooths out a child›s edges to make them more lovable in hindsight. Either way, I have no way of knowing what's mine and what's hers--just that over the years, her version settled into my head like an heirloom I never questioned.

And so, I tell it as I know it.

Even before the sun rose, Mom was shaking me awake against my will. I'd been dreaming of bunnies and teaching them to talk, a recurring and comforting dream, much better from the other one in nightly rotation. In it, I was having my leg chewed off by a hippopotamus--he couldn't talk and I didn't want to teach him.

"Remember, Gramper's coming today to take you fishing."

Although just awake, my question generator was already ticking along.

"Do you think we'll catch the biggest fish in the pond?" I asked.

"Maybe," Mom said, "but only if you get out of bed and put on some clothes."

It was early June, but I was still wearing my bunny foot pajamas instead of summer PJ's. The material was soft and comfy, and the bunnies were all little and friendly. I assumed I'd wear them for the rest of my life.

"Don't fish like pajamas?" I said. "Are they *ascared* of them? Or is it only pajamas with bunnies?"

Mom had a patented "uh-huh" she used to indicate she was aware I was speaking, but wasn't going to respond. After all, I could rattle off questions longer than any human being could answer them.

"Uh-huh."

"If we do catch the biggest fish, we'll have to keep on fishing, 'cause there'll be a new biggest fish, right? Just like Janice used to be the tallest kid in kindergarten but she moved away, so now Warren is. There's always a new biggest fish."

"Uh-huh."

As Mom helped me out of my jammies and into overalls, I pondered my statement, quiet for 30 seconds, long enough for Mom to carry me into the kitchen and put oatmeal with brown sugar in front of me.

"If we catch the biggest fish, then we have to catch the next biggest, 'cause now *it's* the biggest. If we keep going, at the end we'll catch the biggest fish AND the smallest fish at the same time--and it'll be the same fish."

I laughed at the absurdity of a fish simultaneously holding the title of biggest and smallest fish. Mom looked down at me, tousled my hair and gave me the smile that said I was a very smart, but very strange little boy. And that she loved me.

"Gramper loves you very much," she said, "and he also loves fishing. I'm sure the two of you will have a lovely day."

Gramper picked me up at 7 a.m., the smell of gasoline

and damp canvas wafting from the fishing gear in the back of his Buick. His small boat, still dewed from the night, was strapped to the trailer behind us as we drove to Wheelwright Pond. The air had the clean, sharp chill of early morning, the road still damp from the cool night air. The scent of pine trees seeped in through the car vents, mixing with the faintly metallic tang of old leather seats.

This was just a 15-minute drive, but I began a commentary/monologue/inquisition from the second the wheels started turning.

I bounced in the front seat, my bony knees knocking together, small hands gripping the cracked vinyl of the car's dashboard. In those days before seatbelts, I loved climbing from front seat to back, over and other. Not today, though. I was too busy leaning forward, face animated, eyes darting from Gramper to the world outside and back again. My voice was high and rapid, words tumbling over each other.

"Gramper, what do birds think about?"

Gramper's knuckles whitened on the steering wheel, his thin fingers wrapped tightly around the smooth, worn grooves. His face, deeply lined and the color of sunbaked earth, remained impassive, save for a slight tightening at the corners of his mouth. The bristles on his chin, always appearing no matter how closely he shaved, caught the morning light, making his perpetual five o'clock shadow look like iron filings drawn to his skin by some unseen force.

"Have you ever seen a ghost?"

He exhaled through his nose.

"I think Winnie the Pooh is for babies."

His left eye twitched. He kept both eyes on the road, his jaw working like he was chewing something invisible.

"You don't think I'm a baby, do you?"

His only answer was a slow blink, his eyelids heavy and weathered.

"What's your favorite kind of sandwich?"

A muscle jumped in his temple. His shoulders, still broad despite the years, rose slightly as if bracing for impact. The car hit a pothole. My head bounced, but I hardly noticed, already barreling into my next thought.

"Even if Pooh is for babies, I still like Christopher Robin."

Gramper adjusted his grip on the wheel. His hands were rough, thick-veined, the kind that looked built for chopping wood and hauling nets, not navigating a small, chattering boy through the backroads. A muscle in his jaw flexed.

"I'd like to learn to fly."

He cleared his throat.

"Do you know how to fly?"

The sigh he let out this time was long and slow, like air escaping from a cracked tire.

"I wonder what it would be like if Christopher Robin turned into a ghost."

That got a glance. Just for a second, his gray eyes flicked toward me, then back to the road.

"That sure is a big tree."

Could a knuckle turn whiter than white? His looked like chalk. His breath hitched--maybe a suppressed groan, maybe just the sound of a man reevaluating his life choices.

"I like popcorn."

No response. The car rolled on. Gramper said nothing. But I, blissfully unaware of the silent storm brewing in the driver's seat, had plenty more to say.

After this initial quarter-hour, we backed the boat trailer into the water. The lake was still as glass, mist hovering just above the surface, soft ripples spreading outward from the boat's hull. The smell of lake water--mossy, rich, and faintly fishy--rose around us, mingling with the brackish scent of wet wood. The oars knocked gently against the side of the boat as Gramper turned to me, his expression severe.

"The only rule of fishing is NO TALKING! And I mean it!"

A sensible child would have picked up on the subtle implicit message--"Shut the hell up!"--and been quiet. I was not a sensible child.

"Why is that the rule, Gramper? Are you afraid it will scare away the fish? They couldn't even hear us under the water."

My voice was bright and relentless, cutting through the thick summer air. I kicked my feet lightly against the metal frame of the boat trailer, not in impatience but in rhythm, a habit as natural as breathing.

"When I take a bath and put my head under the water, I can only hear nothing."

Gramper stood by the hitch, his broad back to me, arms moving with slow, methodical precision as he secured the boat. His skin, tanned and leathery, stretched tight over the tendons of his forearms. He had the kind of strength that came from years of work rather than effort--nothing showy, just solid, like the trunks of the pines lining the lake.

"How do you know there even are fish here? I don't see any."

He exhaled through his nose, a long, controlled breath. A breath that knew me well. A breath that had learned, long before this moment, that answering would only encourage me.

"What about whispering? Is that okay? Or laughing?"

Gramper's jaw shifted slightly, the muscles in his temple clenching. His hat--sweat-stained, frayed at the brim--sat low over his forehead, but not low enough to hide the vein that had begun to pulse there, a slow, rhythmic beat. I had seen that vein before. I would see it again--on teachers, bosses, girlfriends, anyone who thought they had control over me before realizing they did not. But Gramper had an advantage those others wouldn't: silence.

"If I'm drowning, I think I might talk even if it scares the fish."

His fingers tightened around the crank handle of the winch. His knuckles, thick and ridged like knots in old wood, went pale.

"I wonder if fish laugh when people drown."

The jaw muscle flexed again.

"What language do fish talk, anyway? Do you know how to talk to fish?"

Gramper stepped to the passenger door, opened it and pointed his long, bony finger. He moved slowly, deliberately, like a man handling a fragile object that might explode if jostled.

"Are we leaving," I asked, then continued, "I've heard of flying fish but I don't see any here."

He slid into the seat. The door closed with a solid, final-sounding thunk.

"What kind of snacks do fish like? I wonder if they like butter on their popcorn."

Gramper turned the key in the ignition. The car rumbled to life and lurched forward. I saw his fingers flex against the wheel, the pulsing vein on his forehead keeping time with the road.

He didn't speak. Not once.

So, naturally, I needed to fill the silence.

"Guess they just weren't biting today. Too much talking might have scared them away. But the biggest fish is still there. And the next biggest after that."

At this, Gramper slowed the car down and looked me full in the face. The look was one of astonished annoyance. I felt like he wanted to say something, but only two words came out through his clenched teeth.

"Never mind."

I should have been quiet, of course. But just like everything looks like a nail if all you've got is a hammer, the world and Gramper looked like an audience since all I had was my mouth.

"I wonder if they'll come back later. Should we turn around and see? Or maybe bears ate them all. I don't think real bears are for babies. Just Winnie the Pooh . . . Maybe they were having a snack."

The drive home was silent. Gramper's knuckles stayed white on the wheel, his jaw locked in place, his mouth a thin, unreadable line.

I shifted in my seat. My knee bounced. I thought about asking him something--anything--to break the silence. But for the first time in my life, I had no questions.

I had finally learned the one rule of fishing: no talking.

When we pulled into the driveway, he didn't look at me. He just got out, walked around, opened my door, and pointed to my house. No goodbye. No explanation. Just a silent order: go.

My mother came to the front door, confused to see us back so soon. My grandfather looked at her, his voice quiet but final.

"He's not cut out to be a fisherman."

I looked up at my mother. She smiled and tousled my hair, the way she always did when she wanted to smooth over something rough.

"That's okay," she said. "He's cut out to be something else."

But she didn't say what. And I didn't ask. Maybe I was afraid to hear the answer.

Chapter Six

The Silencing of Chatty Cathy

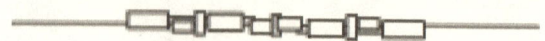

One of writing's most delightful tricks is its ability to transform history into something pliable--a bit of wet clay ready to be squished, stretched, or molded into whatever curious shape the author fancies. I've been as honest as a rascal can be about my youthful mischiefs. Wickedness? Oh yes, plenty of that. I had a knack for breaking things--sometimes to see how they worked, sometimes to test their resilience, and sometimes just because I was curious about the heap of shattered fragments I could create.

The objects of my destruction were as varied as my moods: wooden boxes that smelled faintly of old varnish, perfume bottles whose exotic aromas spilled into the air like tiny acts of rebellion, and, most unforgivably, my parents' tender hearts. To their credit, my parents' hearts healed quickly, but I was industrious, and a fresh offense was usually just around the corner.

Among my many crimes, one stands out--a deed so

shockingly mean-spirited that it rises above mere wickedness. I'll tell you about that moment soon. First, though, let me confess to another, smaller crime of the pen: I've always dreamed of writing a memoir in sonnets.

It would be a grand experiment, wouldn't it? Fourteen neat lines for every memory, each with a bounce like an old pickup on a dirt road. I've toyed with the Petrarchan and Shakespearean forms, though, let's be honest, my talent stops at ambition. Still, I've tried to capture life's messes in their cruelly brief confines. Could I explain why I left a beloved job in fourteen lines? Not a chance. Could I capture the slow unraveling of a friendship? Laughable.

Once, I tried memorializing the moment I'll soon recount. I made it to four lines:

A doll, the jewel of her greedy hoard,

Spoke words she loved--"I love you," "Hold me tight,"

The brother's loss, a string he once adored,

Became his shadow on a guilt-strewn night.

Not exactly Shakespeare. Eventually, I abandoned sonnet form in favor of fairy tales. Memoir sonnets felt too tight, too tidy. Fairy tales, with their forgiveness for exaggeration and their room for magic, seemed the perfect way to recount a childhood crime that still casts its shadow. They're roomy, forgiving, and better suited for unpacking the mess of childhood. So, let me begin with a tale that requires little embellishment: the day I destroyed my sister's Chatty Cathy doll and left it bobbing in the toilet like some tragic heroine. Or lonely turd.

A Fairy Tale

Once upon a time, in a land far, far away--before the world turned bright with unnatural lights and people whispered to mysterious boxes in their hands--there lived a brother and sister in a small cottage on the edge of an ancient forest. The brother was a kind and curious boy, known for his cheerful demeanor, though his worldly possessions were few. His sister, by contrast, was as demanding as an old queen, ruling her kingdom from the confines of an overflowing bedroom.'

Her room was a dragon's hoard, brimming with treasures: stacks of boxes, dolls with unblinking eyes, board games missing half their pieces, and trinkets that glittered in the faintest light. Yet despite her riches, she was seldom content.

"Buy me that!" she'd cry whenever an advertisement flickered across the family's enchanted mirror, her voice sharp as brambles scratching the skin.

Her weary parents would sigh and say, "If it will make her happy..." But happiness, for the sister, was a slippery, fleeting thing.

The brother, on the other hand, lived in a room so small it could have been mistaken for a cupboard. He had little to call his own, but among his treasures was a humble piece of string--a found treasure from the schoolyard. With it, he'd spend hours tying knots, imagining himself a sailor taming the high seas or a magician weaving spells. He loved that string as only a child can love something simple.

One day, the sister stumbled upon her brother in the garden. He was crafting the string into the shape of a bird, its wings poised to take flight. A surge of jealousy, hotter than dragon's breath, filled her heart. How dare he, she thought, find joy in some-

thing so simple when she, with her castle of toys, often felt bored?

"Give me that!" she demanded, her voice sharp.

"But it's my only toy," the boy said softly.

"Mom!" the sister bellowed. "Make him give it to me!"

Their mother's voice drifted in from the next room, heavy with exhaustion. "If it will make her happy, just give it to her."

The boy's heart sank, but he surrendered his string. The sister snatched it gleefully, sticking out her tongue in triumph.

For the first time in his young life, the boy felt a shadow cross his heart.

"This is not fair," he whispered, and something dark began to stir within him.

That night, under the watchful gaze of the stars, the boy crept into his sister's room. There, amid the clutter, sat Chatty Cathy--his sister's favorite doll, a magical creature with a pull-string voice. With trembling hands, he reached for Cathy. "If I cannot have string," he murmured, "neither shall she."

The boy carried Cathy back to his tiny box, heart pounding with a kind of thrill he'd never felt before. This was justice. This was the balancing of the scales. Finally, something in the universe would make sense.

With great ceremony, he put his tattered pillow over the doll's pretty face and yanked the string from Cathy's back. He waited for the feeling of victory, of sweet revenge--

Instead, he felt nothing.

Cathy's last words were faint: "Hold me, Mommy."

And the thrill curdled into something else.

Panicked, the boy concocted a plan. He tied one end of the string to Cathy's foot and the other to the toilet flusher, leaving her head submerged in the bowl. "It will look like she did it herself," he thought, though deep down, he knew how foolish this was.

The next morning, his sister's shriek pierced the cottage. "CHATTTTYYYY!" she wailed, clutching the soggy doll. Their parents stormed in, their faces pale. It didn't take long to uncover the truth--his guilt shone brighter than the morning sun.

"You'll replace her doll," their mother said, firm as steel. The boy surrendered his meager savings and spent weeks scrubbing floors and fetching firewood as punishment. Meanwhile, the sister paraded her new Chatty Cathy around, smug as a cat with cream.

The boy never destroyed anything out of anger again. But sometimes, late at night, as he lay in bed staring at the ceiling, he could still hear that last, faint whisper--"Hold me, Mommy."*

He would turn over, shut his eyes tight, tell himself it was just a doll. But the words would stretch and warp in his mind until they were not Cathy's voice at all. Until they were his own.

And no matter how much he wanted to, he could never quite untangle the knot of what he'd done.

As for his sister? Her demands grew with time, insatiable, unchecked. At first, it was toys. Then clothes. Then the world itself. And one day, years later, the weight of her desires toppled the very foundation of the cottage.

And the boy? He learned that fairness was a story for fools. That wanting was dangerous. That the best way to keep something was to take it before anyone else could.

But that, dear reader, is another story.

Fairy tales are kind to the storyteller. This one is mostly true--though twisted and stretched like the string that started it all. Perhaps that's the real trick of writing: turning memory into something pliable, something almost magical.

Chapter Seven

Plastic and Lies: A Christmas Con

I once believed in Christmas magic. Not in Santa, necessarily--I'd figured that one out early--but in the promise that the right present could change my life.

That belief reached its peak in third grade.

By then, I had graduated from the passive joy of unwrapping whatever my parents had chosen for me. I now understood my right--no, my obligation--to demand, beg, and negotiate for exactly the toy that would make my life perfect. This was the year I mastered The List.

Had I been a child of superior wisdom, I would have consulted my true interests. I loved the woods, simple machines, and the idea of making money. A reasonable, clear-eyed boy would have realized the perfect gift already existed: a rock tumbler.

A rock tumbler is alchemy in a plastic drum. It takes jagged, ordinary stones--the kind you'd barely notice on a walk--

and, through weeks of patient churning, transforms them into polished gems. It's a miniature ocean, a slow-motion magic trick. More importantly, it's a real-life Rumpelstiltskin scenario--minus the child-threatening imp. With zero material costs and infinite potential, I could turn pocket debris into wealth. Within months, I'd be richer than any eight-year-old in New Hampshire.

And yet, despite all this, I did not ask for a rock tumbler.

Instead, I asked for the only gift that mattered--the one every boy in my class had already chosen as the pinnacle of childhood power.

The Fat Cat.

With a name like *Fat Cat*, you might picture a plush feline or a Garfield knockoff. But no. This was a truck. A monstrous, battery-hungry, all-terrain truck that could allegedly crush mountains and inspire awe toward any third-grader lucky enough to own one.

I had never actually enjoyed playing with trucks. My Tonkas sat mostly abandoned in the backyard, gathering rust and regrets. But that wasn't the point. The Fat Cat was different. The Fat Cat was revolutionary. The Fat Cat ruled the world.

At least, that's what the commercials said.

And, by standard childhood logic, commercials were gospel.

Saturday mornings belonged to cartoons.

Cartoons, however, belonged to toy commercials.

The airwaves weren't just delivering entertainment; they were forging destinies--four times an hour, every hour, with the kind of raw spectacle usually reserved for Super Bowl halftime shows or minor Old Testament miracles.

The most powerful of these?

The Fat Cat.

I can't do the advertising justice in print, but here's my memory:

THE FAT CAT -- THE TRUCK THAT RULES THE WORLD

[MUSIC: wailing electric guitar. Drums like thunder on the march. A war cry made of sound.]

ANNOUNCER (booming, apocalyptic):

"BOYS AND BEASTS OF THE SANDBOX --

PREPARE YOURSELVES.

THE FAT CAT HAS ARRIVED."

CUT TO:

A massive sandbox--a golden wasteland of craggy dunes and collapsing cliffs. Wind howls. Dust rises like prophecy.

CLOSE-UP:

Nine-year-old boys, frozen in awe. Eyes wide. Mouths open. Their hands tremble. One of them might be weeping already.

SFX: A DEAFENING ROAR--LIKE A JET ENGINE HAVING A NERVOUS BREAKDOWN.

ENTER: THE FAT CAT.

Not just a toy truck.

A gravel-guzzling, mountain-crushing, thunder-breathing MECHANICAL MONSTER.

Its titanium-all-terrain MEGA-GRIP wheels churn through the sand like a wrecking ball through a birthday cake.

FLASH CUT:

A claw. No--**THE CLAW.** Fire-orange. Hydraulic. Furious.

It scoops up a mound of dirt the size of a baby elephant and launches it skyward.

The kids scream with joy as it rains down like golden ash from an erupting volcano.

ANNOUNCER:

"IT LIFTS.

IT LOADS.

IT DESTROYS."

ZOOM IN:

A glowing red button.

A finger hovers.

Then--

SLAM.

TURBO-THRUST: ENGAGED.

The Fat Cat blasts forward.

A canyon of mud.

A ramp made of fate.

The truck soars through the air, wheels spinning like holy relics.

SLOW MOTION:

It hangs.

Time stops.

Then--

BOOM.

It lands.

The sandbox trembles.

Shockwaves ripple out in every direction like a seismic act of God.

The boys collapse into the sand, overwhelmed. They are laughing, screaming, sobbing.

One clutches his chest like he's just seen the face of God.

ANNOUNCER (now screaming, maybe crying):

"THE FAT CAT--IT. HAULS. HARD."

SFX: EXPLOSION. For no reason. Absolutely none.

FINAL SHOT:

A kid hoists The Fat Cat overhead like a championship belt. His eyes glow with purpose. His mouth forms the words we all already know:

"IT'S SO POWERFUL, I THINK IT CHANGED MY LIFE."

Behind him, fireworks erupt.

Somewhere, an eagle cries.

Somewhere else, time slows for just a second.

TEXT ON SCREEN:

THE FAT CAT -- NOT JUST A TRUCK. A LEGEND.

Batteries not included. (But they should be. Because this thing is unhinged.)

[MUSIC SWELLS -- guitars screaming toward infinity.]

WIDE SHOT:

The Fat Cat tears into the horizon, kicking up a storm of dust.

Behind it, the boys rise, fists pumping, voices rising in chant:

"Fat Cat. Fat Cat. Fat Cat."

By the hundredth time I saw that commercial, it wasn't just an ad.

It was a **summons**.

I had been programed to want--

To ache--

To believe that the only thing separating me from glory

was plastic and packaging.

And I was ready to *believe.*

Rationally, I should have known better. I had never cared about construction equipment. I wasn't the type of kid who played with tools or dreamed of operating a jackhammer. I had no interest in the mechanics of moving dirt.

And yet, I needed the Fat Cat.

It didn't matter that I had never really enjoyed toy cars or trucks. It didn't matter that my previous battery-operated toys had all been disappointments, running out of juice long before the magic wore off. The Fat Cat would be different. The Fat Cat would change me.

And so, for weeks, I launched my campaign. I begged my parents. I wrote Santa pleading letters. I even attempted to manipulate my six-year-old sister into lobbying on my behalf.

By Christmas morning, I was practically vibrating with

anticipation.

The Unraveling of a Dream

The tree sparkled. Wrapping paper littered the floor. My dad, armed with coffee and infinite patience, handed me the present--the one. I clutched it, knowing that once I opened this box, I would ascend to a higher plane of existence.

I ripped off the paper. Fat Cat. Bright yellow box. Just like the commercial.

I whooped. I spun in circles. I made a spectacle of my joy.

And then--

Then I turned it over in my hands.

The plastic felt thin. The oversized tires were... well, just tires. The whole thing was unnervingly light. I knew, even before the first roar of its motor, that I had been lied to.

This was not a legendary machine. This was a toy.

Just a toy.

One that would be forgotten under my bed before the end of Christmas vacation.

The real tragedy wasn't the disappointment--it was the cover-up. My parents were watching me, faces soft with the glow of Christmas happiness. They had worked hard for this moment, and I couldn't bring myself to ruin it.

I swallowed my disillusionment. I thanked them. I performed my joy as convincingly as I could.

And I made a quiet, internal note for next year.

I wouldn't give up on The List. It had worked. I'd gotten

exactly what I wanted.

I just needed to be smarter about what I wanted.

This reckoning could have turned me into a wiser boy, one who recognized that happiness doesn't come in brightly colored boxes with slogans and explosions.

It could have.

But it didn't.

I wasn't a Grinch. Not yet. Maybe a little more cynical. Maybe a little more skeptical of commercials.

But mostly, I had just one thought:

Why didn't I ask for a goddamned electric rock tumbler?

Chapter Eight

Cracking the Unbreakable

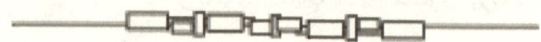

My maternal great-grandfather, Granville Hoffses, built his fortune on sugar pills and shaken water. A Doctor of Homeopathy, he believed that the less of something there was, the more powerful it became--that water, stirred with conviction, could hold the ghost of arsenic in its memory, and that sickness could be bullied into retreat by the barest whisper of the thing that caused it in the first place.

In theory, it was medicine. In practice, it was what happens when science takes a long vacation and comes back wearing a tinfoil hat.

To be fair, Granville wasn't just a diploma-wielding charlatan with an expensive waistcoat. He was a respected physician, honored for his work during the 1918 influenza epidemic, a noted heart specialist, and--somewhat alarmingly--a man who performed actual surgery. He even delivered his own granddaughter, my mother, with hands that had once made the precise, scalpel-clean incision of a trained surgeon.

So, faith and placebos aside, he had skills. But we're getting ahead of ourselves.

My maternal grandmother, Barbie, was born in 1906 and raised in the kind of wealth that meant monogrammed silver and pillowcases pressed smooth by hired hands. She died in 1963 at the age of 57, within days of Kennedy's assassination--though without the grassy knoll, the whispered conspiracies, or Walter Cronkite's voice cracking on live television.

They say bad news comes in threes. The third was me.

I had just turned five, a milestone eclipsed by national mourning and the fact that my face had swollen to twice its size with the mumps. The house reeked of menthol rub, its oily scent clinging to my skin, seeping into my pillowcase. The air itself felt heavy, dense with the weight of sickness and grief.

And worst of all--worse even than the aching glands and the cool, greasy cloth my mother pressed against my throat-- was that my shows were gone. Every channel was the same: a silent, black-and-white parade. A riderless horse. A flag-draped coffin. A little boy saluting, too young to understand why.

Barbie was gone, too, but in a way my fevered mind couldn't quite grasp.

I called her Barbie--I don't know why. Maybe I'd heard someone else say it. Maybe it was because her name matched my sister's doll, though I remember her as neither glamorous nor plastic.

I remember the scent of Woolworth's cold cream and rosewater, the soft crinkle of her housedress when she leaned down to kiss my forehead. The cool, dry press of her hands, feather-light and steady.

I understood she was gone, but not in the way adults meant. *Gone* to me meant someone had canceled my favorite television shows.

What lingered was not grief, but absence--the strange hollow where something should have been but wasn't.

I have two things of hers.

Two small diaries, their covers smooth and paper-thin, the color of old wine. The pages are delicate, thin as pressed leaves. The ink has faded to a ghostly gray, but her cursive remains legible--precise, almost too careful.

1923. 1924.

She was 17, then 18. A student at the University of New Hampshire, commuting back to Manchester on weekends.

I want them to be something grand. A firsthand account of the tension between the lingering shadows of the Great War and the reckless bloom of the Jazz Age. A glimpse of a young woman straddling the space between home, with its coal-smoke warmth and ironed linens, and campus, with its heady swirl of ideas and possibility.

They are none of these things.

They are a catalog of petty annoyances. A psychology professor who was boring. A friend who didn't show up to breakfast. An endless, breathless obsession with a boy named Herbie, who, based on the evidence, was either tragically oblivious or entirely imaginary.

And yet, they are something. A hundred-year-old scrap of driftwood, washed up from the past.

When Barbie died, my grandfather--Gramper--was absorbed into our household like an old, heavy piece of furniture. He sat at the same place at the dinner table each night, his Old Fashioned sweating onto the placemat. The sharp tang of orange peel and bitters clung to him like a second skin.

He was a man of rituals. A splash of water into the whiskey, a slow swirl of the glass, a pause before the first sip. His words, when spoken, were few and deliberate, weighted like fishing sinkers.

He was not given to displays of affection, and I was not the kind of grandson who softened men like him. I was small and loud and full of the kind of questions that made adults flinch.

He did not scowl, exactly. But his gaze had weight. Disapproval, quiet and absolute.

It was a Tuesday. I don't know how I know that. I just do.

The house smelled of pot roast and onions. My mother stood at the stove, steam curling up from the pressure cooker, the high-pitched hiss filling the silence between words.

I, as usual, was filling that silence.

"John McDonald threw up at school today," I announced, dragging my fork through the mashed potatoes. "It made the whole corner of the room smell bad until the janitor came in with a mop and some other smelly stuff. I wonder how one smelly thing can make another smelly thing go away. I think about that a lot."

My mother made a noise somewhere between a sigh and a warning.

"I'm the best reader in kindergarten," I continued. "Mrs. Granger even said so. Then she said if I was half as good at behaving as I am at reading, I'd be an angel. But you have to die to be an angel, right, Mom?"

She didn't look up. She reached for the butter dish.

I thought I was doing well.

"Speaking of dying," I said, turning toward Gramper, "do you think Barbie is ever coming back, or is she dead for good? I kind of miss her."

For the first time in my life, I saw something crack in him.

The air in the room shifted.

His hand--steady, ritualistic--trembled against the edge of the table. His jaw clenched. His breath hitched. And then--

He wept.

Not the dignified, single-tear kind of weeping that men pretend doesn't exist. This was something raw and unguarded, an animal sound pulled from deep within his ribs. His shoulders shook. His breath came in ragged gasps.

My mother was at his side in an instant, arms wrapped around him, whispering something soft and useless. My little sister, three years old, started crying too, unnerved by the sudden collapse of something she had assumed was permanent. My father rose, chair scraping against the floor, and grabbed my wrist, pulling me out of the room.

I did not resist.

I had broken something.

I had made Gramper feel, and that, apparently, was not allowed.

From the dining room, I could still hear the shuddering sound of my grandfather trying to gather himself. The table was still set. His drink sat untouched. The whole house felt suddenly unfamiliar, like the air had shifted, like the walls had seen something they weren't supposed to see. I stood in the hallway, feeling the shape of silence for the first time.

And that's when it hit me.

I had power.

I could shape the world with words alone.

Was that a gift? Or was it something else? Was it cruelty? Or was it just the nature of being five years old?

Either way, it was a lesson.

Words are dangerous things. Even when you don't know what they mean.

Chapter Nine

Warm Blankets, Ice-Cold Terror

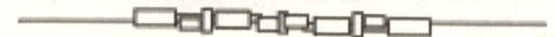

I.   The Age of Theology

Bedtime matters to little boys. From the moment my parents brought me home, they established a bedtime routine. I can't vouch for the earliest days, but by three or four, I had my rituals.

Each evening, my tiny room transformed into a stage for this nightly ceremony. The overhead light clicked off with a sharp snap, leaving only the warm glow of my soft pink nightlight to cast long shadows across the walls. My stuffed animals--Boy, Dog, and Donkey, named with the creative precision of a preschooler--sat in a solemn row on my bed, their worn fur and button eyes illuminated in the dim light. I whispered goodnight to each of them, gently patting their heads as though tucking them into some imaginary slumber.

Next came the prayer. Kneeling beside my bed, the plush carpet pressing into my knees and the coolness of the bedframe steadying my balance, I intertwined my hands. The faint scent of laundry detergent clung to the quilted coverlet, mingling with the lingering sweetness of Johnson's baby powder from my skin. I gazed down at the colorful patchwork squares as though they held some answer to the mystery of the universe.

The prayer started off well enough, the words rolling out in the singsong rhythm of memorization:

"Now I lay me down to sleep. I pray the Lord my soul to keep."

It was soothing, like the soft hum of crickets through the open window or the rhythmic ticking of the bedside clock. But then came the kicker, a line that hit like a crack of thunder in the calm night:

"If I should die before I wake, I pray the Lord my soul to take."

Wait, *what*? My death was on the table? It seemed absurd that this grim contingency would slide into my nightly routine as casually as brushing my teeth. If you find a lifeless Keith, be sure to grab his soul--what a cheerful thought to lull me to sleep. Why didn't we pray before crossing the street or playing with scissors? Why was sleep, of all things, singled out as the nightly gamble with mortality?

When the lights dimmed and the comforting sounds of the house settled into stillness, my thoughts churned. Left alone, I'd squeeze my eyes shut and try to conjure images of bunnies. I pictured their soft fluff, imagined the tickle of their whiskers and the way their warm little bodies would squirm in my arms--a comforting distraction. But my mind, stubborn and insistent, always circled back to death. Would I float away like a helium balloon slipping free into the starry expanse of night? Was my soul tied to my body like a kite, or was it already half-way to heaven, waiting for my body to catch up? Did bunnies have souls? And if they did, did those souls bounce around when their fluffy bodies did?

We went to a liberal Congregational church where theology was about as deep as "God is good" and "Please join us for coffe and pastries afterthe service." I doubt anyone in that sanctuary was secretly harboring Gnostic beliefs, but somehow, I stumbled onto them myself.

Lying in bed, waiting for sleep, I tried to picture my soul--was it already floating beside me lika a rowboat tethered to my sleeping body? If I died in my sleep, would it snap free and float to some cosmic ocean? The idea was comforting, in a way, except that it left my body behind like a forgotten jacket on a playground fence.

I was a Gnostic before I knew the word.

A Gnostic with a touch of bunnies.

II.   The Age of Stories

From my highfalutin theology breakthroughs, I evolved. By the time I was five or six, my bedtime routine had undergone a radical transformation. Saying goodnight to Boy, Dog, and Donkey had been cast aside. They still slept with me, nestled among the tangled blankets and pillows, their soft, worn fur brushing my cheek in the dark. But I figured they were old enough now to handle the night without the babyish rituals. Prayer recitation remained, its familiar cadence a prelude to the real highlight of bedtime: the bedtime story, almost always read by my mom.

The first book I remember hearing in Mom's voice was *Uncle Wiggily's Bedtime Stories for Good Boys and Girls*. The book itself smelled faintly musty, like an old church pew or the inside of an antique trunk--an aroma that hinted at its age and whispered of childhoods long past. Actually, the whisper was of **one** childhood--my mother's. Uncle Wiggily was already almost 40 years old by the time I met him, and the copy mom read was from her childhood in the mid-1930's.

The yellowed pages crackled faintly as Mom turned them, her slender fingers brushing the edges with care. Uncle Wiggily, as I remember him, was a giant rabbit with rheumatism who hobbled around with a cane and dispensed gentle life lessons. His stories followed a comforting rhythm: good boys were justly rewarded for their goodness, while not-so-good or downright BAD boys were, if not punished outright, left to grapple with the consequences of their actions.

My favorite story, "Uncle Wiggily and the Freckled Girl," stands out even now. I had lots of freckles, commented on by everyone--even strangers in the market. I didn't hate them, exactly, but I wanted to be known as more the "the freckle-faced boy."

I can still hear Mom's voice softening as she read about the girl who hated her freckles, her words lilting and full of compassion. Uncle Wiggily, with the wisdom only a giant rabbit could possess, guided the girl to peer into a bird's nest. I imagined the cool shade of a towering tree, the rough bark beneath her fingertips as she steadied herself to look inside. There, she saw a clutch of speckled eggs, their delicate shells glinting in dappled sunlight. A brief excerpt gives a taste of Uncle Wiggily:

"'Oh! Oh!' murmured the girl, clasping her hands as she looked down at the speckled eggs in the nest. 'They have brown spots on, just like my face. They are *freckled eggs*--but, oh, how pretty they are! I never knew that anything freckled could be beautiful! I never knew! Oh, how wonderful.'

"As she stood looking at the eggs, Mr. Bird sang again, a sweeter song than before, and the wind blew softly on the freckled face of the unhappy girl--no, not unhappy now, for she smiled, and there were no more tears in her eyes."

Uncle Wiggily had transformed freckles from a blight to a gift. Voila, the girl loved her freckles, and so, for a time, did I. As a freckle-faced boy, it was a liberation.

Uncle Wiggily was a font of wisdom until he became predictable, the formula showing through from the first line. I grew restless, even rebellious. I didn't want to hear any more tales about a bunny rabbit who always set things right. His lessons were beginning to feel like oatmeal--wholesome but bland. My dismissive label for anything unappealing back then was "babyish," and Uncle Wiggily now wore that label like a too-tight sweater.

I wanted something with more bite, more drama, more... *derring-do*. I wanted adventure. I wanted heroics. I wanted... Winnie the Pooh?

Yes, Pooh. The bear of very little brain. Despite his simplicity, Pooh offered something Uncle Wiggily didn't: real adventure. Christopher Robin, his best friend, was a genuine hero in my eyes. He knew how to do things that mattered--

things like leading an "expotition" to the North Pole. Pooh's world was alive in a way that Uncle Wiggily's never was. I could almost feel the spongy ground of the Hundred Acre Wood beneath my feet, smell the honey dripping from Pooh's pot, and hear the rustling of leaves as Piglet scampered away from a Heffalump.

Pooh, in his own way, is responsible for me learning to read in kindergarten. I had known my letters early, my tiny fingers tracing the shapes on alphabet blocks that smelled faintly of varnished wood. Likely, this was my mother's way of keeping me occupied, channeling my energy into something less disruptive than asking ever-branching series of questions. Over time, I had built a sight-word vocabulary of a few dozen words, a ragged mental collection like mismatched socks in a drawer. But real reading--turning those jumbles of letters into meaning--still eluded me.

Mom changed that. Sitting beside me on my bed, her voice rich and steady, she used Pooh as a primer. The covers of the book felt cool and smooth in my hands, the pages soft from countless readings. Her finger would glide beneath each word as she read, patiently guiding me to follow along. I can still hear the faint creak of the rocking chair in the corner as she shifted her weight, the rhythmic ticking of the bedside clock filling the pauses in her sentences. Slowly, the chaos of tangled letters began to make sense. The puzzle pieces clicked into place, and meaning emerged from the page like a picture sharpening into focus.

Phonics came naturally enough after that, the sounds fitting together like Lego blocks. Soon, I could unstring words together on my own, spinning meaning from pages that had once been mysterious hieroglyphs. Reading became an adventure of its own, the gateway to countless "expotitions" far beyond the North Pole.

III.   The Age of Books

Learning to read was good--great, even. But once I mastered it, my reading habits sprawled out of control, like weeds overrunning the tidy garden of bedtime routines. Mom no longer sat at my bedside with a book in her hands. Her voice, once a soothing nightly lullaby, was now reserved for Jennifer. Jennifer still had Mom's voice, the soft cadence of stories wrapping around her like a lullaby. I had silence--except for the turning of pages.

By the end of first grade, I became a solitary figure in the evening procession, my small feet padding down the hallway's creaky wooden floorboards. The faint hum of Jennifer's bedtime story lingered in the air, a muffled melody through the thin walls.

I'd close my bedroom door with a soft click and slip into my flannel pajamas, their warmth a comfort against the cool night air. Boy, Dog and Donkey no longer shared my bed, but still had pride of place: their own spot in my bookshelf.

The bedside lamp cast a buttery yellow circle on my quilt, its patchwork of reds and blues faded from years of use. I'd stack my books--Encyclopedia Brown, Dr. Dolittle, the Bobbsey Twins--beside me like loyal companions, their spines cracked.

Of all my literary companions, Beverly Cleary was my favorite guide to a world I almost recognized. Her stories didn't shout or bang; they whispered and hummed. Henry Huggins and his dog Ribsy weren't battling villains or escaping certain death. Instead, they fished for Chinook salmon (which I imagined as the golden retrievers of the river), rode bikes through tree-lined streets, and found adventure in scraped knees and paper routes.

Cleary's neighborhoods were alive with sensory details: the sharp scent of rain-soaked sidewalks, the tang of peanut butter sandwiches, and the gentle warmth of sun-dried laundry. Her stories carried no bitterness, no hint of darkness--just lemonade afternoons and the promise that things would be okay. Henry, Beezus, and Ramona faced problems, sure, but they were the sort you could solve by dinnertime.

For a boy whose boredom often erupted into destruction, Cleary's books offered peace. Her chapters unfolded with the satisfying rhythm of eight perfect segments: a setup, a handful of mishaps, and a neat conclusion. Life wasn't like that, of course, but it felt good to pretend it could be.

It's a comforting world to remember--a place where the wickedness was minor and the stakes low. Beverly Cleary taught me that normality is not to be underestimated. It may not sparkle like adventure, but it glows with a steady light, warm and true.

Unlike most kids, my books weren't dog-eared from folded corners. No, my books carried a different kind of mark--one that hinted at either deep literary devotion or mild insanity. At some point--when or why I couldn't tell you--I started tearing off the top corner of every book I read and chewing it like some deranged little rodent. The Durham Library was probably glad when I moved on to bigger books. By then, I needed dental work anyway.

Each book in my room carried its own scent, a blend of musty ink and the faintest trace of wood pulp, grounding me in the physical world even as the stories carried me elsewhere.

The room would grow still, save for the rhythmic turning of pages and the occasional rustle of sheets as I shifted to find a better reading position. Outside, the faint chirp of crickets mingled with a distant rumble in the sky. After 15 or 20 minutes, Mom would appear in the doorway, her silhouette framed by the soft hallway light. "Goodnight," she'd say, her voice low and soothing, before leaning in to flick the switch on my lamp. The darkness that followed wasn't oppressive; it was a cozy blanket that invited sleep--or so it should have been.

Books should have been enough to carry me into sleep, their words a lullaby of their own. But even after the stories ended, my mind wouldn't settle. For a while, books shielded me from the larger, scarier world. But even stories couldn't hold back the growing realization that safety was an illusion.

IV.　　**The Age of the Bomb**

As a toddler, the idea of death felt shocking and improbable, a sudden bolt out of nowhere. But as I grew older, the shadow of mortality began to feel less like a threat and more like a quiet inevitability. Strange as it sounds, I even found a kind of comfort in the thought. Here's why.

At night, as I lay in bed, the sound of distant jets rumbled through my open window, blending with the wind in the trees. Sometimes, I'd picture the pilots--stoic men in crisp uniforms, staring straight ahead, waiting for orders. Where were they going? What were they carrying?

One afternoon, I overheard my father talking with a neighbor. "Those planes," he said, nodding toward the sky. "They're always ready. If the order ever comes, they won't turn back."

I wasn't supposed to hear that. But I did. And suddenly, bedtime took on a different weight. The hum of the jets wasn't just background noise--it was the sound of the world teetering on the edge of something final.

In my mind, the pilots were caught in a grim limbo. I pictured them strapped into their cockpits, faces set in stoic determination, awaiting orders that might never come. If the signal to release their payload was delayed, they'd turn back toward Pease, their engines sighing relief as they landed and refueled for the next shift. I imagined a mirror image of this routine happening in the skies above the Soviet Union. Somewhere out there, Russian planes were circling, their pilots waiting, just like ours, for the go-ahead to end the world.

At night, as I lay in bed, the steady hum of jets overhead became the soundtrack to my own apocalyptic musings. The vibrations seemed to settle into my bones, a low, ever-present reminder that the world teetered on the edge of destruction. I'd stare at the ceiling, tracing the shadows of tree branches swaying in the moonlight, and wonder if I'd make it to morning--or if a sudden, blinding flash would erase everything. Sometimes, I'd chuckle darkly to myself, thinking of the spelling test I might avoid if a Russian bomb found its mark.

In the dark quiet of my room, I conjured vivid scenes: American and Soviet planes crossing paths in the starry night sky. On their way to potential Armageddon, I imagined the pilots shaking their fists at each other, grim and resolute. But on their return flights, having been spared the terrible duty, they'd exchange tired nods, a silent acknowledgment of another day survived.

I was too young to have been drilled in civil defense practices. Ducking under desks and pretending wooden tops could shield us from nuclear fireballs was a relic of the past. Still, I understood that survival wasn't on the menu. If the bombs fell, our fragile little world would vanish

I pictured that end, that explosion, as something like a box of crayons emptied into a hot saucepan. The colors would start melting--bright, vivid blues and reds, swirling together into something sickly and wrong. The wrappers would curl and blacken, tiny flames licking up before sputtering out forever. Then the whole thing would harden into a dull, lifeless brown--solid, permanent. Forever.

Only cockroaches would survive.

Oddly enough, there was something comforting about it all. The jets overhead were like a lullaby of doom, their steady rumble a reminder that the world might not be ending just yet. I'd close my eyes, imagining the warmth of sunlight on my face, the soft fur of my stuffed animals, and the safety of a mother's touch. If everything disappeared before morning, at least it would be quick, painless--a kind of release.

Though I stopped saying bedtime prayers by the time I was five, their echo lingered in my mind, a theological refrain for a child grappling with existential dread. I'd turn my pillow to the cool side, my breath warm against the cotton. I'd mumble.

"Now I lay me down to sleep. I pray the Lord my soul to keep. If I should die before I wake, I pray the Lord my soul to take."

And if He can find my soul in that burned brown crayon, all the better.

Chapter Ten

The Well, the Woods, and the Weight of the Past

Summer 1966 was when my boyhood truly began. Before that, in our house on Faculty Road, I was just a little kid, absorbing the world through the kaleidoscope of the very young. Over this summer, we moved into our new house, the Cape Cod style house Mom and Dad had helped design, then paid to have built.

Now, at seven years old, I was a Big Kid--a promotion as momentous as it was self-bestowed. And I had a new domain to explore: a brand-new neighborhood. Not just new to me, but new to the universe, a collection of ten freshly built houses with driveways so pristine you could still see the chalky tire marks left by the construction trucks. We were the first family to move into Beard's Landing, which, by the unspoken laws of childhood, made me the ruler of this uncharted land. The Biggest Kid. At least for now.

I would be the kid who set all the records in this neighborhood. First kid to climb the lone apple tree? Keith Barton

Howard! Fastest time running from one end to another of our cul-de-sac? Keith Howard! Tallest kid in the neighborhood? Keith again!

Beard's Landing sat on a peninsula embraced by the gentle curves of Beard's Creek, a slow-moving ribbon of water that seemed to shimmer in perpetual twilight. The creek was so still most days that you could count every blade of grass reflected on its glassy surface. When a breeze passed, the ripples moved lazily, as if reluctant to disturb the peace. The air was heavy with the smell of damp earth and sun-warmed water, with an occasional tang of salt wafting up from the Oyster River.

The creek's sluggish pace came courtesy of a wooden-slatted dam that marked its boundary with that tidal estuary. I can still hear the water trickling through those slats, a soft and rhythmic sound that blended with the occasional splash of a muskrat slipping into the water. Their sleek, dark shapes would cut through the creek like miniature submarines, leaving faint ripples behind them. Sometimes they'd surface, their whiskers twitching as they watched me from a safe distance, their eyes glinting like wet marbles in the sunlight.

Our backyard dropped sharply to a shallow pool below, cradled by another dam--this one a stout slab of concrete that looked as though it had been there forever. The surface of the pool was often littered with bits of floating detritus: tufts of cattail fluff, stray leaves, and the occasional drift of algae that shimmered an oily green. On quiet evenings, you could stand on the dam and watch tiny insects skating on the water, their legs dimpling the surface like needle pricks. Sometimes, I'd spot dragonflies flitting above the pool, their gossamer wings catching the light in flashes of blue and green.

Beyond the pool, a hill rose into the forest--fifteen acres of what felt like an endless, enchanted wilderness. The first steps into those woods were always a sensory overload. The air grew cooler and carried the rich, earthy smell of damp leaves and pine resin. Fallen needles formed a soft, springy carpet underfoot, and sunlight filtered through the canopy in fractured beams, dappling everything with gold. Every sound seemed amplified: the crunch of twigs, the caw of a distant crow, the rustle of unseen creatures scurrying through the underbrush.

To my seven-year-old mind, those woods held everything--secrets, dangers, possibilities. The first time I stumbled across the crumbling stone foundation of an old house, I imagined who had lived there. A pioneer family from the 1700s, just trying to eke out a simple living beside the slow-moving creek? A hermit, cast out from the local church for wondering what happened to the communion wine and bread eaten so solemnly Sunday morning, but ignominiously passed in the outhouse Monday morning. A ghost, slain in the ancient 1940s in a bar fight on Bagdad Road? Each visit brought a new story, a new chance to recast the past from a square box of rectangular granite.

And then there was The Well. A dark, circular maw rimmed with crumbling stones, it yawned open like the mouth of some forgotten monster. It was brick lined and only 15 feet or so deep. I called it a well, but there was no water at the bottom, just a lot of pine needles and a few leaves. At different times, the well could be a one-person prison, a hiding place from Nazi agents, a lidless fallout shelter or, most intriguingly, the final resting place for olden-time Durham women who hadn't married by the age of 25, a sort of oubliette for old maids.

A forensic anthropologist, I could spin wonderful yarns in those woods. I'd identify a chipped stone as an arrowhead made by the Iroquois or a related tribe. Having seen Yukon Cornelius in the Christmas special, "Rudolph, the Red-Nosed Reindeer," I'd bite down on the fragment and declare it to have been used in a massacre.

My expertise extended to finding potable water. I made up a personal challenge and tried to skip a rock across the creek. If the rock made it to the other side, the water was safe to drink; if it didn't, the brackish, leaf-filled creek was overrun with bloodsuckers. Even touching one of those evil creatures would lead to a complete blood draining.

Luckily, at seven my arm was way too weak to ever need to take a sip.

This was my world--untamed, unexplored, and brimming with possibilities. Every day brought new discoveries: the path of a muskrat along the creek bank, the skeleton of a bird picked clean by something unseen, the eerie whisper of wind moving through the trees.

Beard's Landing wasn't just a place to live; it was a stage set for adventure, where every sound, smell, and shadow hinted at something bigger, something waiting to be uncovered.

Underneath the thin topsoil of our peninsula was clay--Durham Red Clay, and nothing but. Not just any clay, but a substance that had once been the pride of potters from miles around. In its prime, finished pieces made from Durham clay were compared to porcelain. Under my feet was a local treasure with an international reputation.

By 1966, though, its legacy was just another fact of life. For me, the clay wasn't something to admire--it was a constant nuisance. When wet, it would cling to everything with a stubborn tenacity, coating boots, bike tires, and the soles of bare feet like glue. Once it dried, it hardened to the consistency of concrete, requiring relentless scraping that left a fine red dust clinging to skin and clothes. Even on dry days, the clay seemed alive, waiting to gum up shovels, dull blades, and make any attempt at landscaping an exercise in futility.

The creek carved a lazy arc around our street, wrapping it like a bent elbow for about half a mile. When full, it stretched some 600 feet across, wide enough to make it feel like a miniature lake, especially when the sunlight danced on its surface.

But when we moved in, for the first summer the creek was a shadow of its former self. For reasons I never learned, some civil engineers had removed the wooden slats on the dam, draining the water and leaving behind a muddy, cracked plain crisscrossed with shallow trickles. The mud was a study in textures: in some places, slick and oily; in others, spongy and riddled with tracks--deer, muskrats, and the occasional adventurous kid. In the heat of the summer sun, the exposed clay baked into hard, uneven plates that cracked and curled at the edges, looking like scales on some long-dead dragon.

While the water was low, I was able to be Lewis and

Clark, exploring my new lands. Lewis and Clark with a twist: I spent entire afternoons navigating its banks, imagining dinosaurs lurking in the shadows, making peace with local tribes, and tracking crocodiles with the confidence of a boy who had never seen one in real life.

One day, following the creek all the way to its end, I climbed the hill at Woodman Avenue's end and stumbled upon something extraordinary. The forest gave way to a forgotten graveyard. It wasn't grand or gothic--no towering mausoleums, no stone angels weeping silently into the earth. Just a handful of modest headstones, scattered and half-swallowed by the encroaching moss and ivy. The air was cooler there, with a faint metallic smell that seemed to cling to the stones. Light filtered through the canopy in broken beams, giving the place an otherworldly glow.

The inscriptions on the headstones were barely legible, blurred by more than a century of rain, snow and time. I ran my fingers over the faint grooves of the letters, trying to make out names and dates, piecing together stories I could only imagine. And then, among the unassuming markers, I found one that stopped me cold:

Little Fanny, 1861. Aged 3 months.

Her name was etched so simply, the letters so worn that I had to crouch to be sure I was reading it correctly. Three months. That was all she'd had--a single season. The stone itself was small, barely bigger than a loaf of bread, almost eaten by the earth. Around it, the moss seemed thicker, as if nature itself was trying to cradle the tiny grave, to shelter it from time's relentless march.

For a moment, the world fell quiet. No birds called from

the trees, no wind stirred the leaves. I stood there, staring at the stone, feeling a knot form in my chest. Fanny Woodman. I didn't know her story, and yet, in that moment, I felt like I did. Her brief life seemed to echo in the silence around me, a reminder of how fragile and fleeting everything truly is.

The idea of digging into Durham Red Clay had crossed my mind before, but standing there in that quiet cemetery, the thought took on a new weight. The clay beneath my feet wasn't just ground--it was an adversary, stubborn and unyielding. A casual scrape with the edge of my sneaker revealed its nature immediately: sticky when wet, hard as a rock when dry, and everywhere in between. Even with a proper shovel--and I didn't have one--it would take a long time to dig more than a foot. And that wasn't counting the fine red dust that would coat everything in sight, creeping into the seams of clothes and the cracks of hands.

I'd heard stories about what it was like to dig in this clay. One boy claimed he and his dad tried to plant a tree, only to break the handle of their spade. The idea of someone managing to carve out a grave for Little Fanny here, a century ago, felt like a Herculean feat. I imagined the effort it must have taken: the grueling labor, the aching backs, the quiet sorrow that must have hung over it all.

Did they cry as they dug, the tears mixing with the sweat that turned the clay beneath them slick and unworkable? Or did they work in silence, grim and determined, knowing this was the last thing they could do for her?

I stood there, staring down at the grave, unable to picture what lay beneath. I had no idea how big a three-month-old baby was. In my mind, I pictured her not as a child, but as something smaller, more delicate--a red-winged blackbird, the most common bird along Beard's Creek. They were everywhere in the spring and summer, their flashes of crimson and just a splash of yellow bright against the cattails. I loved to watch them as they flitted between the reeds, their trills rising and falling like tiny songs of triumph.

A baby, though? That was harder to imagine. In my seven-year-old mind, three months was barely enough time to exist. How could she have been real? Did she laugh? Cry? Did she have a favorite lullaby? Or was she more like the birds, a fleeting part of the world that was beautiful and gone before anyone could really hold onto her? The thought made my throat tighten.

I crouched by the grave, brushing my fingers lightly over the mossy stone. The sunlight had shifted, dappling the marker with soft patterns of light and shadow. A breeze stirred the leaves above, sending tiny golden flakes of sunlight dancing around me. I felt the urge to say something, to speak her name aloud, but the words caught in my throat. Instead, I just sat there, listening to the world around me: the faint rustle of leaves, the distant trickle of water from the creek, and the occasional sharp call of a bird in the distance.

Little Fanny, 1861. Aged 3 months.

I read the words again, quietly this time, as if she might hear me. The ground beneath my feet felt heavy, alive with history, and as solid as it was, I imagined it still carried the echoes of those who had walked here before. Her parents. The ones who had laid her to rest. Maybe even a curious boy like me, who'd stumbled across this place long after she was gone.

One evening, as the light waned and the shadows stretched longer, I found myself lingering at her grave, lost in thought. "You've had more years than Fanny got," I told myself, the words settling in the quiet like a stone dropped into still water. "And what have you accomplished?"

I stood there for a moment, the weight of the question pressing down. But then, a smirk tugged at the corner of my mouth.

"Today," I said aloud, as though reporting to some invisible jury, "I identified dinosaur tracks, negotiated peace with the Cherokee, and vanquished a villain of unknown evil."

I straightened my shoulders, letting the declaration ring out in the silence. That would have to suffice.

The air around the cemetery felt alive, humming with possibility. The faint rustle of leaves whispered like an audience stirred by my pronouncement, and I imagined Fanny, somewhere in the ether, smiling at the absurdity of my response. Perhaps she was cheering me on, silently approving of my boyish confidence and boundless imagination.

Little Fanny became my touchstone. My grounding. My first ghost. Even my muse.

As the shadows deepened and the first cool edge of evening crept into the air, I rose and brushed the dirt from my knees. The walk home was quiet, the damp clay clinging to my boots with every step. But for all its weight, the questions and stories I carried with me were somehow light.

She was only three months old.

Chapter Eleven

Cry Havoc and Let Slip the Worm of Memory

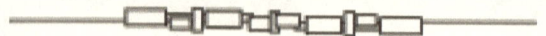

Jonas and I met for lunch at our usual spot, a place called Popovers with overstuffed booths and a waitress who called us both "hon." The place smelled of coffee, bacon grease, and syrup that had been left to caramelize on the griddle. Oh, and the smell of popovers. A host who clearly aspired to maître d'-dom greeted every newcomer, and the murmur of lunchtime conversation blended with the occasional clatter of silverware against ceramic plates.

The food was great, the conversation even better. We talked about end-of-life decisions (cheery), politics (tense), and beards (heated). On this last topic, I have long felt a deep, burning envy of Jonas, who began sprouting facial hair sometime in fifth grade and had a full beard by high school. Today, he stroked it absentmindedly as we talked, the way a villain might in an old black-and-white movie, as though pondering some deliciously sinister plot. Meanwhile, my own attempts at facial hair remain patchy, uneven--a beard that is less "dignified scholar" and more "eighth-grade science experiment gone wrong." Still, I have more hair on top of my head than Jonas does, so I suspect our jealousies run both ways.

We get together every month or two, always relieved to find the other still intact, still tethered to this world by habit and good humor. I love Jonas dearly. But... he remembers some things differently than I do.

And worse, I fear he might be right.

Today, I mentioned our second-grade class, taught by Mrs. Fullam, and how I was writing something about it. Jonas wanted to know more, so I told him I remembered our class newspaper.

"You mean *The Mouth of the Eagle*?" he said. "I think Janet Larson started that. She drew the eagle. John Dunn wrote a piece on the invasion of Czechoslovakia for it. I may still have a copy."

First of all, who the hell remembers those kinds of details? And second--what kind of lunatic still *has* a 60-year-old second-grade newspaper? I don't have anything I've ever written, yet Jonas is apparently the Library of Congress for our childhood. And worse: his version sounds more plausible than mine.

In my memory, *The Mouth of the Eagle*--if that was really its name--existed purely as a strategy to keep me from interrupting class. I had imagined Mrs. Fullam training me like a puppy: rewarding me with ink and paper in exchange for silence. But unless she used a rolled-up copy of the paper to swat me on the nose, my memories seem to be more fog than fact.

Jonas remembers differently. He has names, details, and--God help us--potential documentary evidence. And yet...I still remember it my way. And maybe I'll keep remembering it that way, even if I'm wrong. After all, childhood isn't about truth; it's about the stories we tell ourselves to make sense of who we became. In my version, it went like this...

I am a terrible craftsman, a worse draftsman, and an artist only in soul--or so I like to tell myself. The first part of that sentence is indisputable: my fine-motor skills had sand in the gears, and the gears were missing teeth. Everything my hands attempted--drawing, tying knots, cutting a straight line--looked like the work of a child in the throes of some exotic nerve disorder . My handwriting alone was proof.

A single page of my writing looked like it had been composed during an earthquake, the letters sloshing unevenly across the lines, some stretched thin as if trying to escape, others bunched together--plotting something.

My B's rarely looked the same twice--sometimes resembling a melting snowman, sometimes an eight that had lost the will to live. My S's ranged from elegant curlicues to panicked zigzags. Once I stepped away from an essay, even I had no idea what I'd written. My words became encrypted messages that not even their author could decipher.

Art was even worse.

My stick figures weren't so much figures as warnings--abstract, multi-limbed horrors that suggested I had seen something terrible and was trying, however feebly, either to communicate it or to wipe it from my memory. If someone asked what I was drawing, I learned early to say something vague. "It's a landscape," I'd mumble, and if they squinted, maybe they'd say, "Oh, yeah, I see it now." I took this as a small victory. But if I ever dared to specify--"That's a dog"--the response was always some variation of: "Huh." Or, "If dogs had five legs, sure."

As an adult, I can successfully hide this inability to draw. No one asks a grown man to sketch a dog. But children aren't so lucky. People are always asking kids to draw. Parents beam at their offspring's clumsy creations, teachers demand colorful masterpieces for the bulletin board, and strangers lean down and say, "Oh, sweetie, what are you working on?"

And sometimes, this leads to tragedy.

Or, at least, what passes for tragedy when you're seven.

My second-grade teacher was the sainted Charlotte Fullam. And I don't use that term lightly. Mrs. Fullam was the only teacher who seemed to like me--or at least understand me. She was the first to notice that buried beneath the fidgeting, the interruptions, and the occasional bout of classroom anarchy was something more than just an ill-behaved child.

Other teachers saw only my flaws--easy targets, since I carried them so openly. I was loud, irreverent, incapable of keeping still. I cracked jokes at inappropriate moments. I had a sixth sense for the exact second when a teacher needed a moment of silence and used that moment to stage my loudest outburst. My parents were constantly getting calls about my behavior. The words "disruptive," "undisciplined," and "willful" became as common as my name.

But Mrs. Fullam?

She saw something else. She saw the restlessness, the urge to tell stories, the way I lit up when I found a book I loved. She saw a boy who, if he wasn't trying to be a menace, was actually a pretty decent writer. She told my mother this during one of her calls--calls that, for once, didn't feel like bad news. "He's got leadership potential," she said. "A real gift for interpreting what he reads." She still had to mention my behavior, of course, but that one positive note stuck.

Even when she had every reason to lose patience with me, she didn't.

She had to keep a straight face when I told her I was terribly shy. This, after standing on my chair to get the class's attention.

She didn't snicker when I complained that my voice was too soft, not five minutes after she'd spent the morning competing with my nonstop chatter.

And when I confessed my deepest fear--that one day, I'd be forgotten entirely--she didn't roll her eyes. It's possible she wanted to forget me, but couldn't.

A lesser teacher, an unsanctified teacher, would have sighed deeply, marched me to the class bathroom, and pointed me toward the mirror. "Look at that," she would have said, "a disruptive little hellion. My job is to break you down and build you up into a good citizen. If I don't, you'll end up in prison."

Most of my teachers, principals, and assorted authority figures had given me some version of that speech.

But Mrs. Fullam? She suggested I start a class newspaper.

The idea was radical. Give me an official outlet? Let me channel my energy into something structured? It was like handing a firecracker a match and trusting it wouldn't explode. But Mrs. Fullam had faith.

And it worked.

I threw myself into the newspaper, filling it with jokes, observations, classroom news, and anything else I found interesting. I badgered classmates into contributing.

I insisted we cover "important stories," though what counted as important was up for debate. A spelling bee? Maybe. The discovery that Janet's peanut butter sandwich had a jelly-to-bread ratio of nearly 1:1? Absolutely. Ginger lost a tooth? Banner headline. Jonas puked on his desk? Stop the press!

Of course, there was no press. This was a 1966 second-grade classroom. Before computers, before copy machines, an age when purplish, alcohol-scented dittoes were the only form of schoolwide reproduction.

Since ditto technology didn't allow for revisions, and no classroom had a typewriter, I needed to gather my scrawled stories, edit the very few submitted articles, and find a kid with very good but small handwriting. "Amanuensis" wasn't yet in my vocabulary, but I needed a scribe who would accurately write down my stories as I read them. I struck on Janet, whose handwriting was clear, and who seemed to find me amusing if occasionally nervous-making.

For the first time, my words had a proper place. Instead of interrupting, I could write. Instead of talking over people, I could report. Instead of blurting out whatever came into my head, I could organize my thoughts--at least somewhat.

Mrs. Fullam had done what no teacher had managed before--and would not do again: she found a way to make me focus. At least for brief spurts.

That, I'm convinced, is what makes a saint.

Since there's a lot of jackassery left in this book, you've

probably guessed my reformation didn't last. All I can say is, Charlotte Fullam was a saint, not a seer who could foresee the future.

Mrs. Fullam suggested I have a picture of myself on the masthead. This appealed to my vanity, and I pictured a hedcut portrait of myself, the pointillist style showing a wise and insightful journalist. Before I could talk with her about budget for this portrait, Mrs. Fullam said it needed to be a self-portrait. I pleaded to have one of the *good* artists in class draw me, promised I'd sit still for the portrait. She would have none of it.

"Nonsense, Keith," she said. "This is your newspaper. It will have your picture."

I wanted to generate copy, write the first rough draft of history. Still, I might be the editor, but Mrs. Fullam was the *publisher*. And the teacher.

The Mouth of the Eagle published twice a week. Taking a fresh sheet of purple ditto paper and a Number Two pencil, I drew a lopsided vertical rectangle in the upper left corner.

Janet sat next to me, waiting to turn my fresh copy into a typeset--or at least neatly written--newspaper.

"That box is kind of saggy," she said, doubt in her voice.

"That's how wanted it," I lied, not wanting to start over. "It'll make the picture stand out."

Quickly, I filled the crumpled box, thinking I'd play it safe.

My self-portrait? A worm with two dots for eyes and a shy smile. It was the best I could do, and now I could go back to writing and enjoying life as a media mogul.

Unfortunately, my classmates found my worm... unintentionally hilarious. Snorts turned into giggles, then into gasps of barely-contained laughter. Someone clutched their stomach like they were in actual pain.

"I thought this was The Mouth of the Eagle," one wit snorted. "It's a hungry bird if all it's got is that little worm to eat."

"Hey, Keith," said another. "How you gonna write anything with no hands?"

The worst, though, the coup de gras, was delivered by my so-called friend, Ginger.

"I think it looks just like you," she said, "except it's cuter."

"Practice makes perfect" is one of the standard lies we feed kids. Even at seven I'd recognized no amount of practice would perfect my drawing. Since ditto technology didn't allow for copying and pasting, much less editing, I'd be forced to recreate my self portrait. Twice a week for the rest of the school year, my snaggle-geared fine-motor skills would recreate that same damned picture of myself. I wouldn't move toward perfection; I'd be a small balloon twisting in a tornado--going round and round but never making any progress. By the last day of school, my picture might be recognized as a nightcrawler instead of a flatworm--never as a little boy.

I resigned as editor in chief immediately. The Mouth of the Eagle ceased publication. I returned to the Keith I was apparently fated to be:

A shy, soft-voiced boy who demanded attention at the top of his lungs. A hellion who needed to prove he existed.

As I sit here now, I don't know if any of this happened the way I remember it. Maybe I really did start the class newspaper. Maybe I didn't. Maybe I was just a loud kid who thought he started a class newspaper while Janet Larson and John Dunn actually did all the work.

The problem with memory is that, over time, we become our own unreliable narrators. What we want to believe--about ourselves, about our past--becomes so ingrained that it feels true, even if the facts say otherwise.

Jonas remembers differently. He has the receipts. He has the receipts, but I have the story. For now, I I'll stick with my version.

Loudest kid wins. Always has.

Chapter Twelve

Baptism in Ink and Steam

The world can be divided into an infinite number of two-group sets. (In the previous sentence, "an infinite number of" is pronounced "a lot of.")

Drinkers vs. teetotalers.

The living vs. the dead.

People who bite off the corner of a Hershey bar vs. neurotics who break the bar along the lines.

And then, there was the first great sorting task of my childhood: Marvel vs. DC.

Comic book kids in the late 1960s had to pick a side. DC had the gods--Superman, Batman, Wonder Woman, the Flash. These were statues chiseled from marble, figures of such iconic grandeur that you could almost hear a trumpet fanfare when they appeared on the page.

Marvel had a different vibe. Its heroes were angry, neurotic, and perpetually broke. There was a green monster with daddy issues and a high school kid who got his powers from an insect bite and still couldn't get a date.

The choice was obvious.

At least, it was to me.

Like Superman, I had my own Fortress of Solitude. His was a gleaming ice cathedral at the North Pole, an alien archive where he could brood over the burdens of his power. Mine was warmer. Wetter. And smelled faintly of Ivory soap and damp paperback pages.

When I wanted to disappear, when I needed a place where no one could bother me, I took a bath.

Once I locked the bathroom door, I became untouchable. My sister, a relentless intruder in all other matters, was barred from entry. Even my mother would have needed a life-or-death excuse to violate my sovereign territory. There was something magical about vulnerability--about being a small, damp child, stripped of all armor, yet imbued with absolute authority.

At least once a week, I transformed the bathtub into my personal retreat. I'd march in, arms overloaded with books, comics, and whatever reading material happened to be within grabbing distance. The door shut with a satisfying *click*, sealing me away from the outside world.

Then, the ritual began.

The house pipes groaned as I twisted the hot water knob, unleashing a torrent of near-boiling liquid that crashed against the enamel, sending up clouds of steam. The mirror fogged, the air thickened with the scent of chlorine and minerals, and the pages of my *Superman* comics began to curl before I even touched them.

I undressed with ceremonial precision, peeling off my socks last, savoring the cool tile beneath my feet before stepping onto the damp bathmat. The water shimmered, a liquid portal rippling under the naked bulb overhead.

First, the toes, testing the temperature. Too hot? Perfect. I stepped in, inch by inch, gripping the porcelain edge like an explorer lowering himself into a lava pool. By the time my body was fully submerged, I was weightless, suspended in warmth, the outside world dissolving into nothing but heat and story. I let myself slip deeper, let the water rise just past my ears so the outside world became muffled, distant, dreamlike. The only sound was my own slow breathing, distorted by the liquid, as I drifted between worlds--one printed in ink, the other rising in steam.

I had found my escape vehicle. I didn't know it at the time, but I wasn't just escaping. I was training.

My fingers, slick with steam, reached for a comic.

Superman, arms folded across his impossible chest, surveyed the criminals of Metropolis. His Fortress of Solitude was a frozen palace of alien knowledge.

Mine was a bathtub, rapidly cooling.

But for now--for now--time stood still.

Comic books were 12 cents apiece when I was a kid.

Before younger generations weep at my golden-age fortune, let me establish some perspective: my weekly allowance was a quarter. Twenty-five cents. One thin, fragile coin, just enough to make me feel like a Rockefeller for a day.

Every Saturday, I walked into Young's Donut Shop like a man with capital to invest. The air smelled of old wood, sugar glaze, and the slightly burnt aroma of fried dough. A rotating rack of comics stood near the counter, a kaleidoscope of capes, explosions, and speech bubbles. The pages were thick and slightly grainy under my fingertips, their covers promising entire worlds at my disposal.

I had a system. A comic--carefully chosen. A pack of baseball cards at five cent, the brittle pink slabs of gum inside turning to dust the second they hit my tongue.

And then, there was the final act of financial self-destruction.

No matter how many times I swore I'd be responsible, the candy counter always won. Behind the glass case, the fireballs, root beer barrels, and wax lips called to me. Pez dispensers stood in military formation, their pastel bricks stacked like tiny bars of gold.

My last seven cents vanished in a sugar-fueled frenzy.

The comics, though--those lasted.

They survived the walk home, tucked under my arm like ancient scrolls, protected from the elements as if they contained forbidden knowledge. And later, in the steaming sanctuary of my bath, where the outside world faded into irrelevance, I met myself in those pages.

A kid who, like Jimmy Olsen, was clumsy, underestimated, but always stumbling into adventure.

A kid who, given the right circumstances, might even be a hero.

On the day that would change--or at least strongly influence--the rest of my life, I picked up the latest issue of *Superman's Pal, Jimmy Olsen*.

It was the winter of 1967. I had just turned nine.

As much as I loved Superman and the rest of the Justice League, it was Jimmy I saw myself in. Superman was a god. Batman was a millionaire. Jimmy was a dork. A dork with a press badge and a front-row seat to the action, sure, but still--relatable.

Most of the time, Jimmy was saved by Superman. But in some stories, he lived a normal life, one that felt within reach.

In the first story of the issue, Jimmy, cub reporter, forgot to get the last name of a man he'd interviewed. Perry White, his perpetually enraged editor, turned a shade of red usually reserved for atomic warnings and communist propaganda posters. Jimmy was moments away from being fired.

Then, just as doom seemed imminent, Jimmy reached into his pocket and found the man's name scribbled on a sandwich wrapper. A sandwich that had never been mentioned before. A sandwich that, for all I knew, did not exist.

Still, Jimmy kept his job. I exhaled.

The next story, though--that one was different.

Jimmy had been assigned to interview a group of hippies about their commune. The story must have been written during the Summer of Love, because all they talked about was peace, love, and the Jefferson Airplane. It was mostly meaningless chatter about "the Man" and "the Vibes."

But then, at the end of page three, something happened.

Jimmy asked the prettiest hippie for her number. She smiled, wrote it on a tiny scrap of paper, and handed it to him.

"Memorize it," she said.

Then she told him to swallow it.

And he did.

Then she giggled. "Have a nice trip."

I flipped the page.

And the comic *exploded*.

The straight lines and crisp lettering vanished, replaced by an acid-trip fever dream of electric pinks, twisting greens, and impossible shapes. Jimmy's freckles spun off his face like satellites. His bowtie turned into a Möbius strip looping into infinity. Superman floated in the background, his S-symbol transformed into a writhing blue snake.

I stared, transfixed.

I didn't understand the message. I didn't understand *any* of it.

But I knew one thing.

I wanted to eat a piece of paper from a pretty girl.

I wanted to see my world twist and melt and transform.

Here in my rapidly-cooling ocean of solitude, I pondered this for a long time.

I remember this scene with stunning detail--sensory, intellectual, philosophical.

The kicker? In years of searching, I've never found a single reference to Jimmy Olsen being dosed with acid in 1967 or any other year. Superman has a rabbinical-level following, analyzing particular brush strokes by different colorists. Yet not a word about Jimmy and his trip.

I think I may have torn off the corner of that comic book, put it in my mouth and dreamed the whole thing. Or maybe I just *wanted* it to be real. Maybe I wanted that bad enough to rewrite my own memory.

Seventh Grade, 1971

The gym smelled like sweat, sawdust, and industrial floor cleaner--an unholy trinity of every school assembly. The air was thick with the mingling odors of adolescent bodies, denim stiff from too many starch-heavy washes, and the lingering ghost of whatever mystery meat had been served at lunch.

Rows of seventh and eighth graders slouched on the wooden bleachers, their polyester shirts clinging to their backs, their elbows sticking to the varnished slats. Bell-bottoms draped over scuffed sneakers. Half the boys had their shirts un-buttoned and untucked, Army fatigues they'd probably fished from an older brother's drawer, trying to look like they'd just come back from Da Nang instead of Mrs. Vachon's social stud-ies class.

At the front of the gym, next to a folding table draped with a navy-blue cloth, Mr. Platine tapped the microphone. The mic was a relic--gray and boxy, attached to a stand that had lost its ability to fully tighten, tilting slightly forward as if ex-hausted by years of strained faculty voices.

The PA system screeched, then swallowed itself into a crackling hum. Platine's voice finally emerged, tinny and distort-ed, like an old radio broadcast from the bottom of the ocean.

"Boys! Girls! I know you've heard a lot about drugs . . ."

A few eighth-grade boys, their mustaches wispy and full of ambition, let out low, sarcastic cheers. Platine's head snapped toward them, his sunken eyes drilling into the ring-leader. The would-be rebels melted, suddenly remembering they were still just kids.

"I know you've heard a lot about drugs and how danger-ous they are. President Nixon has declared war on them."

A few students nodded solemnly, absorbing this with the weight of gospel. A few others snickered. Even at twelve, something about the phrase *war on drugs* stuck like a popcorn husk in my brain. How do you go to war against an object? Would there be negotiations? Would a powdered envelope of heroin slide across a table in Geneva? If drugs sued for peace, what would an armistice even look like?

Platine pressed on.

"And I know some of you may think the older generation doesn't know," --he lifted his arms like Nixon, twin peace signs raised, knuckles bent inward, transforming the gesture into air quotes--"'where it's at.'"

A ripple of discomfort rolled through the gym. A few kids winced. Someone in the back let out an audible groan. My insides curled like a burning spider.

"To show that's not true, today we've got Officer McNulty from the New Hampshire State Police. He's going to tell you about the dangers of drugs, about the risks of ex-perimenting. He's also going to show you real drugs, seized from real arrests--some even here in New Hampshire. Not only does Officer McNulty know 'where it's at,' he knows where you should stay away from!"

Platine stepped aside, surrendering the floor to McNulty--a small, wiry man with a weasel's face, his pockmarked skin a roadmap of past acne wars. Even from the bleachers, we could see the scars, small craters that looked like they belonged on the surface of a distant planet.

He leaned toward the microphone.

"Blah blah blah blah blah . . ."

That's not what he actually said, but that's all I heard. Somewhere around minute three, his words dissolved into the droning static of authority. His mouth moved, his hands gestured, but his voice was nothing more than the muffled wah-wah-wah of a Charlie Brown teacher.

Then, suddenly, his tone shifted.

He finished with an urgent crescendo, "Blah BLAH BLAH-BLAH!"--a warning, a command, a dire prophecy. It barely registered. I was already thinking about lunch.

Then came the grand finale.

The display.

We were ushered down by classroom, single file, as if approaching a sacred relic.

And there, beneath the buzzing fluorescent gymnasium lights, was the most breathtaking thing I had ever seen.

The drugs.

They were beautiful.

Pills, capsules, powders--spread out on a velvet-lined display like a jeweler's showcase. Tiny, electric-blue capsules the color of lightning bugs. Fat, sunburst-orange tablets, stacked in neat little rows. Candy-pink pills the size of Tic Tacs, delicate and smooth, each one a promise wrapped in sugar coating.

Ancient, hand-carved hookahs sat at the far end of the table, their brass bodies covered in intricate floral designs, radiating mystery. They looked like something stolen from an Arabian prince's study, their long, curving stems whispering of incense and faraway places where people sat cross-legged in candlelit rooms.

And even *the works*--the needles, the syringes, the tools of ruin--had an eerie elegance. The light from the gym windows caught their glass barrels, bending and refracting, making them shimmer like fragile, hand-blown ornaments in a Christmas window display.

I clenched my hands into fists to keep them still.

If there'd been a ceremonial candle in a votive or seven in a menorah on that holy table, I would have converted to whatever religion they represented.

I should have been scared. I should have felt revulsion. But I didn't.

It was just like that day in the bathtub. Looking at Jimmy Olsen's trip, wanting to know how the world could melt.

I didn't just want to read about it. I wanted in.

Standing there, gazing rapturously, I felt a form of embarrassment. I felt the same way I had when I found my first Playboy--not just fascinated, but restless. Impatient. Watching was no longer enough. I wanted to touch. I wanted to taste. I wanted in.

I needed to be behind that wheel.

Chapter Thirteen

She Smoked, She Spoke, and She Cleared the Air

The Wallpaper of My Childhood

When I was seven in 1966, World War II had ended just 21 years earlier--less distance from today than the Millenium. Back then, The War wasn't just something in textbooks. It lived in the sinews of the men who raised me, coiled in their shoulders, pressed into the set of their jaws. It whispered in the way they stacked woodpiles with exacting precision, in the measured steps they took as they paced their driveways at dusk, hands buried in their pockets. It flickered in their eyes when a car backfired, the barely perceptible flinch of men who once braced for real explosions.

Every evening, as the sky purpled and the air thickened with the scent of cut grass and grill smoke, the fathers of my neighborhood unconsciously enacted the same ritual. They'd step outside, shoulders squared, scanning the perimeters of their modest dominions. They'd check the locks on their garages, peer into the bushes near the porch, then exchange wordless nods before heading back inside to read the paper. They had been trained to secure perimeters, to make sure the night held no threats, and even now--decades after their service--they still did.

Almost every father I knew had served. Some had been grunts, some intelligence officers, some doctors, some pilots, but nearly all had worn the uniform. Bill McDonald, one of my parents' closest friends, had been a paratrooper. He was shot at as he drifted to the ground in Italy--an image that haunted me, even though he never spoke of it.

In his basement, he kept a small castle of C Rations, stacked like sandbags against some future catastrophe. On rare occasions, he let us kids eat one. The powdered lemonade tasted like chalk, and the beef stew smelled like dog food, but we didn't care--it was soldier food.

The only price of admission was handing over the packet of four cigarettes included in each ration box. Bill would tuck them away, wordless, while we pocketed the matches and the P-38 can openers inside. Matches were everywhere, so they carried no prestige. But the P-38--that inch-long, foldable scrap of metal--was a talisman. It could open a can, pry open a door, carve a notch into a stick. It was a piece of the war we could carry in our pockets, a symbol of utility and toughness. I carried mine everywhere. Bill McDonald, because he gave them to us, was a hero.

At the far end of our street lived Dr. and Mrs. Cilley. He had been an Army physician; she, a combat nurse. I was told they met during the war. Maybe it was true, maybe it wasn't, but I believed it. That was the kind of story people told in those days--the war infused everything, even romance.

My own father had served, though not in the way he might have wanted. In high school, he had been a star athlete--a baseball standout, a skiing champion. But Uncle Sam had little use for that. Instead of dodging bullets or commanding troops, Dad was assigned to make dentures for soldiers bound for the front. It was not the glamorous war story a boy longs to hear from his father, but I was still impressed. His handiwork was in military cemeteries all over the world. He shrugged. *"They also serve who only make some teeth,"* he said.

The war was everywhere, soaked into the fabric of our lives like cigarette smoke in a parlor rug. It was in our toys-- tin army men, green plastic paratroopers we lobbed into the air, balsa-wood bombers with rubber-band propellers that we wound up until they snapped. It was in our school plays, where some kid always had to don a paper swastika and lose to the hero. It was even in our television. *McHale's Navy. Combat! Leave It to Beaver*--where Ward, a former Seabee, sometimes slipped a war story into dinner conversation. Even *The Dick Van Dyke Show*, of all things, had its connection--Rob and Laura Petrie had met on a USO tour in the Pacific.

World War II was the wallpaper of my childhood--woven into the air I breathed, as ordinary as green army men scattered across the carpet, as familiar as the scent of gasoline and grill smoke on a warm summer evening. I never questioned it. It was just there.

Even my mother, who had been a twelve-year-old girl when the war started, carried home-front stories in her pockets like spare change. Stories of ration cards, of blackout curtains drawn tight against the night, of Roosevelt's voice crackling over the radio like distant thunder. But by 1966, my mother was no longer a girl pressed up against history--she was a 37-year-old homemaker with a Tupperware party schedule and a phone list smudged with the fingerprints of townie friends. She also had her intellectual set--the kind who drank their coffee black, dog-eared thick books, and debated weighty matters at the kitchen table. And among those friends was Marie Myers.

Marie was Jewish. Marie was German. Marie's parents had slipped through the Nazis' grasp and made their way to Durham, where they began again, folding their old lives into the seams of the new. I knew this as fact, but it sat in my mind like the batting average on the back of a baseball card--something printed, official, but not something I fully grasped. Nazis were bad. Marie's family had escaped. That was enough.

To me, Marie was just another of my mother's friends, another woman with a pack of cigarettes, a tired laugh, and a habit of speaking in low, urgent tones. We'd go to her house, and she and my mother would perch at the kitchen table, their voices slipping between the exhale of cigarette smoke and the gurgle of percolated coffee. The kitchen light was always warm but dim, as if filtering through old lace curtains. The air thick with the scent of tobacco, Maxwell House, and something fried lingering from lunch. I'd be left to my own devices with Robin, Marie's daughter, a girl with straight, dark hair and an expression that could shift between friendly and sullen without warning. Depending on the day, we'd play or sit in silent boredom, a pair of mismatched socks tossed together in the laundry pile of childhood.

The only difference I noticed between the Howards and the Myers seemed minor. In December, we exchanged presents with different families, all part of the same Christmas ritual. The Myers did the same thing, except the gifts were called Hanukkah presents, and instead of just unwrapping them, there was a dreidel, a spinning top marked with Hebrew letters, and gold-foil-wrapped chocolate coins. I was bored by the former--it was no Matchbox car, no action figure--but the chocolate was fine. Not top-shelf, but not bad either. Afterward, the adults would smoke and drink, and Robin and I would retreat to her room to test out new toys.

But my first memory of Marie Myers alone, without the buffer of my mother, took place at Yoken's, a seafood restaurant with a towering neon whale outside, its belly flashing *Thar She Blows!* against the night. I was their guest and, should have been grateful. But I was six and likely overtired, a combination that made me declarative and foolish. Once seated, I announced that I hated fish. When pressed on what I did like, I offered veal--though I'd never tasted it. My order arrived, a pale slab drowning in glistening brown gravy, and Marie, cutting into her meal, casually informed me that veal was calf--baby cow.

Baby.

The word lodged in my throat. The veal was soft, its juices pooling like something freshly wept, and I pushed it around my plate with my fork, my stomach curling into knots. I wasn't a picky eater--I loved anything salty, anything sweet--but the idea of *baby* sat heavy in my gut. I nibbled at the edges, my appetite extinguished.

But my second memory of Marie Myers--that was different. That one altered something fundamental in my bones.

It was night, and we were driving along the north side

of Lake Winnipesaukee, the road curving like a lazy snake beside the water. The lake swallowed the moonlight whole, its surface slick as oil, unbroken except for the occasional ripple from something unseen. The air in the car smelled of damp towels and lake water, with a faint undercurrent of Marie's cigarettes and the salt of dried sweat.

Marie drove, her cigarette dangling from her lips, the ember flaring in the darkness like a firefly caught in a jar. Robin and my sister, Jennifer, were curled in the backseat, small and warm beneath a pile of sun-dried beach towels. I was up front, wide awake, my seven-year-old mouth a runaway train.

I leapt from topic to topic, words filling the car like popcorn exploding in a pan. I gave a full review of *My Mother the Car*, explaining how Jerry Van Dyke's mother had been reincarnated into a 1928 Porter Touring Wagon and spoke to him through the radio. I launched into a spirited homage to *Bewitched*, *Flipper*, *Gidget*, *Gomer Pyle*.

And then I landed on *Hogan's Heroes*. I rattled off how funny I thought Sergeant Schultz and Colonel Klink were. How they were bumbling idiots, always outwitted by the clever Americans.

Marie tightened her grip on the steering wheel, rolled down her window, then rolled it up again. In a moment, she lifted her foot from the gas. The car slowed. She snapped the turn signal, pulled off onto the gravel shoulder, and let the car settle into silence.

The cigarette, still clutched between her fingers, burned low. She inhaled deeply, then snapped her wrist and flicked it out the window. The ember burst apart on the asphalt, glowing for a moment before fading into the night.

She sat still, staring through the windshield, her hands loose on the wheel. Then, with careful deliberation, she took another cigarette from her pack, struck a match, and lit it. The flare of the flame threw sharp lines across her face, and for a moment, she looked older than I had ever seen her--ancient, weathered, filled with something I did not understand.

She exhaled, long and slow, then turned on the dome light.

Her face, usually soft with laughter, had gone still. The shadows stretched across her cheekbones, pooling beneath her eyes. When she spoke, her voice was quiet but sharp enough to cut.

"Keith," she said. "You like me, right?"

I blinked. "'Course," I said, confused.

"And Robin's your friend, right?"

I nodded, but I could feel something shifting. Something I didn't quite understand but sensed was important.

Marie took another drag, held it, then let the smoke drift between her lips in a slow, deliberate stream.

"And we like you," she continued. "Our family loves your family."

Her tone was different now. Measured. Heavy.

The only time adults spoke like this in stories was when something terrible was about to happen. When the child was about to be led into the forest and left there. I knew I was too big at seven to be made into a veal cutlet, but I also knew I was too young to die. My throat tightened.

"Did I do something wrong?" I asked, my voice small.

Marie's eyes flicked toward me. "Wrong?" she echoed. She took a slow drag, let the silence stretch, then exhaled. "You?"

Her gaze moved past me, out into the night, into something farther than the lake, farther than anything I could see.

"Keith, you didn't do anything wrong." She paused. A pause so long I thought she might not speak again. And then, very softly--soft, but sharp as a blade--she said,

"But they did."

The *they* landed hard, heavier than anything I had ever heard. It wasn't a whisper. It wasn't a shout. But it carried a weight that made the air in the car feel too thick to breathe.

Marie flicked her cigarette out the window. It arced through the night, landed, scattered into sparks. Then, with the same quiet deliberation, she pulled another from the pack.

She sat back. Inhaled.

And I sat there, staring at her, knowing something was about to change.

"The two characters you mentioned from that show--Schulz and Klink--are not funny," she said. "They were serious, and they were evil. They were Nazis who wanted to kill me and Robin and every Jew you know. The Nazis wanted to kill my parents. That's why we came to America. And no TV show should portray them as anything but monsters. Remember who they are. Remember what they wanted. Remember this: the Nazis wanted to kill your friends."

But Sergeant Schultz *is* funny, I wanted to say, like when he says, "I know nothing." Sergeant Schultz had always been funny--his bumbling, his doughy, harmless face. But

Marie's voice was different now. Sharper. It wasn't just a history lesson--it was personal. I wanted to argue, but something in Marie's face--something dark and old and hurt--made my words shrivel before they reached my mouth.

I swallowed hard. My mouth tasted like the peanut butter and jelly sandwich I'd eaten hours ago, now sour and gluey. I looked down at my hands, suddenly aware of how small they were in my lap. I wanted to say something, but my mouth was too small. It was big enough to disrupt a class, big enough to ask a million questions, big enough to talk endlessly about TV shows.

But my mouth wasn't big enough now to say a single word.

I nodded.

Marie smoked, looked out the window, then looked back at me. Her gaze didn't feel like judgement, at least not judgement of me.

"Mrs. Myers?" I said after a minute of silence.

"You can call me Marie." She threw her latest cigarette out the window, lit another. "What did you want to say?"

I wanted to tell her I was sorry. Sorry about her parents, sorry about the Nazis, sorry about her needing to escape, sorry I wasn't a better friend to Robin. But those ideas were too big for my small mouth.

"I won't watch that show any more."

She gulped down a sob, took my hand and gave me the most powerful blessing I'd ever received.

"Keith, you are a good boy."

"Sometimes," I said, and we both laughed.

Marie flicked away her cigarette, its ember flaring once before vanishing into the dark. In the silence that followed, I felt something settle inside me--small, like a P-38 in my pocket, but heavy all the same. Something that would last.

Chapter Fourteen

A Portrait of the Artist as a Total Fraud

When I was a kid, my big goal was to stay small. Or at least short enough to be called a midget, which was still the term back then. From kindergarten on, I'd been the shortest kid in every class--I at least wanted it to mean something. Like many childhood dreams, this one had two components: misunderstanding and delusion.

I saw midgetdom as a sure path to fame. And money. The only little people I ever saw were on TV or in movies. Reasoning from this data set, it was clear that all little people were destined to be actors--stars, or at least recurring characters like Dr. Miguelito Quixote Loveless, a regular on *The Wild Wild West*. Loveless may have been a villain, but he was a damned memorable and clever bad guy, inventing airplanes, penicillin, and even a device that let people walk into paintings--all in the Old West of the 1800s. People remembered him. He was a little guy I could look up to. Unfortunately, while DNA would never make me tall, it prevented me from being short enough for that life.

After I grew out of little-people potential, I wanted, like every other boy I knew, to be a major league baseball player. But since I was only the second-best catcher in my little town, I realized my reach might exceed my grasp. Still, my love of baseball could lead to a career as an umpire--until I learned potential umps had to be at least 5'10" just to get into umpire school. Dream one was destroyed by growing. Dream two was destroyed by assuming I'd never grow enough.

By sixth grade, I'd discovered the thrilling, anarchic world of Abbie Hoffman through his underground classic *Steal This Book!*--a rebellious how-to manual that mixed street-level activism with countercultural mischief. Hoffman, co-founder of the Youth International Party--better known as the Yippies--blended political protest with theatrical pranks, aiming to upend the establishment with humor, media savvy, and guerrilla tactics. The Yippies demanded an end to war, capitalism, and conformity, staging headline-grabbing stunts like nominating a pig ("Pigasus") for president and attempting to levitate the Pentagon.

I took it all very seriously. My revolution mostly consisted of reading, talking, and proudly identifying with the movement, but I believed I was part of something urgent and real. Shoplifting became an act of defiance, as did figuring out how to cheat the phone company--Yippie-approved tactics for disrupting a corrupt system. That posture lingered through high school, but last I checked, the United States remained stubbornly unrevolutioned.

Still, I had plenty of other goals to miss out on--minor ones, the kind that look cute on paper but feel life-or-death when you're a kid. For example: I wanted a girl--any girl, really--to want to kiss me. Or at least hold my hand. I was good at generating my own crushes, but love, for me, was like trying to bounce a tennis ball off a snowbank. No girl ever bounced it back. The ball just sank.

And then there was art.

All I wanted was to make one drawing--just one--that didn't look like a duck with paint on its feet had wandered across my paper and called it a day. I'd swear, every time, this would be the one. If I drew a horse, I'd stick to the essentials: head, four legs, mane. I didn't know Plato, but I understood his Ideals. I could feel horseness in my mind. I could see it. But somewhere between the idea and the execution, between the motion and the act, what fell wasn't a shadow--it was a full-scale artistic catastrophe.

"Horseness" collapsed into a void, and my paper became a scattered collection of disjointed parts--a Picasso nightmare if Pablo had never learned to draw. One eye where an ear should be. A tail detached and floating off in the corner. Nothing connected.

I knew I'd failed. That part didn't surprise me. What hurt were the comments:

"What's that supposed to be?" "It's a horse." "Horses have four legs." "I know, but I didn't have room, so I made the third one fat."

I learned early that no helpful art critique begins with the words, *What's that supposed to be?*

But the questions came anyway. And the comments.

"Was there a nuclear attack?"

"Is it melting?"

But worse than my drawings of horses were my attempts to depict my family. Dad in profile, a pipe hanging out of what might have been a mouth. Mom with a stiff triangle of a skirt, sharp enough to puncture Jennifer, who looked like a tomato with curly pigtails. And out of modesty, my self-portrait would be a snakelike creature slithering out of the picture.

If any teacher had referred me to an art therapist, I'd never have escaped the bin. You can't fail at art and be considered well-adjusted. Maybe my brain saw myself with four nostrils and mismatched eyes; maybe I saw beauty in the random.

Or maybe I just couldn't draw. Or paint. Or glue pictures into a collage.

Then there was Jeff.

Jeff was the kid who knew how to do everything right: sketching, sculpting, silk-screening. Whatever we touched in art class, Jeff turned to gold. Me? I'd make a sad blob of clay that even the teacher struggled to comment on.

One day, we were given copper sheets to etch. I was happy to have made an if-you-squint-you-can-see-it houselike structure. Jeff? Without even trying, he created a Roman soldier in profile, one so real you could tell the soldier had seen some hard combat and was now relaxing in old age, having put on his gear just to sit for this portrait.

Jeff's soldier belonged in a museum.

And then, at the end of class, Jeff shrugged, glanced at his work, and threw it in the trash.

I couldn't believe it. That was *art*. It didn't deserve to be treated like an apple core--it deserved gallery space, or even a whole museum wing. I reached in, pulled it out, and slipped it into my book bag.

Only, it never made it to my room.

At home, my mom spotted the etching.

"Oh, Keith," she said, beaming. "I didn't know you could do something like this."

I couldn't. And I still can't. But I couldn't take that look off her face. Not after all the calls from teachers about my "attitude," the notes on my "lack of focus," the stories about how I could be "so much more."

So I just looked at my shoes.

She put Jeff's Roman soldier up on the mantelpiece.

And just like that, I became an artistic genius.

Oh, I tried to live up to my false reputation. Knowing I couldn't do it with my drafting ability, my painting ability, or any other hypothetical skill, I did what all hacks with more chutzpah than talent do--I briefly became a *conceptual artist.*

From the Gallery of Keith:

1. **Nuclearized Snowmen** – Three marshmallows stacked on a hot plate. At first, they sat there, pristine and puffy, their soft white curves reflecting the kitchen light. Then, as the heat seeped up, their bellies sagged, their smooth surfaces glistening. A faint caramel scent curled into the air, sweet but wrong. Within seconds, they slumped into a sticky, bubbling mass, darkening to an angry brown, then black, the sugar crisping and crackling. The smell shifted--first like over-toasted marshmallows, then like something synthetic burning, an acrid sting that made me cough. *A profound statement on the arms race,* I thought.

"Keith! What's that *smell*?" Mom yelled from the other room.

A fire hazard, she decided.

Philistine, I muttered.

2. **A Burning Statement on Vietnam** – I spent the afternoon constructing my masterpiece, an elaborate house of cards on the living room floor. Each card whispered against the next as I placed it, my breath held in tight suspense. The finished structure was delicate but perfect. Around it, I positioned my little green Army men, their rigid plastic rifles raised, their flat feet pressed into the carpet. One soldier stood apart. That was the plan.

"I need some matches," I told Mom. My voice was casual. Too casual.

"Why?" she asked, her tone instantly suspicious.

"Well," I said, shifting from foot to foot, "I'm going to light this guy on fire, and then--wwwwhhhhhooooossssh--the flames will spread and take out the whole village. Just like napalm."

I gestured toward the delicate paper walls, the soldiers frozen in eternal plastic alertness.

"It's an anti-war piece."

Mom turned from the sink, still drying a plate. She stared at me, her hands pausing mid-motion. Her eyes went wide. Her mouth fell open slightly, and for a second, all I could hear was the hum of the refrigerator. That was the moment I realized *maybe* I'd miscalculated my audience. I backpedaled immediately.

"Just kidding, Mom," I lied, my voice a little too bright. "I just wanted to see what you'd say."

She exhaled sharply and shook her head. "I'd say don't ever make jokes like that again." She put the plate down with a decisive *clank*. "The thought of it! Burning the house down."

I loved Mom, of course. But when it came to high art, she lacked vision.

3.   **The Doll Stares Back** – I placed one of Jennifer's dolls on the table, her frilly pink dress stiff with starch, her glossy plastic curls catching the afternoon light.

"Just sit," I told Jennifer, guiding her into the chair opposite. "And stare into her eyes until she looks back."

Jennifer squirmed but did as I said, fixing her gaze on the doll's wide blue eyes--too bright, too empty, a little too knowing. The longer she stared, the more the air in the room seemed to change, thickening like before a thunderstorm. The house was silent except for the soft *tick tick tick* of the kitchen clock. Jennifer sniffled. Her breathing quickened. The doll's glossy lips seemed to part *just* a little. And then Jennifer screamed. She bolted from the chair, her socks sliding on the linoleum as she took off down the hall.

"Mom!" she wailed. "Keith's being weird again!"

I leaned toward the doll, studying its glassy stare. I figured Jennifer just wasn't ready for what the doll had to say.

After a while, I got tired of being a conceptual artist. If anything could be art, and everything the artist labeled as art was art, then nothing was art. It was exhausting. I stopped pretending to have grand ideas and went back to what I did best--doing crazy things for no reason at all. No explanations necessary.

Still, for the next three years, Jeff's Roman soldier sat on our mantel, getting oohed and ahhhhed over by every family member and party guest who walked in. My aunts, my uncles, neighbors--they'd take one look, nod approvingly, and say something like, "Kid's got talent."

And I'd stand there, my face burning, my throat dry, pasting on the most convincing half-smile I could manage.

By eighth grade, my "issues" had fully blossomed--now the phone calls home from school were always about my behavior, not my wasted potential. Apparently, I'd become a horse chestnut--hard, spiky on the outside, hiding something smooth and fragile within.

Jennifer's artwork had taken the soldier's place, and my mother had finally put him away.

One afternoon, when no one was watching, I snuck into the drawer, pulled it out, and folded it in half. The copper cracked. I folded it again. And again. Then I dropped it into the trash, pressing it down under the coffee grounds and eggshells.

It belonged there. Maybe I wasn't worth keeping either..

But I wasn't ready to throw myself away. Not yet.

Chapter Fifteen

The Alchemy of Bad Ideas

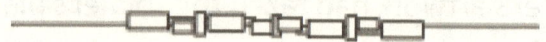

I've never been much of a believer in fate, but every now and then, something happens that makes me wonder if the universe isn't just some old-school Greek dramatist, hunched over a desk, setting me up for a spectacular downfall.

The Greeks had a name for this kind of thing. Aristotle--who apparently had time to think about these matters while not inventing science or ruining people's fun--laid down the rules of tragedy, and we've more or less stuck with them ever since.

Bad things don't just happen; they happen because of some fatal flaw in a person's character. The hero, or at least the guy we're rooting for, makes one bad choice--pride, arrogance, trusting the wrong person, forgetting to check the expiration date on the milk--and suddenly the wheels are in motion. The disaster isn't immediate. No, that would be too easy. First, the hero almost wins. Almost claws his way out. And then--only then--does the whole thing collapse like a bad soufflé. That's what makes it a tragedy.

But the Greeks weren't above cheating, either. When things got too tangled to resolve, they just dropped in a god. Literally. They called this *deus ex machina*, or "the god from the machine," and we still pull the same trick. The cavalry rides in at the last second. The long-lost love turns up just in time to stop the wedding. We like justice. We like resolution. And we like our stories wrapped up neatly, like a burrito with no filling spilling out.

Chekhov had his own rule about this kind of thing: If there's a gun on the wall in Act I, somebody's firing it by Act III. Meaning, we expect things to matter. If you introduce a detail, it needs to pay off. So much so that we don't even think about it--we just assume it's how stories work. It's how life works.

Except, a thousand years ago, nobody thought this way. The idea that a person's choices determined their fate would have sounded as ridiculous to a medieval Englishman as trying to predict the stock market by dissecting a goat does to us. They had a different system--the *Rota Fortuna*, or the Wheel of Fortune. Not the kind where you win a new microwave, but the one that randomly tossed people up or down. One day you're king, the next you're in a dungeon, and there's nothing you can do about it. The idea of deserving anything, one way or the other, was absurd. Thomas à Kempis, a 14th-century mystic, summed it up best: "Man proposeth, but God disposeth." Meaning, you can plan all you want, but the universe has other ideas.

Then, of course, the Renaissance came along and flipped the whole thing on its head. Copernicus demoted Earth; humanists promoted us. Suddenly, we were back to Aristotle--our choices mattered. Actions have consequences, characters have flaws, and if something goes wrong, well, buddy, that's on you. Ironically, if the Wheel of Fortune was still running the show, this kind of reversal was inevitable.

I don't know which version I prefer. I'd like to believe my mistakes are my own, that I get to shape my own story, that I'm the hero in my own tragicomedy. But then again, some days, I think I'm just a cork bobbing in the ocean, a medieval peasant at heart.

The Greeks believed fate delivered its blows through character flaws. If so, my flaw in this tale was scientific hubris, and my downfall was smoldering in my basement crawl space, waiting for its moment.

Before I tell you about the basement crawl space, let me be clear: my parents were good parents. This is important because, by all rights, they should have been arrested for allowing their seven-year-old son to conduct unsupervised chemistry experiments in an unventilated cement cell. Not that they *let* me do it. They just... didn›t ask too many questions. Lucky for them, they're long gone--beyond the reach of any retroactive child welfare investigations.

Besides, it's not like I burned the house down or poisoned the neighborhood.

At seven, I was strange. We had just moved onto Beards Landing, and everything about it felt oversized: the sprawling front yard where grass refused to grow, the endless woods behind it that smelled like sap and damp earth, and my cavernous bedroom with its deep, yawning closets that seemed eager to swallow me whole.

That first summer, I had the woods to myself. I scrambled up a rock face so sheer I got vertigo halfway up, crept across a crumbling old dam with a creek gurgling below, and dragged a rickety wooden ladder to the mouth of an abandoned well just to see what lay at the bottom. (*Spoiler: mostly mud and dead leaves.*)

But then November arrived, and adventure lost its appeal. The trees turned brittle, the ground froze, and my fingers numbed too quickly to climb, balance, or investigate. That's when I discovered the basement crawl space.

At first glance, the basement had nothing to offer beyond cold cement and the occasional smell of heating oil. One side held a ping-pong table--clean, safe, and no fun for one kid.

The other side, however, was a different world entirely.

Tucked in the far back corner, beside the oil tank and washer-dryer, was a rough, four-foot-wide hole in the wall. It sat just high enough off the ground that I had to drag a wobbly kitchen chair over to climb in.

The opening's edges were still gritty from construction, and the air that seeped out smelled like damp stone and something metallic, like a ghost breathing through a mouthful of pennies. I ducked inside, and instantly, the outside world disappeared, as if covered by an invisible but powerful cloak.

The space was an eight-by-eight cement box, just tall enough for a short seven-year-old to stand without hitting the ceiling. Lucky me. If I'd been even an inch taller, the rows of nails poking down from the underfloor of the family room would have left puncture wounds.

I never figured out why, but every so often I'd see a

shadow or even a wraith--then have it disappear when I tried to look full-on. I'd like to attribute this to magic or haunting, but this is a scientific study, so I'll leave conjecture aside.

Still, it was freaky.

A dirty, mud-flecked 4 X 2 window allowed no light--and provided complete privacy. The only illumination came from a single dangling 75-watt bulb, its pull-chain swaying slightly when I moved. If I jostled it too hard, the glow flickered, giving the whole place the feel of a mad scientist's lair.

Which, in short order, it became.

My dad was a dental technician. His lab smelled like minty plaster, hot metal, and the faintly medicinal scent of acrylic teeth. He sculpted dentures with a careful hand, filing and polishing until they gleamed. I had no interest in the finished products, but the scraps--oh, the scraps--were treasures. He let me take home wax sheets, extra teeth, and whatever odds and ends he didn't need.

Down in my crawl space, I'd press the wax into monstrous shapes, creating nightmare dentures that would have sent any orthodontist into cardiac arrest. The light bulb became my kiln, melting the wax until it left greasy, translucent streaks on the glass, dimming its glow into a mysterious, orange haze.

Every now and then, I'd mess with the light bulb, though I never figured out exactly how. The bulb would flare brightly, then go out, followed instantly by the entire basement's plunge into darkness. This meant the washing machine would stop, the only thing Mom would care about.

I held a flashlight for Mom and watched closely the first

time she healed the basement blackout. I memorized the steps: flip the fourth circuit on the right-hand side, restart the washer. Just like that, I was self-sufficient in home repair.-- and keeping prying eyes--and their inevitable questions--at bay.

If those early, eerie, toothsome sculptures had ever left the basement and made it into my bookbag and then to school, I would have spent less time in the principal's office and a lot of time with the school district psychologist.

I might even have become a syndrome.

Then came Christmas.

At seven, I didn't care about the size of the haul--Christmas was magic because the whole world transformed overnight. The house smelled of pine needles and something sweet baking in the oven, cinnamon and vanilla thick in the air. The tree, a noble fir, stood glowing with tiny glass ornaments, each reflecting the lights like frozen fireworks.

Rules disappeared for the day. Pajamas until noon? Allowed. A candy cane before breakfast? Encouraged. Relatives we barely saw arrived with tins of homemade fudge, their coats dusted with snow, shaking off the cold as they stepped inside. Laughter mixed with the crackle of the fireplace, and somewhere in the background, Bing Crosby crooned from the record player.

By Christmas afternoon, the floor was buried in shredded wrapping paper and ribbons curled like question marks. Empty boxes stood like abandoned fortresses, Scotch tape clung to socks, and the air held that strange mix of excitement and exhaustion unique to Christmas Day.

Then came the moment of quiet--the Christmas night

hush--when the chaos settled, and I could take stock of my loot. And this year, my basement lab had hit the jackpot: a chemistry set with powders and vials that practically whispered *mad science*, and--better still--a Creepy-Crawly machine. The possibilities shimmered before me, bubbling with promise.

For the uninitiated, the Creepy-Crawly machine was a tiny hot plate that came with metal molds and bottles of something called Plasti-Goop--a viscous, liquid that could be baked into rubbery spiders, lizards, and other grotesque critters. The box was plastered with warnings about fire hazards and the need for adult supervision. These warnings lasted about as long as the wrapping paper. By December 26, the entire setup had vanished into my crawl space.

The chemistry set followed.

Now, when I use the word *experiments*, don't picture the scientific method. I wasn't formulating hypotheses or recording observations. My entire process boiled down to:

• Step 1: Grab two or more substances.

• Step 2: Mix them together.

• Step 3: Apply heat and see what happens.

This approach led to several critical discoveries:

1.   Plasti-Goop, when overcooked, releases a smell not unlike burning tires.

2.   Heating unknown chemicals over a bare light bulb produces smoke that might--hypothetically--set off a fire alarm. Thankfully, such devices weren't common.

3.   Potassium nitrate and sugar, when combined in

the right proportions and heated, make a decent smoke bomb.

That last one almost got me killed.

One late-afternoon, I got the mixture just right, held it to the bulb, and watched in awe as a thick, gray plume curled toward the ceiling like some malevolent genie escaping its lamp. At first, it was mesmerizing--the way the tendrils of smoke twisted and bloomed in the dim glow. Then, almost instantly, the laboratory transformed into a suffocating gray void. My eyes burned. My throat seized. I took one breath and immediately regretted it--the air was dense, acrid, and hot, as if I'd just inhaled the ghost of a car fire.

Panic hit fast. Burning eyes. Pain-pierced lungs. Need to escape. First--oxygen. Crawling toward tiny, grime-encrusted window. Never once opened.

My fingers scrabbled at the latch, slick with sweat, as my lungs shrieked for oxygen. My head pounded. My vision blurred.

Then--finally--movement. No god descended from the rafters to save me. Just one sticky window latch and the sweet, sweet hand of freezing air. I shoved the window open with the desperation of a drowning man clawing for the surface. A gust of frigid, 25-degree air slapped me in the face, and I gulped it down like water, my chest heaving, my pulse hammering in my ears.

For a few minutes, I just stood there, coughing up who knew what carcinogens, shivering, my head stuck out into the night like a cartoon burglar caught in the act. The smoke curled behind me, sluggish now, drifting toward the opening like an exorcised demon slinking back to hell.

Eventually, my breathing steadied. My coughing became intermittent. My vision cleared. My crawl space--my sanctuary, my laboratory--looked like a crime scene. I was covered in sooty dust just thick enough to see. The air still reeked of charred dreams and something sharp and chemical. But miraculously, nothing had caught fire. The bulb still glowed, flickering slightly as if deciding whether it wanted to finish me off.

I had survived.

And more importantly--my secrets were safe.

It's amazing I lived. Between the toxic fumes, the exposed wiring, and my wildly unqualified approach to chemistry, my childhood could have ended in an obituary that read *Cause of Death: Scientific Inquiry.*

By the following November, though, my luck finally ran out--not in an explosion, but in an unexpected growth spurt. To perform my scientific duties, I'd need to walk hunched over like Igor. Oh, the ignominy! One moment, I was a brilliant young scientist on the verge of unlocking the universe's secrets. The next, I was a kid with a scalp full of scratches, reevaluating his career choices.

And so, at eight years old, I hung up my lab coat--or at least the soot-streaked T-shirt that served as one. My genius was no match for growing up. The crawl space was abandoned, left to whatever ghosts or carbon monoxide fumes still lingered.

To this day, I wonder what would have happened if I'd been just a little shorter, just a little less flammable, just a little better at chemistry. Would I have gone on to revolutionize science? Or would I have simply been found one day, fossilized in melted Plasti-Goop, covered with teeth and clutching a still-smoking light bulb?

That was the end of my scientific career. Maybe I was never meant for the lab coat. Maybe my fate was always to be the guy telling the story rather than the one making the discoveries.

Either way, Rota Fortuna kept me turning, smoke-stained but unburned.

Chapter Sixteen

Shooting a Chickadee

George Orwell wrote an essay, set during his days as a policeman in colonial Burma, about having to shoot an elephant, a beast that, by the time Orwell arrived with his gun, was doing no one any harm. Orwell, as the armed white man representing the Crown, knew he *must* do something. He fired, repeatedly, into the elephant's heart and down his throat, but the creature was unable to move or to die. It's a great piece of writing, and I'd recommend you read it. I'd love to have written it. But I didn't.

Orwell had his elephant. I just had a chickadee.

When I was a boy, guns were around the house. My dad had a couple rifles for hunting deer and a shotgun for birds. They weren't locked up, but they were kept on the top shelf in my parents' bedroom closet, which might just as well have been a safe when I was 11. In my memory, I never went into that space.

I had my own gun, nowhere near as powerful as my father's, but impressive in my young hands. An air-powered pellet gun I needed to repeatedly pump by hand, it fired metal pellets the size of a pencil eraser. Honestly, it could do more serious damage than my parents must have imagined when they gave it to me. Its barrel wasn't rifled, so its range was limited and its ammo came out without a spin, lacking the ability of rifle ammo to go in one part of a body and come out somewhere completely different. To my 11-year-old mind, though, it was a sniper's rifle. I was a kid, and probably shouldn't have been given a weapon capable of putting holes in a body where no holes should be.

Whether I should or shouldn't have had it, I did, and I practiced in our backyard, shooting at hand-drawn targets, empty cans, my sister's dolls and, once, a discarded radio. I'd drawn a firing line and set up the targets under the hanging birdfeeder it was my job to fill with seeds every three or four days.

It was fun to look over the damage I'd inflicted on the moment's target, empty sunflower seed shells under my feet, and I'd morph from Daniel Boone to GI Joe to John Wayne while plunking away.

By and by, I became a pretty good shot and took pride in that. Even the chickadees, looking down from the feeder, had gotten used to the phhhhsssst sound of the air rifle and the tiiiiiinnnngggg of the bullet hitting the target. With their black-masked heads, chickadees are hard to read, but I think they were impressed with my aim. I know their bright white chests seemed to swell up with pride that the boy who fed them was such a good shot.

For whatever reason, playing with my gun was a solitary pursuit, and I'd happily put it away for a game of catch or kick-the-can or pepper.

I know my parents didn't *buy* me the gun. Not because I was somehow deprived as a child, but even at 11 I could tell the gun was old--not antique-it-might-be-worth-a-fortune old, but old enough that it wasn't new. Things just appeared sometimes, the result of someone moving away or getting tired of a possession. The gun was an item the tide of good fortune had left behind.

In the same way objects drifted in and out of our life, so with people. My parents had friends who were always around, friends who were there for a season or three and friends who might not come around often but whose stories I knew because they'd been part of my mom or dad's childhood--that ancient time when the earth was just beginning to cool.

The Hansen family was one of those. Mrs. Hansen had been my mother's childhood friend, and though I barely knew them, their stories had been folded into our family history. They had three kids, all older than me, and whenever we visited their lake house, at least one of them tried to teach me something--how to dive, how to snorkel, how to water ski--the things I'd need to be a big kid. Their kindness might have been genuine, but at 11, all I knew was that failing to dive, snorkel, or water ski just meant proving, again and again, how much smaller I was than they.

In my world, the only thing stronger than a Big Kid's judgment was an even Bigger Kid's. With three kids way bigger than me, the Hansen clan's opinion of me mattered. A lot. If I could have found a way to impress them on the water or lakeside, I would have risked almost anything to do so. The most impressive thing I could do was worship them and follow their directions in everything. Their opinions weren't going to be changed by my ability to poorly imitate them, a dance partner always a beat behind.

The year I was 11, the Hansen clan came for Thanksgiving. I don't know why. As a kid, things sometimes just happened. When they got to our house, the older Hansen kids adopted the boredom masks teenagers carry in a back pocket for such events. Not wanting a group of *Big Kids* to be bored on my watch, I asked them if they wanted to shoot my gun. At first, they were unimpressed--or hadn't had a chance to put away their masks, but with a bit of wheedling, they all agreed to come into the backyard.

I encouraged the two Big Girls and Big Boy to hold the gun and sight down it. Then I set up empty cranberry sauce and evaporated milk cans for each of them to shoot at. Because of my hours of practice, I was much better than they, a first for me. Imagine--being better than Big Kids at shooting! This Thanksgiving was turning out to be a red-letter day in the life of Keith.

Not content with demonstrating my marksmanship skills on pieces of trash, I searched for something else to shoot. While the windows in the house were tempting, they wouldn't demonstrate my pinpoint accuracy, even if they would have shown I was one tough hombre. (Here, the phrase "one tough hombre" is sometimes translated "lunatic.") I looked up into the trees, but shooting a branch or pine cone wouldn't have the *oomph* I wanted. And then I saw it--the way to prove I was one of them. The perfect shot.

I raised the rifle's stock to my right shoulder, sighted down the black barrel at my target five feet above the ground. I adjusted my grip, my finger hovering over the trigger. The chickadee bobbed its tiny head, completely unaware.

I hesitated. Then, just like I had so many times before, I took a slow breath, let it out, and squeezed

The chickadee crumpled like a punctured balloon, a soft thud against the frozen ground. A split-second of weightless silence. The gun was still warm in my hands. The shot rang in my ears.

Then I saw it--The tiny body, the blood spreading across the snow like spilled ink. The glass feeder, cracked, hemorrhaging sunflower seeds onto the ground.

Then, finally, I felt it--something slipping down my throat, thick and sour. A fist of regret curling inside my ribs. The Big Kids hadn't moved yet. But I already knew what they would say, what any human being would say.

Then, almost involuntarily, one of them stepped back-- as if I had become something dangerous.

I could feel the weight of their judgment pressing down, heavier than the gun still in my hands.

For a second, complete silence. The Big Kids didn't move. I could take a breath. Then, slowly the Big Kids looked down at the body on the ground, the birdfeeder above, the gun and, after another pause, at me.

The biggest of the Big Kids spoke first.

"What's wrong with you?"

I had no answer but to let my eyes drop to the ground,

focusing on anything other than the miniature carcass.

The other Big Kids spoke, moral outrage dripping from their mouths and eyes.

"You're crazy!"

"What kind of monster shoots a little bird?"

"It's a chickadee," I said, wanting to salvage some pride in my ornithological knowledge.

"It WAS a chickadee!" said Big Boy. "Now it's a nothing."

He was right. The tiny bird's head had been destroyed by the shot. Its white feathers were smeared red, like a torn swab from a botched surgery. Barely recognizable as a bird, the dead chickadee didn't move at all on the frozen ground. The shot, after killing the chickadee, had shattered the glass front of the bird feeder, so sunflower seeds flowed slowly to the ground around the fresh bird corpse.

The Big Kids stared in horror at me, and I wanted to join them. I wanted to be part of the mob judging me, finding me barely human, and driving me off into the forest. Unfortunately, no matter how much self-loathing we monsters feel, we cannot join the band of humanity, at least until the tribe has a chance to forget.

That Thanksgiving, I had much for which to be ashamed and even more for which to be thankful, most of all that my mother called us all in right then and, for reasons I never understood, the Big Kids didn't say a word about my killing a chickadee.

Perhaps they remembered horrible things they'd done as little kids.

Perhaps they wanted me to suffer silently for the rest of the day, wondering when they'd reveal my evil.

Most likely, they'd never imagined a sweet kid like me could *really* have done what I'd really done. For whatever reasons, they kept quiet.

After the Hansens left, I went to the back yard, picked up the dead chickadee and threw it into the bushes. I took down the bird feeder, so my father could buy new sheets of glass for it. I put the pellet gun away in my closet, until I was older. Then I said a prayer for the bird, and vowed I'd never shoot another animal again.

And I haven't.

Come every winter, I look for chickadees and make sure they have seeds.

When they turn their heads sideways, I know they haven't forgotten a thing.

Chapter Seventeen

Tone Deaf at Full Volume

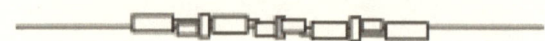

Music flowed through my childhood, skipping and crackling like the scratchy vinyl on our living room hi-fi. As a kid, I'd sprawl across the carpet, my cheek pressed to the rough weave, soaking in the melodies. The room smelled faintly of furniture polish and mothballs, a scent that somehow felt like home.

I didn't listen to babyish or little kid music--we didn't have any. Before I was born, my parents had been members of the Columbia Record Club, which asked members to check their favorite genres. Mom was a serious piano player, so Classical must have been given a check, and both my parents liked the wit of Broadway Musicals. Those were the only choices for music in our house.

I avoided Mom's classical collection.

We went to a plain old mainstream Protestant church, lacking any of the religious gewgaws found in Catholic churches. The Durham Community church worshiped the same way its members drank: Scotch or Bourbon straight up and in conservative moderation. No blood, no wounds and no bodies on the cross--the Catholics were welcome to that. Our cross resembled a lower case "t" in Times New Roman Font. Likewise, our home was kept neat and tidy with no Palestinian corpse figurines cluttering up the place.

Mom, though, was a secret pagan. The hi-fi was her altar, and the objects of reverence were classical music discs. Her household gods? Bruno Walter, Eugene Ormandy, Arturo Toscanini, Otto Klemperer and other high-priest conductors of sacred symphonies. For me to touch a classical musical disc would be like an ancient Jewish kid breaking in to the Holy of Holies to use Aaron's rod for a game of stickball.

Mom, for once, needn't have worried. I didn't stay away from Mahler or Mozart because of their sacredness. It was the music itself. If there's an antonym to the second word in "music appreciation," that's what I felt.

The show tunes, though, offered great opportunities for me to join right in. I knew all the words to dozens of musical theater classics, from the majesty of "Oklahoma" to "South Pacific's" inspiring "You've Got to be Taught" to the sickly sentimentality of "The Fantasticks" "Try to Remember." I could sing along all afternoon.

Except . . . I couldn't sing.

Technically, that's not true. I could and can make musical sounds with my voice. I just can't do so consistently and certainly not with a set tune. I would not be a prisoner to melody or rhythm or any other hobgoblin of little musical minds. Still, I would chant loudly and happily along.

Show tunes filled the air and my ears, their dramatic highs and syrupy lows weaving around me as if they were a warm quilt on a winter evening. The lilting refrains of *Lil' Abner* or the swelling crescendos of *Carousel* didn't just play--they enveloped me. Each crackle, each pop of the vinyl, felt alive, like the music was telling me secrets only I could hear.

Looking back at the mid-60's, it's laughable how out of sync I was with the world. While other kids were going crazy for the Beatles or, for the Hipper than Thou Crowd, Dave Brubeck, I was lost in a Broadway dreamscape, enchanted by over-the-top dramatics and glittering orchestral flourishes. I could almost smell the greasepaint of imaginary stages, feel the phantom spotlight warming my skin. It was as though the music had claimed me, shaping my eccentric, melodramatic tendencies long before I knew the word "eccentric" existed.

The living room was the beating heart of our musical life, a brightly-lit space cluttered with overstuffed chairs, dog-eared sheet music, and the imposing silhouette of our baby grand piano.

My mother had excellent taste, which makes her decision to paint our white piano the color of a green avocado even more inexplicable. To my knowledge, she never suffered any blows to the head. A graceful musical instrument was transformed into a huge baby turd in our living room.

Despite being the same color as all our kitchen appliances, the piano was kept in our front window, gleaming in the golden afternoon light that spilled through the lace curtains. My mother gave piano lessons there, her voice alternately encouraging and exasperated as she guided neighborhood girls through scales and sonatas.

But to me, the piano was more than an instrument--it was a forbidden treasure and a setting for musical experiments.

I'd never heard of John Cage as a kid, but I was his unwitting acolyte. As you may know, Cage was either a genius avant-garde composer and music theorist or a complete charlatan and fraud. One of his techniques was "preparing" a piano by placing nuts, screws, wrenches, etc. between the keys before performing. For all I know, apple pie a la mode may have been eaten out of the piano body. A properly prepared piano can be "unprepared" by removing the foreign objects.

Cage, I'm sure, had an intriguing and confusing explanation for this process. After all, his most famous piece is 4'33", which instructs the pianist to sit at the instrument that long, but not play a single note. Only ambient sound fills the concert venue. Ambient sound and quiet outrage as the audience starts calculating ticket costs and how much per second they're paying for nothing.

Whenever my mother wasn't looking, I'd sneak up to the piano, my fingers hovering over the cool ivory keys. Inevitably, I'd succumb to mischief. A Hot Wheels car would find its way onto the soundboard, tumbling through the tangle of strings, or GI Joe would stage a daring mission inside its cavernous belly. The chaotic clang of disrupted chords thrilled me until my mother would swoop in, shooing me away with the stern finality of a judge issuing a verdict. The piano was verboten. Period. At least for me.

Still, on rare evenings, the piano became a centerpiece for our family sing-alongs. My mother's nimble fingers danced over the keys, her playing as smooth and effortless as the gentle hum of summer cicadas outside the window. Dad, who had been a soloist in his hometown church, had a voice like hot fudge--a bass-baritone that was rich and thin at the same time. He was not Paul Robeson, of course--this was small-town New Hampshire--but when Dad sang "Ol' Man River" you could close your eyes and pretend.

Jennifer was not an extraordinary singer--but she didn't need to be. She was cute as a button and well-behaved, so her treble was perfectly adequate. Also, she was born with a sense of what music should sound like and how her voice fit in. She could join Dad on a song and provide exactly what was need-ed. That may be the basis of all choral singing, but I wouldn't know that. I was exclusively a lead singer . . . with no followers.

Dad and Jennifer sang harmonies with varying degrees of success, their voices threading through the music like del-icate embroidery. And then there was me--off-key, off-tem-po, and unashamedly loud. My only strength as a singer was volume. I was not self-conscious about being too loud. I was no prisoner to melody . . . or rhythm . . . or any other so-called element of music. As long as words flowed out of my throat and overwhelmed every other voice in the room, I would leave it to others to figure out where I was going and do their best to meet me there. I was unconsciously godawful while believing I was extraordinarily gifted. Call it the Dunning Kruger Effect for the musically inept.

When we sang "Who Put the Overalls in Mistress Mur-phy's Chowder?" or "I Don't Want to Play in Your Yard," songs that were old even when Mom and Dad were kids, I bellowed with unrestrained enthusiasm. My voice was a clumsy battering ram, crashing through melodies and demolishing any pretense of harmony. Jennifer's face would crumple in dismay, her teary protests blending with my mother's weary sigh as she closed the piano lid, declaring the concert over. Jennifer, sensitive to her role as my mother's protégée, would inevitably burst into tears, partly because it was supposed to be her time with the family and partly, I suspect, because my singing grated on her eardrums.

Jennifer, red-eyed and indignant, would glare at me and declare,

"I can't wait until you go to college so we can sing like a real family. Finally!"

The joke was on her, of course; even at that age, it was obvious to everyone that I wasn't college-bound. No way was I letting my lack of study habits and penchant for mischief take me to a place where people took their futures seriously.

And there I'd be, left alone in the room, free to murder song after song to my heart's content.

By the time I reached junior high, my enthusiasm for music hadn't dimmed, even if my talent remained nonexistent. Oh, at various music teacher's requests/demands I'd learned to lip synch my way through a Christmas concert or a spring chorale. I am even listed on a recording of the school's production of "Oliver," performing the parts of Workhouse Waif #3 and Pickpocket #2. Even on that record, though, I was not allowed to make a sound. The only consolation I had was a sense John Cage would be proud of me. After all, I'd been silent for more than 10 times longer than his signature piece.

Although I realized the audience for my singing was small--composed, I'm afraid of the person I saw in the mirror each morning--I could still conquer the world of music as an instrumentalist. In third grade, I thought I'd found the steed I'd ride to greatness: the flutophone.

The flutophone dates to the 1940s, an era when plastics emerged as the miracle material that would one day transform the world into the paradise we now enjoy. Resembling a pint-sized clarinet, the flutophone was designed to fit snugly in children's hands, promising to turn us into master flautists--or so the marketing insisted. With its glossy white barrel and festive red mouthpiece, I now see it as a Christmas-themed adult novelty.

But to a third grader, the flutophone had a far nobler purpose: an unbreakable sword, a pirate's cutlass, a knight's dagger. Many legendary battles were fought with these plastic weapons as we waited for the music teacher to arrive, the air filled with the clash of flutophones and the occasional dull *thunk* of a well-aimed jab to the ribs.

In theory, all 24 of us would steadily progress in our flutophone training, and after two months of diligent practice, we'd deliver a concert that would leave parents and siblings dabbing their eyes, overwhelmed by the unexpected beauty of plastic woodwinds. And in theory, that's exactly what happened--for 23 of us. Guess who was number 24.

While my classmates learned to shape their breath, glide their fingers over the raised holes, and coax actual music from their instruments, I hyperventilated, stabbing at the finger holes like I was trying to crack a stubborn safe. My notes didn't soar or flow--they shrieked. They wheezed. They came out in strangled bursts, like a robin choking on a peanut.

Before long, the room filled with the sweet, honeyed notes of *Little Brown Jug*, the melody rising and falling in a warm, golden hum. My classmates played together in near-perfect unison, the sound blending into something smooth, something whole. I, on the other hand, produced nothing but bitter, acrid notes that turned their honey rancid. Even when, by some miracle, I blew and fingered properly at the same time, I never found the current of music. Their collective melody was a wide, rushing river of molten steel--I manufactured BBs of noise, tiny metallic plinks that fell straight to the floor, useless and hollow.

It didn't take long for the music teacher to take me aside and gently suggest that I "sit this one out." And by "one," she meant an entire year.

At the concert, while my classmates sat in neat rows, flutophones poised like miniature oboes, I entertained myself--and a few amused parents--by tossing mine higher and higher, watching it spin in the stage lights. By the end of the night, I was the world's first flutophone major, specializing in aerial performance.

Later, in sixth grade, all my friends decided to take music lessons and learn instruments. At first, I assumed this was just a fad, and not one I needed to join. After a month or so, though, when all the guys were still strumming, blowing, plucking and banging away, I reconsidered. By that time, all the best secret society tickets for instruments were gone. Except for one.

I became a tubist, or is it tubaist? Either way, that last sentence is a lie. I didn't play the tuba, I took it hostage and tortured sounds out of it and into the ears of anyone near me. That gleaming brass behemoth dwarfed me and made my head look a rat's struggling to swim in a strong undertow. The cold metal of the mouthpiece tasted faintly of pennies, and the instrument's bulk rested against my chest like a reluctant dance partner.

My arms strained to lift it, the valves sticking under my fingers as though the instrument itself was rebelling against my touch. The first note I managed was less music and more guttural roar, a sound so jarring it made the girl next to me drop her clarinet. I flushed, a hot wave of embarrassment creeping up my neck, but I pressed on, convinced I could tame the beast.

I couldn't.

The tuba became an amplifier for my shortcomings. Every offbeat note, every mangled rhythm, blared through the band room like a siren, drawing winces and side-eyes from my classmates. Before I began my tuba studies, I would have believed a loud, annoying instrument would be right up my alley. The tuba, though, would not, could not be bent to my will. Whatever sound it produced came straight from the bowels of hell--I was merely a middle-man. Somewhere, John Cage might have called it a bold new frontier in avant-garde composition. The band director called it 'a problem.'

The band director, a wiry man with ears sharper than a bat's, finally pulled me aside. His tone was kind, but his words landed with the weight of a funeral dirge: "Maybe music isn't your calling. Or at least not playing it." I nodded, relieved. Then he added, "For every 40 symphony musicians, there are 4,000 audience members. Maybe that's where you belong."

It was the perfect sendoff.

I never played music again. I'd been silenced by teachers,

outshone by my sister, and betrayed by an instrument shaped like a brass toilet. But I wasn't angry. Not really. Some people make music. Some people ruin it. And some people sit in the back of the hall with their arms crossed, scribbling in a notebook, muttering, *"Well, that was disappointing."*

That's where I live now. In the back row. Judging. Not because I'm bitter. Because I finally found a role where no one expects me to stay on key.

Chapter Eighteen

Crushes, Catechism, and a Minnow's Martyrdom

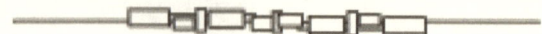

Crushes came easily to me as a boy, like bruises on a kid who runs too fast on hot asphalt--sudden, inevitable, and mostly one-sided. Unfortunately, no girl ever reciprocated. Not even by accident.

Looking back, this made perfect sense. I was always the shortest boy in class, with knees like knobby knobs under scab-crusted shins, my T-shirts smeared with peanut butter and playground dirt, my voice pitched somewhere between a mosquito and a teakettle. I had the look of someone per-manently startled--hair flattened on one side, collar flipped, sneakers untied, socks never matching. My mouth never shut. My brain sprinted ahead of every conversation, trailing tangled parachutes of unfinished thoughts. I could not, would not, let a thought die unspoken.

Had I been capable of stillness--of mystery, silence, shad-ows--I might have stood a chance. But no girl in her right mind longed for the boy who narrated his own lunch chewing or tried to make a fart sound with his armpit in music class.

With real-life love a guaranteed failure, I sensibly turned to the distant and divine. The unattainable. The exquisitely out of reach.

My first true love arrived when I was six.

She was already in her fifties.

Her name was Kitty Carlisle, and she sat, gleaming like royalty, at the panelist table on *To Tell the Truth*, a game show my father watched with the grim attention of a weatherman tracking a tropical depression.

Kitty had cheekbones like temple carvings, lips painted into a precise bow of coral-red, and hair lacquered into a helmet of raven-black armor. Her bouffant shimmered like obsidian under the studio lights. She spoke in crystal chords, her voice chiming like fine glassware being tapped by a silver spoon--each word deliberate, precise, expensive.

She didn't sit; she *perched*. Poised, eternal, the way you imagine a duchess might settle into a chaise after fencing lessons.

I was besotted.

Every afternoon, I retreated to the backyard, to the warped, splintered porch where spiders nested between nail heads and the wood smelled of heat and sap. I'd clutch a sun-bleached two-by-four, its edges frayed and grain rising like old skin, and press it to my cheek like a telephone.

"Kitty," I whispered into the wood's soft belly, tasting salt from my own sweat on my upper lip. "You are radiant. You are everything."

A squirrel skittered up the fence and froze, tail twitching in disdain. Wind sighed through the laundry line, sending one of my father's boxer shorts ballooning into a sky so blue it hurt to look at. The elastic snapped with each gust, clapping like slow applause.

In my head, Kitty's voice drifted through the static of our imagined connection.

"Oh, darling," she cooed, as though reclining on a velvet settee. "I've been waiting for you to call."

Hard to believe no little girl developed a crush on a boy who whispered sweet nothings to discarded lumber.

Eventually, I moved on. I was nothing if not practical.

If Kitty Carlisle and I were doomed by time itself, my next love would be--well, only slightly less impossible.

In the late 1960s, *The Today Show* was hosted by Hugh Downs, Joe Garagiola, and--be still my buttered toast--Barbara Walters.

Barbara wasn't just beautiful. She was composed. Dignified. Radiating the kind of power that made grown men clear their throats and straighten their ties.

Her voice floated across the living room like steam from a teacup--controlled, aromatic, just a little dangerous. Each sentence arrived like a sealed envelope: crisp, meaningful, impossible to ignore. She wore tailored dresses the color of dusk, pearl earrings that winked when she turned her head, and she looked straight into the camera, past the lens, *through* the screen, directly at me.

I sat cross-legged in front of the television, knees popping, my before-school bowl of Cheerios softening into pale glue. Her eyes said: I see you. Her mouth said: You matter.

I was hers. She was mine. The rest of America could go scratch.

Never mind that she'd been born in 1929--the same year as my mother.

Even years later, when *Saturday Night Live* parodied her round-mouthed R's and anchor-matron frostiness, I stayed loyal. Her syllables still landed like velvet hammers in my heart.

If she's still alive and single... well. Call me.

Hard to believe no little girl developed a crush on a boy who had a shrine to Barbara Walters in his heart.

By seventh grade, I had accepted the truth: remote, adult celebrities weren't going to respond to my silent longing. I needed someone accessible. Someone who could physically turn me down.

I chose Carol.

Carol was not a girl. She was an oracle in bell bottoms. She moved like a feather duster in human form--soft, swaying, smelling faintly of citrus shampoo and bubblegum. Her hair was parted dead-center, a perfect highway of scalp running between smooth, glossy flanks that shimmered when she walked past.

She was funny without trying. Smart without showing off. Her laugh bubbled from the back of her throat like soda fizz. I knew, with the absolute certainty of twelve-year-old prophecy, that we were destined for one another.

She knew, with the same certainty, that I was a walking misfire of a boy.

This did not deter me.

One afternoon in science class, as fluorescent lights hummed and the classroom smelled of chalk dust, gum wrappers, and aquarium funk, I made my move.

From the tank near the radiator, I scooped a live sea minnow, its small body slick and urgent in my hand. It writhed against my palm like a living nerve, its silver scales flashing under the buzzing overhead lights. Cold water dripped from my elbow, spattering the floor like Morse code.

Carol was hunched over her notebook, sketching something focused and serious. A flower? A diagram? The future? Apparently, there was schoolwork to be done. I hadn't been informed.

I cleared my throat. The minnow twitched like it wanted to leap from my grasp and flee this unfolding disaster.

"Carol," I said, holding the fish inches from her cheek, "if you won't go to the dance with me... this fish is a goner."

She looked up.

Her gaze was flat and unimpressed. Her hair caught the light like wheat at harvest. She crossed her arms, her face a wall of casual contempt.

She was calling my bluff.

The minnow thrashed, opening and closing its mouth in frantic, airless pleas.

Seconds passed.

Carol did not blink.

The minnow did not survive.

Nor did my dignity.

I went to the dance alone, the ghost of that tiny fish haunting my damp palm for the rest of the night.

But I wasn't finished making a fool of myself for love.

Carol was Catholic. My best friend, John, was Catholic. I was... not Catholic, but I was willing to fake it.

One Thursday, I followed John to catechism, stepping into St. Thomas More Church. The air was thick with old incense and candle smoke, a smell like burnt sugar and secrets. The pews creaked. The altar glowed. Light spilled through stained glass in buttery reds and ocean blues.

John dipped his fingers into a heavy stone basin and traced a cross on his forehead.

I hovered nearby. The water's surface trembled, alive with reflected light. It looked holy. Expensive. Electrified.

I hesitated.

If I touched the water but failed to sign correctly, I'd be exposed. If I avoided it, I'd be branded a godless fraud.

I reached forward.

My elbow caught the edge of the basin.

It tipped.

The Holy Water surged over the rim and cascaded down in a biblical flood, sluicing across the marble floor, pooling beneath pews, soaking hymnals, baptizing my sneakers.

John turned pale. "That water had to be brought in from the Jordan River," he whispered. "That's expensive... and a mortal sin. You don't even know the Hail Mary. You can't be forgiven."

I stood ankle-deep in sacred runoff, blinking through

colored light.

Carol turned.

She sighed. A long, slow sigh, like she was personally bearing the burden of all human disappointment.

"Go away," she said.

And for once, I had nothing to say.

Hard to believe no little girl developed a crush on a boy who accidentally bankrupted the Church.

Chapter Nineteen

A Slow, Lazy Fire: The Science of Smartassery

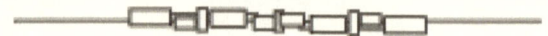

I was not an evil child, but I was wicked, and trust me, the distinction matters--like the difference between a wildfire and a grease fire in your mom's pristine kitchen. Evil is that unstoppable force of nature, charging in with all the subtlety of a demolition crew. Wickedness? It's more like flicking a match into the air just to see where it lands. Evil has a mission statement. Wickedness prefers to improvise.

Where evil sharpens its horns and plots world domination, wickedness leans back with a grin and says, "I wonder what'll happen if I..." It's not trying to torch the house; it's just curious if the sprinklers work. My wickedness was never about destroying--it was about disrupting, a little chaos here, a little confusion there, all with the air of an amateur magician testing tricks that weren't quite ready for the big stage.

Today, I'd like to think I've outgrown all that, but who really knows? The faint whiff of sulfur still clings to my old antics. Sparks might burn out, but memories--and scorched curtains--

tend to linger.

The thing about being wicked is that you don't always get to decide what people remember about you. Years later, I'd learn that some of my mischief had left a lasting impression. I ran into Dianne, an old schoolmate, at our high school reunion.

She was a professor now, full of poise, with the kind of calm self-assurance I imagined her students admire--or fear. After lying to each other about how great we looked, Dianne suddenly leaned forward, her face lighting up as if she'd just discovered an old diary.

"Keith," she said, "I tell a story my students about you every semester."

I blinked, surprised. "Oh yeah? What kind of story?"

She grinned, savoring the reveal. "Do you remember the time you hijacked an entire classroom with your laugh?"

I tilted my head, trying to recall. "You might need to be more specific. Chaos came easily to me back then."

"No, no. This one was legendary," she said, her voice picking up speed. "We were in sixth grade. You were acting up--shocker--and the teacher finally snapped. She pointed at you, her finger trembling like it might combust, and yelled, 'Keith Howard, go to the office!'"

I had and still have no real memory of this, but I started manufacturing one from Dianne's recollection, blurry at first, then sharp.

The classroom air had been stuffy, tinged with the sour tang of wet boots drying on the radiator. Sunlight slanted in through streaky windows, catching the floating dust motes. Desks creaked as kids shifted nervously, pencils paused mid-scratch. And teacher's voice--sharp, brittle, like a snapped ruler--sliced through it all.

Dianne continued, "At first, you stayed in your seat, just smiling at her. That's not what kids do when they're sent to the office. Time slowed down as you gazed at her, and we could feel tension rising. Students don't act like this – they go to the office right away. Without warning, you stood up so fast your chair screeched across the floor. I thought, 'He's going to do it. He's going to the office. Normality will be restored.'"

She leaned in closer, her smile widening. "But then you didn't. You stood there for a few seconds, and then--oh my God--you started laughing."

It hit me like a phantom echo: my laugh, loud and uncontrollable, the kind that started in my chest and exploded out of me like fireworks. I could almost hear it again, bouncing off the chalkboard, ricocheting around the linoleum-floored room.

"At first, we all froze," Dianne said, her voice dropping conspiratorially. "It was like a ripple went through the room. Kids looked at each other like, 'Is this really happening?' And then the teacher lost it. 'Stop that! I said go to the office!'"

She was right--I could picture the teacher, her face flushing a furious red, the veins in her neck like taut strings on a violin. Her fingers curled into fists at her sides as if sheer willpower could force me to obey. And me? I was gone, shoulders shaking, barely able to stand under the weight of my own hilarity.

"She yelled louder, but that only made it worse," Dianne said, almost giddy with the memory. "Your laugh got bigger, louder--like you were trying to fill the room with it. And then, like dominoes, the rest of us couldn't hold it in anymore."

I imagined it clearly now: the muffled giggles breaking free, spreading across the rows of desks like wildfire. One kid snorted so loudly his pencil shot off his desk. Another slapped a hand over her mouth, trying and failing to stay quiet. The sound of laughter swelled, echoing off the high ceiling, spilling out into the hallway.

"And the poor teacher," Dianne said, shaking her head, "she looked like she might combust. Her foot was stomping on the floor, like she thought she could physically stamp out the laughter."

I could see her jaw clenching, her hands shooting up to her temples as if the sheer volume of our chaos might split her skull. But then, something unexpected happened.

"She cracked," Dianne said. "You could see it--her lips twitching, her shoulders starting to shake. And then, boom. She was laughing too. She couldn't stop any more than we could. She was beaten

"She threw her hands up and said, 'Fine! Sit down! Forget the office!'"

My new memory flashed in an instant. The teacher's laugh had started hesitant, almost grudging, before bursting out fully, her frustration melting into something almost joyful. And me? I'd collapsed back into my chair, triumphant, surrounded by the remnants of a storm I'd created out of wickedness and chutzpah.

Dianne was laughing now, tears glinting in the corners of her eyes.

"Keith, I tell that story to my students every semester.

It's my favorite example of how unpredictable people are. How one moment--one laugh--can completely change the energy of a room."

I believe in autonomy, so I won't question Dianne's right to use her memory to illustrate any point she'd like. After all, that's what I'm doing here. Still, my takeaway is a bit different than hers.

I see contempt for power as an effective catalyst for change. Or at least a way to get out of going to the office.

Sometimes, a single laugh can upend an entire classroom. Other times, it takes a little more creativity--like turning a science lesson into a battle of wits over oxidation. But no matter the method, my wickedness always thrived on one thing: the thrill of seeing what would happen next. Case in point: my relentless pursuit of scientific "truth" in Mr. Lefave's sixth-grade classroom.

Mr. Lefave was a kind man, a smart man, a patient man. He had the easy smile of someone who believed teaching junior high science was his calling, not his penance. His dark-rimmed glasses perched neatly on his nose, and his neatly combed salt-and-pepper hair gave him an air of affable dignity. He dressed in the standard-issue teacher uniform of the time: button-down shirts in muted tones, always tucked into khaki pants. He even smelled like a teacher--chalk dust and faint hints of soap--as if he'd been molded for this exact role.

In other words, he was precisely the kind of teacher I wanted to upset.

I don't know what it was about kindness and patience that stirred my mischief, but it did. Maybe it was the challenge, like trying to catch a butterfly in a hurricane. Mr. Lefave seemed unflappable, and I wanted to see his feathers fly.

My first attempts were crude, scattershot efforts--the kind of juvenile rebellion that involved working bodily fluids into scientific discussions.

During a lesson on nutrition, I raised my hand with mock sincerity. "Mr. Lefave, is it possible to extract vitamins from feces after digestion? You know, like recycling nutrients?"

The class exploded into groans and giggles. The girl, sitting two seats to my left turned beet red and covered her face with her hands. A boy snorted so hard it send him into a coughing fit. Mr. Lefave's smile faltered, just for a second. His fingers adjusted his glasses, his professional calm barely wobbling.

"Keith," he said, his voice measured, "we'll save that question for another day."

Encouraged, I escalated. If we were discussing viscosity, I inquired about measuring the stickiness of mucus as it dried. During experiments with calcium chloride's absorbency, my lab report included urine in the variables and included specific observations about odor. Each time, my classmates erupted, and Mr. Lefave sighed, pinched the bridge of his nose, and moved on. His patience was vast, but I was determined to find its limits.

Then came the great oxidation debate.

It started innocently enough. Mr. Lefave was explaining rust--how it's a slow form of oxidation, requiring oxygen and moisture. He added that combustion was a rapid form of oxidation, igniting the kindling of my mischievous mind.

"So," I said, "rusting is slow burning?"

He paused, mid-gesture with the piece of chalk in his hand. His eyes narrowed, not in anger but in calculation--the way a chess master evaluates a move.

"No, Keith," he said. "Rusting and combustion are different processes."

"But they're both oxidation," I countered, my tone feigning innocence.

"Yes, they're both oxidation, but rusting is a chemical reaction requiring oxygen and moisture, while combustion--"

"Is faster. Got it," I interrupted. "So rusting is just fire slowed down by water."

A ripple of laughter coursed through the room. A kid whispered, "Oh man, he's gonna blow."

"No, Keith!" Mr. Lefave's voice rose slightly, his chalk squeaking against the blackboard. "Rusting and burning are not the same thing!"

"But they're both oxidations," I said, my tone edging toward triumph. "So, logically, rusting is just slow burning."

"That's NOT logical!" His voice cracked like a whip. "Rusting doesn't release energy like combustion does. It's a completely different process!"

"Sure, sure," I said, drawing out the words. "But if you think about it, it's kind of like..." I paused, savoring the moment, "a really lazy fire."

The classroom erupted. Even the kids who usually kept their heads down were stifling laughter. some crying tears of suppressed mirth, and one kid was doubled over, pounding his desk.

Mr. Lefave's face turned crimson, his voice climbing into an octave rarely heard in adult men.

"Keith! Rusting and burning are not--NOT--the same thing!!" His hand slammed the desk for emphasis, sending a stack of lab papers flying.

I grinned, feeling the sweet, terrible thrill of victory. "Thanks, Mr. Lefave. I'll make sure to note in my report that rusting is just a slow, lazy fire. Appreciate the clarification."

"THAT IS NOT A CLARIFICATION!" he bellowed. The sound echoed through the room like a thunderclap, leaving a stunned silence in its wake.

That silence broke when a girl's high-pitched giggle escaped, setting off another round of laughter. Even Mr. Lefave's shoulders shook--though whether in laughter or frustration, I couldn't tell.

He drew a deep breath, closed his eyes for a moment, and then... the thumb. His hand shot up, fist clenched, thumb raised high. It was the universal sign for "Out of my classroom."

The laughter followed me down the hall to Mr. Platine's office, where I received my standard detention. Sitting outside his door, I reflected on the encounter.

I'd finally cracked Mr. Lefave, but as the echo of his bellow faded, I felt a pang of guilt. He hadn't deserved it. He was a good man, after all--maybe too good for the likes of me.

Having now confessed my sins, I hope we can agree on two things. First, I was not just a stinker, but a goddamned verbally manipulative stinker. And second, even so, it's pretty satisfying to know that a sixth grader with nothing but a shaky argument could rattle a grown man armed with the rest of the universe.

I was a 12-year-old armed with a skewed sense of logic, a thirst for chaos and the pent-up energy of wickedness, I didn't care. I'd found his weak spot. Oxidation. Who knew science could be so combustible?

Years later, I see these moments differently. They weren't just about testing boundaries; they were about learning how laughter and irreverence could puncture pretense, shift power dynamics, and leave a lasting mark. Whether it was a laugh that dissolved a teacher's fury or a debate that pushed a patient man to his limit, my wickedness wasn't evil. It was curiosity set ablaze.

If wickedness was my spark, the junior high auditorium became the bonfire. It was there, under the fluorescent lights, that I first tested the limits of irreverence on a stage. Running for student council wasn't about leadership; it was about an audience. My speeches weren't campaigns--they were performances.

I ran for office a few times--not because I wanted to lead, but because I loved the sound of my own voice reverberating through an auditorium. While Francis of Assisi sermonized to birds, I had no such constraints. Free speech, to me, meant mocking convention, slaying sacred cows, and fabricating truths with a straight face.

I'm not sure which of my political addresses are taught in school these days, but I'd like to share one from my memory.

Remarks to the Citizens of Oyster River Junior High School--October, 1970

Good afternoon. I'm Keith Howard, candidate for Student

Council Vice President. You may know me as the kid who disrupts class. Guilty as charged. You've seen me sitting outside the principal's office, awaiting his judgment. Absolutely true. You've witnessed my relentless assault on logic, convention, and the patience of every teacher I've ever met.

You've enjoyed these performances, haven't you? So have I.

But today, I'm not here as a clown or an agitator. I stand before you as a revolutionary. Through my sharp political analysis, undeniable charm, and devastating good looks, I present a vision for a brighter future--a future free from the drudgery of junior high, the tyranny of pedagogy, and the defilement of democracy.

I offer you a three-part plan, one that will transform Oyster River Junior High from a mere school into a beacon of freedom, equality, and laughter.

Point 1: Equality in Bra-Snapping

Let's begin with a pressing issue that has divided this school for too long. After consulting with the boys, it's clear that one of their favorite pastimes is the noble sport of bra-snapping. However, upon consulting the girls, I discovered a shocking truth: they do not share the same enthusiasm.

This, my friends, is an asymmetrical battle of the sexes, and it must end. Therefore, I propose a revolutionary solution: henceforth, all boys--students and teachers alike--will be required to wear brassieres during school hours. This bold move will ensure that girls have equal access to the joys of bra-snapping, creating a school where fairness reigns supreme. Together, we will snap our way to justice!

Point 2: Disciplinary Reform

But equality is not just about undergarments; it's about power. And right now, power at Oyster River Junior High is terribly unbalanced. Detention is a privilege reserved for students alone, while teachers roam free, unchecked and unpunished. This, my friends, is an outrage.

Under my leadership, we will reform this broken system. Every student will receive a book of detention slips and the authority to issue them to misbehaving teachers.

Did Mr. Johnson assign homework on a Friday? Detention.

Did Mrs. Smith mark you tardy even though her watch is five minutes fast? Detention.

Together, we will create a school where everyone--students and teachers alike--can experience the quiet reflection that detention provides.

Point 3: The Democratic Republic of Oyster River

Finally, my pièce de résistance: a complete rebranding of our institution. No longer will we be shackled by the mundane name "Oyster River Junior High." Instead, we shall rise as the Democratic Republic of Oyster River!

In this new regime, every decision will be made by plebiscite. Cafeteria menus, homework policies, and even the length of gym class will be decided by majority vote. Every voice--student or faculty--will carry equal weight: 30 votes for teachers, 300 for students. This is democracy in its purest form, a shining example for the world to follow.

I warn you, however: revolutions are not for the faint of heart. There will be challenges, resistance, perhaps even pop quizzes. But if we stand together, there is no detention we cannot endure, no standardized test we cannot overthrow.

So, my friends, I ask you: are you content with the status quo? Or will you join me in building a school that dares to dream? Together, we can snap bras, detain teachers, and revolutionize Oyster River Junior High. Vote for Keith Howard--your Vice President of Revolution--or resign yourself to another year of mediocrity.

Thank you, and may the revolution begin!

The students stared at me, their faces a tableau of confusion and delight. I spotted one teacher in the back furiously scribbling in what I imagined was my Permanent Record. My speech had landed like a paper airplane in a storm--wobbly, but noticed.

Although my speech wasn't a campaign trail success, it was a personal triumph. It cemented my belief that irreverence could puncture pretense and that laughter, even confused laughter, could shake the foundations of power. I didn't just enjoy laughter--I weaponized it.

Some kids threw punches; I threw punchlines. If I could get a teacher to crack a smile, even against their better judgment, that was a win.

Laughter isn't just noise--it's a shift in power. It takes a room from authority's grip and hands it to the mob, even if only for a moment. And once you see that shift, you never forget it.

That sixth-grade oxidation debate? That was more than just me being a wiseass. It was a trial run for what I'd later do in bars, classrooms, and newspaper columns--poking at the walls of authority to see where the cracks might be.

Chapter Twenty

Stupidity: A Case Study

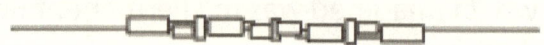

On a beautiful May Saturday afternoon when I was 11, I was in trouble--again. Trouble wasn't just an occasional visitor; it lived with me, like a mischievous twin whispering bad ideas in my ear. Trouble meant being grounded and groundation meant I couldn't leave our property until I'd expiated my sins. To my parents, no theologians, the forgiveness of sins required the shedding of fun. Even though it was a beautiful spring day, a day of which all other early summer days were but pale imitations, I would be imprisoned.

That day, trouble had come in a severe letter from school. That week I'd distributed my own creation: Cheezit Christ's, crackers in a baggy with a picture of The Man Himself promising the forgiveness of sins and a rebirth of snacking.

Honestly, it could have been anything. Trouble wasn't picky.

The important thing was how to get out of it.

My parents and Jennifer were at the high school soccer field at the end of the street. As a prisoner, I was left home. Standing in the kitchen, I racked my brain for a plan. I needed something big. Not just an apology or a token good deed, but a grand gesture--something so dazzling that my parents would have no choice but to forgive and forget.

I scanned the room for ideas. Dishes? Too mundane, and I was supposed to do them anyway. Vacuuming? Not dramatic enough. My thoughts drifted to the garage, and there it was: the Oldsmobile, gleaming faintly in the sunlight that streamed through the dusty garage windows. Washing the car. Perfect.

I could picture the response. *"Oh Keith! We're so proud of you! What other 11-year-old would be so thoughtful. Washing the car--it's a miracle. And so are you! You're just a misunderstood kid and now you've made things right! Forget being grounded-- and here's three dollars. Buy some comic books and candy!"*

A wave of confidence washed over me. *Yes, this will work. They'll come home, see the car sparkling like it just rolled off the lot, and they'll forget all about my latest crime. I'll be a hero-- and never be punished again.*

I strode into the garage, imagining the scene: my mom's delighted gasp, my dad's grudging nod of approval. As the thought blossomed, I felt a swell of pride. *Why didn't I think of this sooner? Heck, they might even not care when report cards come out next month. I envisioned the Beard's Landing Parade that would be held to honor me.*

The garage smelled like oil, paint, and a faint trace of sawdust--a scent that felt heavy with possibility. I grabbed the extra set of car keys from their usual spot in Dad's old cigar box. The keys jingled in my hand, a thrilling sound that seemed to hum with potential. I'd snuck the keys out a few times before when my parents were gone, turning on the engine, pumping the gas and warning Mario Andretti he'd have competition in a few years.

Sliding in, I let a new fantasy take over. What if I took it for a spin? *I've started it before--how hard could it be to put it in reverse, go down the driveway, then go for a drive? Not far--just down the street. I'd pull back in, no one would ever know, and maybe, maybe the Boy girls would happen to see me. "Keith Howard driving?" they'd say, impressed.*

I grinned at the thought. But the reality of my parents' wrath brought me back to earth. The mission was to wipe away old sins, not produce new ones. *Stick to the plan. The future's a big place with plenty of time to drive. Gotta stay focused.*

The cracked leather of the seat was warm under me, and the steering wheel felt enormous in my hands, its texture rough against my sweaty palms. I turned the key just enough to hear the engine growl to life. The sound sent a thrill through me. *It's like the car knows I'm in charge now.*

But as I sat there, I realized something. The car couldn't stay in the garage if I wanted to wash it properly. It needed to be out in the open, where the hose and soapy water could do their magic. I thought again of reversing it onto the driveway, and rejected it. I knew me and knew if I tasted movement from behind the wheel, I couldn't avoid the open road. I shut off the engine and thought.

This is a science problem, so I've gotta find a scientific solution. Let me start by defining the problem: how to move a huge lumbering vehicle 25 feet without using the engine? What are the resources at hand?

I don't know if a lightbulb actually went off in my head, but I immediately thought of social studies class. The Incas built empires without the wheel. I had four right in front of me--I just had to use them right. All I have to do is shift the car into neutral and push it out. It'll show how responsible I am--taking care not to start the engine, saving gas, thinking ahead. Plus, I can handle it. How hard could it be?

Sliding the shifter smoothly into neutral, I hopped out and positioned myself deep in the garage. I looked at the front gill of the car. Piece of cake. The metal of the hood was cool against my hands, and I braced myself to push.

Nothing happened.

The Oldsmobile stood its ground like a stubborn giant. I pushed harder, planting my sneakers against the concrete floor for leverage. My arms trembled with the effort. We'd learned about inertia in science class--a body at rest tends to stay at rest . . . blah, blah, blah. Throwing all my 60 pounds into the task, I'd teach inertia a think or two!

Come on, you stupid thing. You can't be this heavy. I've seen Dad push it a little when he needs to. If he can do it, so can I.

At first, the Oldsmobile refused to budge, a stubborn monument to Detroit's golden age of steel and chrome. My breath came out in short, frustrated huffs, carrying the faint tang of peanut butter from my forgotten lunch. I planted my feet more firmly, the garage floor chilling my ankles through the thin rubber soles of my sneakers. Slowly, with a groan that seemed to come from the depths of the car itself, it moved--just an inch, but it moved. Triumph surged through me.

I'm doing it! I'm actually doing it! Stupid inertia! It's a piece of cake. Why didn't I think of doing this before?

But as the car began to move, I realized my miscalculation. The car was moving slowly, true, but when I tried to slow it down, I remembered the flip side of inertia: a body in motion tends to stay in motion. Gravity was no longer my ally--it had turned traitor. The driveway wasn't flat. It sloped. And the Oldsmobile, emboldened by momentum, wasn't about to stop.

Oh no. Oh no no no. Stop! Stop!

At first, the slow roll was almost hypnotic. The tires crunched softly over the loose gravel just outside the garage, and I marveled at how easy it all seemed. But then the slope grew steeper. A faint metallic squeal from the undercarriage broke the calm, followed by a deeper groan as the car's speed began to pick up.

"Wait--no!" I shouted, the words barely audible over the growing crunch of the wheels. I darted to the front, my heart hammering in my chest, the blood rushing so loudly in my ears that it muffled everything else.

The back bumper loomed above me, its chrome bars gleaming in the afternoon sunlight. I grabbed for it, fingers slipping against the polished metal that felt warm and unforgiving under my hands. A lazy inevitability was in the driver's seat now.

This isn't happening. I coulda gotten run over. This cannot be happening. I'll go to the back and hold on for dear life. It'll work. It has to!

But it didn't. The car was no more slowed by me than it would have been by a dragonfly on the windshield. It slowly, inexorably tore at my fingers, popping them off the bumper one by one, like rivets off a steam engine getting ready to blow.

I'll just jump in and hit the brake. Yes, that's what I'll do. I'll run to the front, jump in the driver's side and slam my foot down. It'll all work out.

It didn't.

By the time I reached the door handle, the car was slowly gaining speed. Slowly, but at an increasing rate. There was nothing more to do than observe a practical application of basic physics: a boy in trouble tends to stay in trouble.

Rolling backward, the car may never have gone more than three or four miles an hour. Speed doesn't make a juggernaut, mass does. Almost two tons of rolling steel slowly rolled down the driveway. It rolled across the street with dreadful grace, and before I could fully process what was happening, it met a relatively immovable object: a wooden light pole across the street. Then and there it remained at rest.

The sound was deafening--a crack that seemed to echo forever. For a moment, everything froze. I stood at the top of the driveway, my heart pounding so loudly it drowned out the world. The car's trunk was crumpled into a jagged mess, glass shards scattered across the pavement like cruel little stars.

Oh God. Oh God oh God oh God. What have I done?

They're going to kill me. They're actually going to kill me. This is it. This is the end of my life.

Tears burned my eyes as I took in the damage. The pole swayed ominously, but it held. Or most of it did. The light fixture at the top broke of and dropped directly onto the front windshield. The Oldsmobile looked like a casualty of war.

And I felt like one.

Think. Think! THINK! What can you do?

My first thought was to find someone else to pin it on.

Mom, Dad, these bad guys were trying to steal our car! They had masks on and they were swearing--really bad swears! Luckily, I thought fast and got Dad's rifle out of the closet and ran downstairs. As I got there, they were backing down the driveway. They saw my gun and jumped out of the car and ran away. Then the car crashed.

Even with my emotions overloaded, I recognized this story as Swiss cheese. Guys in masks walking down Beard's Landing? Did any neighbors see them? See them escape? See me standing in our driveway pointing a rifle? It was a bunkish non-starter

Mom, Dad, I don't know what happened. I was inside vacuuming the floor so I couldn't hear anything. I emptied the vacuum bag to take the trash out and the car was crumpled up at the bottom of the driveway.

They'd never buy that either. I mean the car independently rolling down the driveway was implausible, but the idea of me vacuuming and emptying the trash without being asked was impossible.

I'll run away. Only cowards stay and face the music. I'm

no coward! I'll grab the seven dollars I've got in my sock drawer, plus the money in Dad's change jar on his bureau. I can put some food in my sleeping bag and head out into the woods until this all blows over.

This may have been the dumbest one of all. Unexplained smashed cars don't "blow over," and living alone in the woods, eating graham crackers and peanut butter would get old by dinner time. Anyway, Monday was a school day.

I know. I'll be honest and fess up to what I did. Honesty's the best policy. They might even forgive me right away. I bet they will--they'll be so proud of me.

Without thinking any more, I turned and ran. Up the street, past the rows of houses, to where my parents were watching the soccer game. Each new step filled me with resolve. I would be the George Washington of my generation. I didn't cut down a stupid cherry tree--I wrecked a car and wouldn't lie about it.

My breath came in gasping sobs, my shirt clinging to my back with sweat. People turned to stare as I stumbled into the crowd.

The pride bubbled up and filled me--even overfilled me. Then it popped.

"I didn't do it!" I wailed, throwing myself into Mom's arms. "Mommy! Daddy! It wasn't me!"

Usually, when I'd exasperated her, Mom would take three deep breaths before saying anything. Today, I stopped counting when she got to breath eleven. Then her words came one at a time.

She stared at me, her expression unreadable, her lips pressed into a tight line. Finally, she spoke, her voice sharp enough to cut through my tears.

"What. Exactly. Didn't. You. Do?" Pause. very long pause. "And I want the truth!"

"I didn't do the dishes," I mumbled, staring at the grass as my cheeks burned with shame.

"And what else?"

"I didn't vacuum."

"And . . . "

Ten seconds of silence.

I've explained that I was a wicked boy, but not evil.

Another 10.

Here is the strongest evidence I can present.

Five more seconds of silence.

"I kind of wrecked the car."

My mom's lips pressed into a tight line, her eyes drilling into me like lasers.

"You *kind of* wrecked the car?" she repeated, each word enunciated with surgical precision.

"Well, I mean, technically you could still drive it," I offered weakly.

Her stare didn't waver. My dad, who had arrived mid-confession, pinched the bridge of his nose, muttering something about Darwinism.

That night, I wasn't just grounded. I was excommunicated from fun. I was buried in a dungeon of despair. I was sentenced to eternal groundation, with no hope of parole.

But as I sat in my room, replaying the disaster in my mind, one thought kept me warm: at least I hadn't tried to blame it on masked burglars. I wasn't *that* kind of kid. Not yet.

Chapter Twenty-One

Rubber Boots and Reckless Ambition

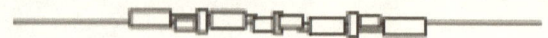

Our garage on Beard's Landing was a portal--not to other worlds, maybe, but to forgotten pasts and undiscovered futures. I never knew what I'd find in its dim, dusty depths. Some discoveries were thrilling, others unsettling, but all of them irresistible. My rule was simple: anything I found was mine. Like a beachcomber with a metal detector, I lived by the law of salvage--if it had been abandoned, it was free for the taking.

One April morning, I had a singular mission: to find my baseball glove. The season had finally arrived, and I was eager to demonstrate a winter of maniacally throwing a tennis ball against our concrete basement wall had improved my throwing, catching, hitting and spitting ability.

But fate had other plans.

As I shifted a pile of sun-bleached cardboard boxes, something long and green and rubber tumbled out, flopping onto the concrete floor like a beached sea creature. I'd never seen their kind before, but I instantly identified them. They were boots, of course, but not just boots. These weren't the kind of rain boots kids wore to splash through puddles.

They were hip waders--taller than my ten-year-old crotch, the rubber stiff with age, exhaling the musty scent of damp decay. The moment I touched them, a ghostly residue clung to my fingertips, an amalgam of stale pond water and something more primal--something that whispered of unseen creatures lurking in dark, brackish depths. I'd never seen waders before, but their purpose was clear. These were tools of conquest, designed to carry their wearer into places no land-bound boy had dared go before.

Beard's Creek was waiting.

And not just Beard's Creek, but the unexplored source of the creek. Just as the Amazon had denied adventurers a peek at whence it sprang, so Beard's Creek had hidden its source from white men.

If you weren't paying attention when you studied the great explorers in sixth grade, I'll give you a thumbnail sketch.

Beard's Creek had changed over the years. When we moved to Beard's Landing, the sluice gate draining into the estuarial Oyster River had been left open, drying the main creek bed into a cracked desert of red Durham clay, its surface fractured into brittle, dinner-plate-sized shards. I had explored those dry lands, turning over rocks in search of stranded fish skeletons, imagining myself a pioneer discovering a long-lost canyon.

But even in those barren seasons, a small body of

water had remained, thanks to a small concrete dam--built, I believed, by either the Iroquois or the Egyptians--had endured--and right behind our house! . I believed I was the only person aware of that dam; I'd sure never seen anyone else on there.

Howard's Pond--my name for the basketball-court sized pool-- remained dark, brackish, and completely unexplored.

To my knowledge, no one alive had ever set foot in its deep, secret waters.

I would be the first.

If I survived.

I stuffed the waders into a burlap sack--another relic from the garage, its coarse fibers scratching my arms, releasing a musty smell of mildew, old potatoes, and something indefinably rotten. Slinging the bag over my shoulder like a shipwrecked pirate lugging stolen treasure, I made my way through the woods, down the steep hill behind our house, and stashed it behind the towering pine where I hid all my most valuable contraband. From the back windows of the house, no parent would ever spot it.

Perfect.

Despite the chill--early spring in New Hampshire, maybe 55 degrees at best--I ran upstairs to prepare. Stripping down, I pulled on shorts beneath my jeans, a strategic move for when I inevitably had to wade into deeper, colder water. Then I assembled my supplies:

• A metal pasta strainer from the kitchen, now repurposed as a makeshift fishing net for the monstrous catfish I was certain lurked in the murky depths.

• A small hammer, for breaking through unknown obstacles.

• My Cub Scout pocketknife, an essential defense against giant snapping turtles, rabid muskrats, or whatever else might challenge my dominance of Beard's Creek.

• And finally, Dad's heavy field binoculars--because any real explorer needs a good view of the unknown.

I made one final reconnaissance check--Dad hunched over the dining room table, lost in a tangle of tax forms, Mom absorbed in her book. The coast was clear.

The grand adventure could begin.

For no particular reason, I zigzagged down the hill like a soldier under fire. Maybe it was instinct, a leftover reflex from my last imaginary battle. I was not just an explorer--I was a spy, slipping past enemy lines, evading both the Nazis and the Japanese. Just another layer of icing for the fantasy cake I was baking. By the time I reached the water's edge, I had fully transformed from a kid in Durham to a daring adventurer poised at the brink of discovery.

When I reached the water's edge, I raised the binoculars to my eagle-sharp eyes, scanning the distant shore like a captain searching for land across an endless sea. A quick calculation suggested it was somewhere between 100 feet and 3,500 miles away. Using my keen navigational knowledge, I mentally split the difference--about 1,500 miles from my backyard to the far shore. I needed to be prepared for anything. And I was.

I took off my shoes, socks, shirt and pants, folding

them as neatly as my excitement would allow. I put on the waders over my shorts. They were heavier than I expected, stiff and unwieldy, the rubber clinging to my legs like thick, damp skin. Knowing the dangers ahead, I brought only the essentials: a hammer in my belt loop, my knife clipped to my shorts, and my colander, ready for deep-sea samples.

I placed the binocs safely in the tree crook. If I didn't return, I didn't want Dad mad at me for losing them.

I gave the expedition my green light and set off.

The first few steps were easy. Like Columbus looking back at Spain, I could see what I was leaving behind while unaware of what lay before me. The rocky bottom stretched about ten feet from shore, solid underfoot, giving me dangerous confidence. The water was cold but hadn't overcome the wader's height.

I was invincible.

Then, without warning, the bottom disappeared.

A sickening lurch, a rush of cold up my spine, and then--nothing. The ground was gone. One step--solid ground. The next--nothing. My foot sank into something soft and shifting, and before I could react, the creek wanted to swallow me whole.

You may think of clay as a thick, moldable substance used in pottery. And it is--when solid. But submerged under water, red Durham clay transforms into something else entirely. It turns to quicksand, dissolving into a soupy, bottomless trap. Without so much as a yellow warning light, the rocky shoreline vanished beneath me, replaced by wet, sucking mud. My waders plunged a foot deeper.

Ice-cold water surged in, racing up my legs, wrapping around me like a frozen second skin. The cold hit me like a punch, knocking the breath from my lungs. My chest clenched. My limbs locked up, slow and sluggish in the frozen water

I was no longer an explorer. No longer an adventurer. No longer a soldier behind enemy lines.

I was a very wet, very cold, very scared ten-year-old.

And then I saw it.

A muskrat.

Gliding effortlessly across the water, its slick brown fur unbothered by the icy chill, it locked eyes with me. It knew. It knew I was doomed. It knew I had no business being here. It paddled a slow, judgmental circle around me, whiskers twitching. I could hear the tiny plop of water dripping from its tail, see the ripple it left behind, feel its beady-eyed scrutiny drilling into my soul. Then, without a sound, it vanished into the reeds.

I was something of an expert on muskrats. And I knew what this meant.

It had gone for reinforcements.

Frozen in place, watching my life slip away, I recalled everything I knew about muskrats:

- Muskrats eat five times their weight daily.

- Their diet consists of fish, bears, wolves, and under-prepared children.

- They grow up to 11 feet tall and weigh 235 pounds.

- All muskrats are rabid.

- If you are attacked by muskrats, try to die quickly. If you somehow survive, doctors will inject you with anti-rabies serum for 20 agonizing days.

- It won't save you.

I'd gone from invincible to doomed.

A less courageous boy might have whimpered, crying out for his mother.

A less resourceful boy might have thought he was finished.

A less resilient boy might have assumed he was fated for a short, tragic life of feeding turtles and catfish.

I was none of those boys.

But a less foolhardy, less headstrong boy?

He would never have put himself in this position.

And I wasn't that boy either.

At that moment, what kind of boy I was didn't matter. I just needed to get out--of my boots, of the water, of this mess.

All I knew was, "I am here. It is now. Everything else is beside the point." If I'd paid attention when we'd studied Greek mythology, I might have called upon Tethys, the goddess of fresh water. I hadn't, so I didn't.

I was on my own with no divine intervention possible.

I tried using my hands to pull up my waders. No matter what Horatio Alger suggests, pulling yourself up by your own bootstraps is impossible. All I got was cold, wet arms. *I was sinking. The waders, once my glorious ticket to adventure, were now iron weights pulling me deeper. And the water wasn't done with me yet.*

Panic was creeping in, a sinister force whispering that this was how it ended. But I wasn't ready to surrender. I tried pulling my feet free, but the vacuum of the mud tightened its grip. My hands plunged into the freezing water, clawing at the waders, but they were lead weights, anchoring me in place.

I knew what I had to do.

With numb fingers, I worked at the straps, loosening them, tugging, shaking my legs as best I could. The waders resisted, reluctant to release their prize. But I was relentless. I wriggled, twisted, fought. And then--

POP.

My feet burst free, my body lurching forward, half-stumbling, half-crawling toward solid ground. Water-logged and shivering, I collapsed onto the shore, gasping, limbs trembling, heart hammering against my ribs. My glorious, treacherous waders were gone, a sacrifice to the hungry creek.

I may have made some miscalculations.

But the expedition was far from over.

First, I did a thorough inventory of my supplies.

• Thank God the binoculars had not been touched. Dad would still love me.

• I'd jettisoned the colander when I'd been plunged into the deep. A shame. I liked spaghetti.

• The hammer, which had been in my belt loop, must have fallen out in the turmoil. It would deserve a funeral someday to commemorate its being lost at sea.

• My Cub Scout knife remained clipped to my shorts. "Be prepared," indeed. I'd probably get an award of some kind for this mission.

I remembered an often-overlooked part of being prepared--disposing of evidence. The waders were safely underwater for at least 300 years and the colander and the hammer, now on the sea floor, would rust away to nothing by Monday. The only incriminating materials left--my shorts and underpants--could safely be left in the woods. Birds would make nests of their tattered remains.

Now that my life had been spared and I'd covered my tracks, I felt the late-morning sun warming my skin. That meant I'd regained my sense of touch after the frigid onslaught!

To celebrate my return from the dead, I stripped off the wet shorts and underpants and put on my clothes, now almost toasty from sitting in the sun. My knife made shredding the wet clothes a breeze, and I felt downright Francis of Assisi at my kindness to the birds.

Wanting to return my knife to my bedroom, I walked past Dad, face still buried in tax schedules and forms and other grownup stuff.

"Where you been?" he asked, not looking up. He didn't have a clue.

"Just looking for my baseball glove," I said. "Some of the guys are gonna shag balls and stuff."

Dad turned and looked me straight in the face. My recently warmed body went cold. Was he on to me?

"Keith, Keith, Keith," Dad said. "Don't you remember

you used it as a goalie's glove when you guys were playing hockey? It's still in my trunk."

He pushed away from the dining room table and walked toward the garage.

I watched him go. Time for a brief after-action report.

Mission Accomplished with Highest Honors and Distinction and a Bronze Star with a cherry on top.

Chapter Twenty-Two

I Loved the Library. The Library Tolerated Me.

I can't remember my first trip to the library--it feels like it's always been part of my life. Every journey began with me climbing into an old red wagon, its chipped paint and squeaky wheels making the short walk feel like an adventure.

We'd stroll up a quiet street, sunlight filtering through maple and oak branches, scattering shadows on the pavement. The smell of fresh-cut grass mingled with diesel fumes from school buses. Crossing Mill Road felt daring as we dodged shirtless fraternity brothers tossing footballs, their laughter adding to the thrill of the journey.

When we reached the University of New Hampshire campus, its gravel paths crunching underfoot, the world seemed to open up. As we approached the campus, the brick buildings seemed to hum with secrets and discoveries waiting inside. To four-year-old me, this wasn't just a walk--it was a pilgrimage. Dimond Library rose like a grand citadel, where all 6,000 of us in Durham could borrow books alongside university scholars.

As we reached the steps of the library, my mother tightened her grip on the wagon handle and leaned forward, pulling me up the stone stairs with deliberate effort. The wheels bumped and clattered, the wagon lurching like a stubborn mule refusing to climb. I gripped the sides, my excitement mounting as the heavy doors loomed ahead.

My mother paused to catch her breath, brushing a stray strand of hair from her forehead, then pushed the door open with a creak that echoed through the quiet entryway. The cool air rushed out to meet us, bringing with it the faint scent of ink and polished wood.

"All right, Keith," she said, her voice both encouraging and commanding. "Let's see what treasures we can find."

To my young mind, the library's red-brick walls and white-trimmed windows were ancient, as though they'd been built by hands much older and wiser than ours. In reality, the building was just a few months older than me, having opened in late 1958. But I liked to imagine the books had lived somewhere mysterious before the library existed--a hidden trove of treasures waiting to be unearthed.

Inside, the cool air wrapped around us, carrying the faint scent of ink, waxed floors, and old paper. The library had six stories, an elevator, and an entire world beyond what I knew. But I only needed one room: the children's section--my personal kingdom.

I darted ahead, my feet skidding slightly on the smooth, waxed floor, as I made my way toward the picture books. The shelves stretched around me like a fortress, each book a brick containing its own world. I walked quickly along the aisles, running my hand lightly over the spines, their cloth covers rough against my fingertips. One book slipped loose and tumbled to the floor with a satisfying thud. I crouched down to pick it up, glancing over my shoulder to make sure no one had noticed, then hugged it to my chest as if I'd found buried treasure.

Sunlight warmed the yellow walls, and low shelves filled with picture books stretched like a colorful maze. Cracking open a library-bound book felt like unlocking a treasure chest. *Make Way for Ducklings* and *The 500 Hats of Bartholomew Cubbins* carried me into ponds and hat collections, while my mother gently guided me, encouraging me to explore.

I carried my chosen books to a small table in the corner of the room, where sunlight spilled across the polished surface in golden streaks. Climbing into a chair, I spread the books out like a feast, my fingers tracing the illustrations on the covers.

Before I could decide where to start, a soft voice interrupted me.

"Would you like me to read that one to you?" I looked up to see a smiling college student, her hair pulled back in a neat ponytail. Without waiting for an answer, she pulled out a chair beside me and opened *Make Way for Ducklings*. Her voice rose and fell with the rhythm of the story, drawing me in as I leaned forward, completely absorbed.

The children's room wasn't just for kids. Female college students often lingered in the children's room. They swooped on kids, practicing reading out loud with picture books. Their soft voices and encouraging smiles made them magical to me. I basked in their attention, convinced I was their favorite.

One of them would settle into a low chair, holding up a book with the practiced poise of a storyteller. Her voice had the rhythmic cadence of Dr. Seuss, making every word sound like a personal performance.

Another might lean in close, chin resting on her hand, her gaze fixed on me like I was the most interesting person in the room. The faint floral notes of their perfume mingled with the musty tang of old books, creating an atmosphere I can still recall vividly.

"Why is Mrs. Mallard afraid of turtles?" I'd ask, my brow furrowed in genuine curiosity. "Turtles are nice."

"Snapping turtles aren't nice--they'd eat baby ducks."

"Those are ducklings," I'd say, my tone serious as I nodded in agreement, eager to show my understanding. The coed would laugh, a light and musical sound, and reach out to ruffle my hair.

"Keith, you are very smart."

"I know," I'd say, then return my attention to the book.

While the coeds entertained me, Mom had her own sacred ritual of diving into books--a practice that would shape my own approach to reading. After a brief word with one of the coeds, she'd kneel until her face was level with mine, her hands resting lightly on my shoulders. "I'm going to look at grown-up books now," she'd say, her voice warm and reassuring. Then she'd nod toward Kathleen, Linda, or Barbara--whoever had taken up the mantle that day. "She's going to stay with you and read until I come back."

Kathleen--or whichever future teacher had been assigned to me--would pat her lap with a playful smile. I'd grab a couple of books from the nearest shelf and crawl into her perfumed embrace. The fabric of her dress felt smooth against my arms, and the rhythmic sound of her voice as she read about Little Bear's adventures seemed to vibrate through me. *Little Bear* was one of my favorites, especially the story about his trip to the moon.

"Do you think he really went to the moon?" she'd ask, her tone curious, trying to coax me into thinking deeper.

"It's probably pretend," I'd admit, "but it's *brave* pretend."

With no transition, I'd look up into her eyes. "Do you think I look like Little Bear? I do."

My reader would look down, evaluation in her eyes.

"I can see a family resemblance,"

At some point during these visits, the urge to test boundaries would strike me. Once, while the coed was focused on reading, I quietly slid off her lap and crawled beneath a nearby table, taking one of my books with me.

"Where did you go?" her voice called, light but confused. I stifled a giggle, peeking out just enough to catch her glancing around.

When she spotted me, crouched like a turtle under the table, she laughed and said, "Are you hiding like Little Bear on the moon?"

Pleased with myself, I crawled back out, grinning. "No, I was practicing being brave."

Eventually, Mom would return, her arms stacked high with books. She'd sink into a nearby chair with a sigh of satisfaction, the faint scent of mildew and ink rising from the pages. Watching her disappear into a book felt like seeing magic--her face softening as she journeyed to a place I couldn't yet follow.

Even then, I understood the power of books to transform the mundane into the extraordinary.

Mom's love for reading was boundless. She devoured everything--literary fiction, detective novels, gothic romances--her appetite as varied as it was insatiable. To her, books weren't trophies to display but doors to be opened. I learned early that it didn't matter whether the door was gilded or battered; what mattered was what lay beyond. It's no wonder I grew up the same way, with one small difference.

For Mom, opening a book was a commitment--each one a train she'd follow to the end. I, however, saw books as apples in a boundless orchard, sampling and discarding them as I pleased. Even now, I rarely remember how most of them end. But I've never forgotten how they made me feel.

I left the library after every visit with my arms full of books and my head buzzing with stories. To my young mind, I was the center of the universe, a boy who had charmed both the coeds and the library itself. Surely the world, I thought, had turned its full attention to me.

As it should.

By the time I was in second grade, we'd moved to Beard's Landing, making the walk to the library a solid 15 minutes instead of five. For a "certified big kid"--and yes, six- and seven-year-olds were big kids in those days--this new distance meant more independence. I could walk to the library with friends after school, clutching my book bag.

None of us carried rucksacks or backpacks--those were for camping. Instead, we dragged around oversized, waterproof pillowcases with drawstrings, looking like tiny sailors heading to sea. While they were supposed to sling casually over your shoulder, I usually dragged mine along the ground. This worked fine until a hole wore through the bottom, which inevitably happened, leaving a trail of books or crayons in my wake.

Although my friends *enjoyed* the library, they never *needed* it the way I did. Like normal drinkers could have a beer on a hot Saturday afternoon or a Bloody Mary with Sunday brunch, my friends saw books as a nice accessory to a trip to the library; for me, books, and signing them out, were the whole, all-encompassing reason. Scott or Gary might sign out a couple books. Or not. I needed at least a half-dozen to make sure I had access to a proper supply.

The freedom to visit the library on my own was momentous. When I first got my library card, I stuck to the usual second- and third-grade fare. But I read fast--too fast for the limited selection I could carry home in my fraying book bag.

Like my mom, I'd discovered an insatiable appetite for reading, but mine came with its own quirks. While she read in more conventional places--the couch, the table, or her bed--I claimed the bathtub as my literary throne. I'd draw a hot bath and stay there until I was prunified, a stack of books balanced on the rim. Dinner was often announced with a loud knock on the door and my mom's exasperated voice: "Keith! You're not a sponge. Get out of there!"

Even at that age, I had what I considered a sophisticated approach to reading. I hated the frustration of picking up a book and realizing I'd already read it, so I made a point of reading everything by an author in order. Hugh Lofting's *Doctor Dolittle* books were my first great literary conquest. From *The*

Voyages of Doctor Dolittle to *Doctor Dolittle's Puddleby Adventures*, I worked my way through every title, each smelling faintly of dust and old cardboard boxes.

Other series followed. *The Chronicles of Narnia*, which, even at nine I felt was too heavy-handed with the religious stuff, although I did love Reepicheep. All of Beverly Cleary, naturally. And one of my favorites: Encyclopedia Brown, the boy detective. Before I was halfway through most of the stories I'd figured out the mistake the villain, large or small, had made. Each series had its own feel and each book its own world.

And then, there was the taste. Most readers wouldn't understand, but books from the 1920s and 1930s had a flavor that newer ones lacked. This wasn't some abstract idea--I knew this firsthand.

I had developed the habit of tearing tiny corners off the pages as I read, rolling them into little wads, and chewing them like gum. It was a bad habit, sure, but one I indulged until I was old enough to realize the librarians might use dental records track me down and take away my borrowing privileges . Years later, I'd revisit those books and see my handiwork: rodent-like indentations in the corners of well-thumbed pages. I'd run my fingers over the bite marks and marvel at my younger self's strange, tactile connection to stories.

By fourth grade, I had outgrown the children's room. I'd read my way through its low shelves and cheerful walls and set my sights on the Browsing Room. Twice the size of the kids' section, it was filled with recent adult purchases and perennial fiction favorites, all neatly arranged on taller, more intimidating shelves. Walking in felt like entering a foreign country--a place where I didn't quite belong but desperately wanted to explore.

The Browsing Room helped me get way over my literary skis. At 11, I devoured *The Catcher in the Rye, Franny and Zooey* and *Rabbit, Run*. I had no idea what masturbation or infidelity were, but I read with the conviction of someone certain he was unraveling life's mysteries. Salinger's Holden Caulfield became a kindred spirit, though I doubt I understood half of his complaints. Updike's Harry Angsrom? He was just as fascinating, though I probably read most of the book with my head tilted like a confused puppy.

I remember an older man once spotted me reading *Catch-22* and asked, "Do you even know what a catch-22 is?"

I smiled and nodded, then contradicted my outside self-assurance. "Not exactly," I admitted.

"Neither do I," he laughed, and walked away.

"Another phony," I thought, "just like Holden Caulfield talks about."

As I sat there, nose buried in books far beyond my years, I occasionally caught glances from the college students working at the checkout desk. In my mind, they were impressed by my precociousness, admiring this small boy fearlessly navigating adult literature. Looking back, they were probably wondering why a fifth-grader was reading *Portnoy's Complaint* and whether someone should step in.

One day, as I returned *Rabbit, Run* to the counter, one of the coeds leaned over and asked, "You're really reading these?"

"Of course," I replied, trying to sound nonchalant.

"Do you... like them?"

"They're okay," I said, shrugging. "I mean, I read all the Encyclopedia Browns."

She laughed, a genuine sound that made me feel both proud and slightly ridiculous. I probably puffed up with pride at her attention, but there was also a flicker of self-awareness-- maybe I wasn't quite the literary genius I pretended to be.

These moments, small as they were, left an impression. The library was more than just a building full of books; it was a stage where I could test out different versions of myself. A child reading beyond his years. A connoisseur of old novels. Whether I was chewing corners of *Doctor Dolittle* or pretending to understand *Portnoy's Complaint*, I felt like the library was a place where anything was possible. There, I was a boy who believed every librarian and coed was secretly rooting for me-- even if they thought I was a little weird.

Time passes. Eventually, I left home. My parents moved from Durham to Lee, a tiny adjacent town, and my mom switched her literary allegiance from the vast ocean of the UNH Library to the smaller pond of the Lee Library. She loved it. The librarian knew her taste--anything that could be read-- and would keep new purchases tucked under the counter until Mom stopped by every Thursday afternoon on her way home from work.

Now, when I drive through Durham, I sometimes detour into the past, memory pressing against the windshield like mist on a fall morning. Once, on my way to meet my high school best friend Jonas, I stopped at the Lee Library on a whim. I wasn't looking for a specific book or title--just something, some faint connection.

When Mom died in the winter of 2001, instantly and painlessly from an acute brain hemorrhage, my family asked that donations in her memory be made to the Lee Library. It seemed fitting--she'd spent so many hours there, immersed in the worlds within books, always coming home with more than she could possibly finish in a week. Dad, always one for gestures, brought a framed photograph of Mom and her younger brother to the library, asking that it be placed on the wall.

The photograph was taken by my Gramper around 1937. In it, Mom sits like a little princess, a book open on her lap, while her younger brother gazes at the pages as though trying to decipher their meaning. To me, he looks less like a reader and more like a vassal, dutifully waiting for orders. It's easy to read too much into an image--especially one as playful as this--but it's undeniably perfect for a small-town library. Granted, she's reading *The Bobbsey Twins in a Radio Play*, not one of the classic titles about Freddie, Flossie, Bert, and Nan. (And, yes, even if admitting it costs me my dignity, I've read into the Bobbsey oeuvre myself.)

After a couple decades, I assumed the photograph had been taken down, packed into a box, and likely sent to the dump. But when I walked into the library that day and mumbled something about "a picture of my mother and uncle from the '30s," the desk librarian knew exactly what I was talking about. Without hesitation, she led me around a corner to the reading room, where the photograph still hung, pride of place.

The librarian remembered everything. She remembered Dad bringing in the photograph and telling her stories about Mom. How she'd been delivered into the world by her grandfather, a country doctor. How she spent her early years in Colebrook, where her father was the schoolmaster, before moving to Weare when he became principal. How, at seven, she came to Durham, where her father became the founder and first director of the Thompson School. The librarian even remembered Barton Hall, the ugliest building on the UNH campus, which was named after my grandfather when he retired.

And she remembered Mom.

I stood in the quiet reading room, staring at the photograph, the years collapsing into a single breath. Mom wasn't just a memory. She was still here, tucked between the shelves, waiting in the pages. The librarian's memory was like a bridge, spanning decades and connecting me to Mom in a way I hadn't expected. It struck me that libraries, like photographs, are keepers of stories--some written, some told, and some only hinted at in the details we notice when we stop long enough to look.

As I left the library, I realized the photograph wasn't just a tribute to my mom's love of reading; it was a testament to the way she lived. She wasn't someone who displayed her books or talked about what she'd read to impress anyone. To her, reading wasn't an escape--it was an act of curiosity, a quiet insistence that the world was bigger and more interesting than it sometimes seemed.

The picture remains on the wall, and in some ways, so does she.

Chapter Twenty-Three

The Freight Train and the Baby Carrot of Shame

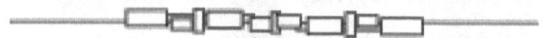

Kids all over the world have coming-of-age ceremonies, trials they must overcome to prove they're ready for adulthood. These aren't just festival showpieces--you remain a child until you complete them.

Among the Satere-Mawe people of Brazil, boyhood ends in the most excruciating way imaginable: with your hands shoved into gloves filled with bullet ants. These aren't your average picnic invaders--they pack one of the most painful stings on the planet, said to rival a gunshot. Boys as young as 12 endure the agony for more than 10 minutes, their bodies wracked with venom-induced convulsions. Why? Because pain is the price of manhood. Survive this, and you prove yourself strong enough for adult responsibilities--hunting, protection, survival.

For the Hamar people of Ethiopia, the path to manhood isn't about enduring pain but demonstrating agility, balance, and courage--by running across the backs of a line of bulls. Friends, family, and potential future in-laws gather to watch as the boy strips naked and takes his leap, hoping to reach the other side without slipping. A successful crossing earns him the status of an adult. Fail, and, well... better luck next time.

Then there's the Fulani, a vast, nomadic people spread across west and central Africa. Their initiation into manhood isn't just painful--it's a battle. Boys around 12 or 13 must face off in a public duel, each armed with a whip of his own making. There's no dodging, no retreat. The goal is to strike, to draw blood, to endure without flinching. But most importantly, to win over the crowd. Because in the end, it's not just about taking the hits--it's about standing tall, commanding respect, and proving that you're ready for the burdens of adulthood.

Manhood, across cultures, often comes down to this: pain, perseverance, and the willingness to endure what should break you.

Most kids in the United States don't get trials of fire and pain. But I was lucky. I grew up in Durham. We proved our manhood by jumping off an incredibly high railroad trestle. Into a river of unknown death. A river that might be filled with lamprey eels--a deadly nonfish/noneel creatures that could suck the life out of you.

Thanks to the Lamprey River, I know I'm a man--if only because I survived.

I remember the day I became a man like it was yesterday.

The ride to the trestle passed in silence--four miles of

steady pedaling, the sun pressing down on our backs, the asphalt shimmering with heat. Every now and then, the crack of gravel under our tires broke the rhythm, but mostly it was just breathing, legs pumping, thoughts drifting.

At Bennett Road, we veered off, coasting the last quarter mile to the dogleg where we ditched our bikes in the bushes. The road had been empty--no cars, no farm trucks--so no one saw us stash them.

Scott tried to walk the ties but couldn't find a rhythm, stumbling like a drunk, muttering curses under his breath before giving up and shifting onto the gravel.

Gary and I had it down--step, half-step, step, half-step--keeping our weight centered, our balance steady. The sun was still low in the morning sky, but the air was thick, the kind that soaked through our t-shirts, gluing them to our backs.

Then we rounded the bend and saw them--dozens of crows, packed tight on the rails, glossy black heads jerking up and down as they tore at something.

The smell hit a second later, hot and sweet and wrong, the unmistakable stink of wet fur and old blood, like the inside of a skinned knee.

We stepped closer, and the crows lifted in a slow, ragged cloud, black wings beating against the thick, humid air. They didn't go far. Just enough to let us take our turn at the carcass.

A beaver. Or half of one.

Its body lay between the rails, a mess of fur and torn flesh, its big, flat tail ten feet away, like the train had sheared it clean off. Blood streaked the gravel, soaking into the wooden ties, dark and sticky in the fading light.

"They're not dumb, though," Gary said, softer than usual. "How'd it not hear the train?"

I stared at what was left of its tail, at the shredded place where it had been.

"Maybe it did," I said. "Maybe it was too busy working to care."

Because that's what beavers do.

Something knocks down their dam, they rebuild.

Water rises, they reinforce.

A flood washes everything away, they start over.

And sometimes, that's how they die.

Not from hunger. Not from old age.

Just because they wouldn't quit.

We walked until we reached the bridge.

And as I stood at the edge of the trestle, the Lamprey River below, the steel beam beneath my sneakers, I realized something:

I wanted to be a beaver.

Either so I wouldn't quit--or so I wouldn't have to jump.

The thought of jumping--falling, really--forty feet into a river named after lampreys with their sucking and deadly mouths, these things suddenly seemed stupid.

I imagined hitting the water, surfacing, then feeling that cold, sucker-mouth clamp onto my leg, teeth rasping away at my skin before I could even get back to shore.

That was nightmare territory for sure.

I stood between the railroad tracks, looking up. Above me, the trestle loomed, a tangled maze of rusted beams, ancient bolts, and weathered wood. The scent of hot creosote rose from the planks, mingling with the sharp tang of river water below.

Scott and Gary stood beside me, squinting at the noon sun. The air shimmered with heat.

"Guess I'll go first," I said, peeling off my t-shirt and balling it up before tossing it onto the cinders. I kicked off my sneakers and sent them after it.

"Let's do it," I added, forcing a grin. My gut cramped--a dense, molten warning from the Pop-Tart I'd wolfed down an hour ago. I prayed it was just nerves. But deep down, I knew: something unnatural was coming.

The first step of the jump was, in some ways, the worst. Once you were out on the beam, there was no climbing back. The only way down was forty feet through empty air.

Crawling out from the railroad bed onto the scaffolding meant perching for a moment, body suspended in space, gripping steel while gravity whispered, One wrong move, and you're mine.

If I slipped, I might get lucky and clear the guide wires--just a belly flop from hell. If I hit them, though, I could lose a hand. A foot. Get knocked out and sink like a rock.

Still, I was a man. And men did the things set before them.

I got on my belly, swung my legs over the edge, and clung to the end of a railroad tie, stretching my feet into the void. The girder was three feet out and four feet down.

Think, man.

"A-squared plus B-squared equals C-squared," I muttered. "I'm the hypotenuse of a right triangle. Mr. Stoykovich would be so proud."

Scott and Gary crouched on the tracks, tracking my progress.

"Your right foot's almost there," Gary said. "Couple more inches."

I stretched, toes groping for the steel. My foot landed. I shifted my weight onto it, muscles screaming. Then the left. Got it. Now, I had to roll sideways, reach the outer beam, and pull myself out.

I rolled, caught the beam, and hugged it like a scared kid clinging to his dad's leg.

I was ready.

I was not ready for what happened next.

My fingers gripped the beam, slick with sweat. My legs trembled, the river below looking somehow closer and farther away at the same time. Then--something changed.

A deep, slow vibration hummed through the steel. Not in the beam. In my bones. The air grew thick, charged, like before a thunderstorm. Then--God help me--I heard it.

The whistle.

A train was coming.

Gary and Scott leapt to the far side of the tracks. My heart jackhammered. I wanted to jump--God, I wanted to jump--but I couldn't.

The whistle blasted, slicing through my bones. I could feel the beam tremble beneath my feet, the deep-throated roar of the engine closing in.

I couldn't go up. Couldn't go sideways.

Just me, a four-inch-wide beam, and a goddamn locomotive bearing down.

The engine exploded into view, thirty feet away.

The ground shook. The air burned with heat rolling off the steel. The whistle screamed, not like the soft, distant lull I'd heard at night but the shriek of an owl diving for prey.

I clenched the beam like a lifeline.

The train roared past, each car rattling my spine. My teeth clattered. I had to keep my mouth open to keep from biting my tongue.

I thought of the groundhog I'd once seen carried off by a hawk, twitching helplessly in the talons. I shuddered.

Thirty cars.

A new fear hit me.

I was about to die.

A freight train was screaming toward me at 60 miles an hour. My friends were watching in horror.

And yet, during all this, my body decided that the real emergency wasn't the train, or the jump, or the imminent, gory death. No. It was the half-digested Pop-Tart in my stomach. This was my true rite of passage. The moment I realized manhood is less about bravery and more about finding yourself in the middle of an existential crisis and worrying about your bowels.

To distract myself from my digestion, I tried to picture something calming--a bunny. But the bunny vanished, leaving behind something worse.

A cow.

On a train.

Staring at me through an open door. It chewed its cud slowly, with the unsettling patience of something that had seen too much. It didn't blink. I wanted to ask if it would jump--but I already knew the answer.

It would jump.

Would it land beside me? Yep.

We would drown together, followed by a tragic headline:

"Boy and Cow Perish in River--Town Mourns One of Them."

That thought made me laugh--unfortunately, it also made me fart.

Then, worse.

I felt it. A small, solid, cheese-dense turd. It slipped between my butt cheeks, wedged in my bathing suit.

I stared blankly at the moving train.

Great. I was going to die with a baby carrot of shame in my trunks.

The train kept coming. I pictured it derailing, knocking me loose, sweeping me under. At least that would be quick.

Thirty-five cars.

Forty.

Still, I clung to the beam.

I had to live. If not for me, then for the poor bastard who would have to wipe my corpse's ass.

Then--finally--the caboose.

I didn't hesitate.

I kicked off the beam and sprang forward like it was a damned trampoline.

The river raced toward me, the sky swinging upward. My arms shot over my head. The rush of air roared in my ears.

Then--impact.

A full-body slap, then silence.

I plunged deep, sinking fifteen feet before I even realized I was underwater.

I spread my arms, kicking hard, desperate for the surface. As I swam, I reached between my cheeks and pinched the turd like it was a goddamned crime scene clue.

In the clean, cold water, it felt like clay.

I dropped it.

I imagined a catfish gobbling it up.

I gagged, kicking harder.

Breaking the surface, I gasped, sucking in hot summer air.

I wiped my face, checking for lampreys. Nothing. I was alive.

Somewhere upstream, another beaver was probably rebuilding its dam, because that's what beavers do.

They don't stop. They don't hesitate.

They don't question why they do the things that will

probably get them killed.

I wasn't sure if that made me a beaver. But I'd jumped. I'd survived.

I left something behind in that river, and it wasn't just the baby carrot of shame.

Whatever I was before--less. Whatever I was now--more.

And that was enough.

Chapter Twenty-Four

Catcher with Speed

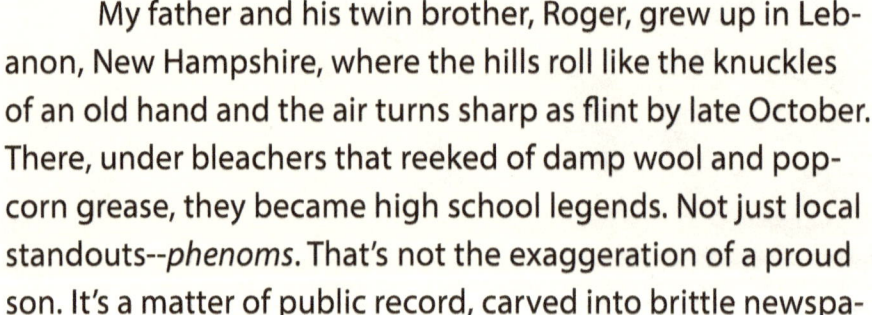

My father and his twin brother, Roger, grew up in Lebanon, New Hampshire, where the hills roll like the knuckles of an old hand and the air turns sharp as flint by late October. There, under bleachers that reeked of damp wool and popcorn grease, they became high school legends. Not just local standouts--*phenoms*. That's not the exaggeration of a proud son. It's a matter of public record, carved into brittle newspaper clippings and the fading memories of the Upper Valley's oldest residents.

They were mirror images: my father, a left-handed pitcher with a windup smooth as river water; Roger, his right-handed twin, crouched behind the plate like a coiled spring. When my father's curveball snapped through the air, Roger's glove popped like a firecracker on the Fourth of July. They carved their names into three seasons--scorching turf in fall, chewing ice and powder in winter, and filling the muggy summer dusk with the crack of ash wood on leather.

In the winters, they ruled the slopes of Dartmouth Skiway and Storrs Hill. Mornings smelled of wax and thermos-steamed cocoa, skis strapped to the tops of wood-paneled station wagons, the bindings still flecked with bark from backyard practice runs. Downhill, they flew like rumor--packed powder crunching beneath them, wind screaming in their ears, cheeks raw with cold and pride.

But being a three-sport star in 1939 guaranteed little. College scholarships were rare. Professional scouts, rarer still. The applause faded with the snowmelt. They played on for UNH, until Pearl Harbor called. The war swallowed them up.

Their father--my grandfather--and his brother Winky built Howard Brothers' Groceries from the ground up, in a time when floorboards creaked under every step and the air inside a general store held a hundred layered scents.

The place sat on a main drag in the Upper Valley, wood-framed and weathered, with front windows fogged in winter and propped open in summer. The sign above the door bore their name in black paint, faded now in every photograph I've seen.

Inside, the store smelled of sawdust scattered to trap the day's dust, of cinnamon bark and nutmeg pods in wide-mouth jars, of coffee ground to order and stacked burlap sacks leaking flour onto the floor like slow-dripping hourglasses.

-There was the tang of vinegar from the pickle barrel, the blood-iron scent of butchered meat wrapped in waxed paper, and the sweet smoke of hams hanging from ceiling hooks like edible pendulums.

Customers entered beneath a cowbell that clanged with

authority. They carried paper lists folded and smudged, written in stubby pencil, and left with brown bags that rustled against their coats--the sharp corners of tins pressing into ribs, apples thudding gently against bread.

It was the Depression, yes. But hunger was a stranger to our family. My grandfather and Winky made sure of that. They extended credit on handshakes and nods. Not out of charity--though there was some of that--but because they understood something elemental: *people need to eat.* You could always square up later. When the harvest came in. When your boy got work at the mill. When the government checks arrived.

And then, in 1951, the Atlantic and Pacific Tea Company came to town, and everything began to rot.

A&P didn't smell like cinnamon or ham. It smelled like polished linoleum, chemical wax, cold air piped from industrial compressors, and bread so uniform it had no scent at all.

It gleamed with chrome fixtures and humming fluorescents. The shelves stood tall and impersonal, everything boxed, wrapped, and labeled in bright colors that promised nothing and delivered less.

At first, it was just a few cents here and there. Potatoes at Howard Brothers? Fifteen cents a pound. At A&P? Eleven. Baking soda, canned peaches, toothpaste--nickels mattered.

But A&P understood shame.

At Howard Brothers, you might find yourself face to face with the man your father still owed fifty cents from 1935. The man who wrapped your Christmas roast. The man who knew your family story.

At A&P, you were just a wallet with wheels. You could

glide down aisles, drop things in your cart, and never meet a pair of human eyes.

No guilt. No debts. No past.

My grandfather and Winky saw it coming. They could have fought for a while. Cut prices. Extended hours. Bought neon signs and piped in music. But their money had limits. Their pride, too. They were merchants of the old world--slow, relational, analog. They believed in inventory you could count by hand, in ledgers scrawled in pencil, in saying thank you without printing it on a receipt.

And so the store closed in 1952.

On the final day, they swept the floors in silence. They packed up the jars and the hooks. They turned the "Howard Brothers' Groceries" sign face down. The keys clicked in the lock. The air inside turned still. The scent of cinnamon faded beneath the slow, permanent smell of dust and time.

My grandfather, once the king of his own corner of the world, put on a butcher's apron and went to work at Dartmouth College. Every morning he walked across the loading dock into a refrigerated room lit by flickering fluorescents, the tiles underfoot slick with fat and frost. He carved roasts with the same hands that once wrote credit in a ledger. He trimmed steaks for faculty dining rooms where no one knew his name.

Dad never spoke of it. Not once. Not in anger. Not in sadness. But it lived in him.

He had no patience for complaints about fairness.

"Things are what they are," he'd say, with finality.

But he also never worshipped the cold efficiencies that gutted his father's life. He didn't romanticize suffering. He just believed: *people need to eat.*

For what it's worth, A&P didn't stay either. After crushing the competition, they raised their prices--past what Howard Brothers had charged. And then, one day--quietly, efficiently--they left.

No fanfare. No sign. Just gone.

For all his belief in grit and effort, my father never pushed me into sports. Encouraged? Yes. Supported? Without fail. But he never lectured or demanded. He didn't need to.

From the moment I first touched a baseball--a real one, scuffed and buttery from years in a garage bin--I was in love. I loved the sharp leather tang of glove oil, the sting of a ball smacking palm, the dusty vanilla scent of sunbaked chalk lines. I wanted to be like him: to wear a number on my back, to sweat through the seams, to feel the puck slide under my stick on frozen ponds, to run until my lungs burned and my legs hummed with fatigue.

Love, though, is no guarantee of talent.

I was a generalist. A try-hard. I played hockey, baseball, soccer. In pond hockey games, I was fast--but I had hands like wooden spoons. I could catch an opponent, corner him--and then fumble the puck like I was holding a trout. My passes wobbled like wet soap bars.

Baseball was my favorite. Always. I threw like a duck and hit like a bumblebee, but I could run. I was quick on the bases--aggressive, fearless, messy. I was a catcher with speed, which is like being a motorcycle with snow tires: interesting, maybe, but not what anyone asked for.

If there was one place I almost shined, it was track.

I ran the old-school 800 meters--the half mile--on cinder tracks that turned your socks black and left grit in your teeth. The starting line always smelled of sunscreen and spit. There was a silence before the starter pistol, like air being held underwater. Then the crack, the scramble of spikes on stone, the immediate ache of lactic acid in your thighs. Two laps around, arms pumping like pistons, lungs catching fire by the final turn.

I qualified for the state meet more than once. But never won. Never placed.

Did my father dream I'd follow in his footsteps?

Probably.

I would have.

But he never showed disappointment. Not once.

He came to everything. Games where I struck out twice. Meets where I barely finished in the top ten. Soccer games where I'd pray we'd score enough to signal garbage time. He stood on sidelines with a paper cup of coffee, the steam rising past his face like a votive offering.

He cheered like I mattered.

Not just the athlete he once was--but the son I actually was.

That kind of support doesn't always survive the death of a dream. But it did in him.

Dad rarely talked about the store. Never spoke Roger's name with anything but affection.

After college, Roger moved to Virginia. He and Dad kept up what seemed like magical long-distance communication--phone calls that always came at just the right moment,

birthday cards in the same uneven script, letters I wasn't supposed to see but sometimes did. They were twins with a tether
you couldn't trace but couldn't deny. When Roger died in 1994,
Dad cried in a way I'd never seen.

I think the fall of Howard Brothers settled into his bones,
the way cold settles into knees before a storm. He didn't say it
was unfair. He didn't even say it was sad. If pressed, I imagine
he'd shrug.

"It was business," he'd say. "Things change."

But deep down?

I think he knew better.

And I think, in the quiet way he showed up for me--not
for the star I never became, but the boy I was--he made peace
with it.

Quietly, steadily--just by showing up.

PART TWO

Glimmers of Light from the Dark Carnival

Chapter Twenty-Five

Heal Yourself: The Untold Story of the Peace, Love, and Death Cult

I started a religious movement once.

"Movement" may be gilding the lily. I threw a stone into the spiritual broth of the 1970s. Some ripples ensued, only to drift away like incense in a windy chapel.

Still, how many teenagers do you know who have even tried to start a cult?

Despite my dramatic self-healing--an armpit-chafing, crutch-flinging spectacle--and even a sort-of-kind-of *crucem resurrectionis*, the Peace, Love, and Death Cult never spread. My small but enthusiastic band of followers took immediately to our slogan:

"Eliminate the Middleman: Heal Yourself."

But the masses, the clueless many, turned a deaf ear to our insights.

In my mind, all the pieces were in place--doctrine, spectacle, fervor--but somehow, lift-off never came. I was sixteen, standing atop Durham's modest but mythic Mount Sinai, having lugged enough firewood up its slope to signal the divine. I stood there, waiting for lightning.

It never struck.

Eventually, I got distracted and wandered off. Story of my life.

Still, the people of the future deserve to be told of this brief, shining moment in ecclesiastical history.

It all began in the nurse's office at Oyster River High School, a little-visited hole that smelled of rubbing alcohol, floor polish, and faint resignation. The cabinets held bandages, cotton balls, and a thermometer I was convinced hadn't been sterilized since the Eisenhower administration. Occasionally, a school nurse appeared--when she wasn't in the teacher's lounge chain-smoking Pall Malls and muttering about kids these days.

That day, I found the crutches.

They were ancient, with peeling varnish and the splintered texture of something used in a World War I field hospital. My leftist political phase was in full swing, so I saw their existence as a metaphor for oppression, or maybe just as an irresistible opportunity for performance art. Either way, I liberated them--okay, stole them--and swung my way down the hall, mastering the rhythm like a born medieval beggar.

Clearly, this was a sign.

Like all good universe-changing ideas, it arrived as a half-baked outline, with no exit strategy--just overwhelming conviction.

The library smelled of old pages and teenage anxiety. Fluorescent lights buzzed overhead like a swarm of mechanical bees, their flickering giving the space a vaguely apocalyptic feel. A murmur of whispering students and the occasional squeak of sneakers on polished tile underscored the tension of a hundred unfinished term papers.

Heads lifted as I hobbled in, performing my best saintly suffering face. Some students glanced at each other, already amused. A few stiffened, sensing an impending disruption. Behind the circulation desk, Mrs. Dewey--a relic of an age when librarians were feared, not befriended--adjusted her bifocals and narrowed her eyes.

I climbed atop the nearest table, crutches under my arms like twin pillars of agony.

The murmurs stopped.

I let the crutches fly.

One smacked against a bookshelf, sending a cascade of paperbacks to the floor. The other crashed onto a neighboring table, where a sophomore gasped, clutching his heart as if he'd just witnessed a minor miracle.

A beat of silence.

Then, arms wide, I bellowed:

"I'M HEALED! I HAVE HEALED MYSELF! ELIMINATE THE MIDDLEMAN! JOIN THE PEACE, LOVE, AND DEATH CULT!"

A moment of perfect stillness.

Then laughter--genuine, disbelieving, delighted. My fellow anarchists, the ones who respected stunts the way lesser mortals respected varsity athletes, clapped and cheered. A few juniors at a nearby table muttered *Jesus Christ* under their breath, shaking their heads in admiration.

But across the room, a girl in a gingham dress sat frozen, her hands clenched in fists of righteous horror.

Debbie Randall. Fundamentalist.

Her face, usually as pink and smooth as a child's balloon, had gone white. I might as well have turned water into LSD.

"You--you mock the Lord?" she hissed.

"I channel the Lord," I said, spreading my arms magnanimously. "And so can you. Eliminate the middleman. Heal yourself."

"You are damned," she whispered.

"Maybe," I conceded, hopping off the table, "but at least I'm entertaining."

Debbie stormed off, presumably to alert the assistant principal.

After my miraculous recovery, I performed another.

Between classes, I stopped a senior girl I'd never spoken to and gazed into her eyes.

"You don't know me," I said solemnly. "But I know you've been troubled by those warts on your hands."

She recoiled. "I don't have warts anywhere!"

"Of course, you don't, my child," I said in a soft, fatherly voice. "I've removed them through your faith. Because you believe, your warts are gone."

A pause. A little longer.

Then, in my best late-night TV adman voice:

"Eliminate the middleman. Join the Peace, Love, and Death Cult."

"You're a weirdo," she said, marching toward the office.

"A weirdo of wisdom," I called after her.

Then the assistant principal walked out.

This led to yet another sit-down with Mr. Shapiro, who spent most of the meeting rubbing his temples. He studied me across his desk, weighing whether my latest stunt was a boyish prank (which he tolerated) or assault, blasphemy, and disrespect (which he did not).

"I suppose," I said solemnly, "that flinging the crutches could have hit someone in the eye. That would have been unfortunate."

His brow softened. He appreciated contrition.

"But," I added, "if that had happened, it would have been another opportunity for me to demonstrate my healing power."

His temple vein pulsed.

In the third miracle of the day, the end-of-school-day bell rang. I was free.

That afternoon, I gathered three disciples--okay, three friends--and prepared my next miracle.

I scaled the chain-link backstop of the baseball field, stopping halfway to stretch my arms in a mock crucifixion pose. A small crowd gathered.

"YOU DON'T KNOW WHAT YOU'RE DOING! I FORGIVE YOU! I FORGIVE MYSELF! ELIMINATE THE MIDDLEMAN! JOIN THE PEACE, LOVE, AND DEATH CULT!"

Then I pushed off the fence.

It was a five-foot drop.

I flubbed the landing. My ankle twisted, my knee buckled, and I went sprawling onto the grass.

I lay there, staring at the sky. The clouds swirled in that *yes, you're an idiot* kind of way.

Then, summoning every ounce of theatrical instinct I possessed, I rolled onto my back, sprang up, and threw my arms wide.

"I HAVE RISEN!"

Laughter. Applause.

Debbie Randall, who had appeared on the periphery, got down on her knees in prayer, presumably for my soul. Or for the ability to get grass stains out of her starched skirt.

And that was the high point of the Peace, Love, and Death Cult.

Looking back, my biggest mistake wasn't the name. *Peace* and *Love* were fine. *Death* was the problem. Nobody wants to join a religion where death isn't metaphorical. I had thought it gave us an edge--something mysterious, something dangerous. But it turns out, when you promise people resurrection, they'd rather not risk the first part. Everybody wants to go to heaven, but nobody wants to die.

But my *real* fatal error was calling it a cult.

Cults don't call themselves cults. That's a label imposed by outsiders--the ones who need to draw a line between their sacred truths and someone else's dangerous delusions.

A movement only works if people believe the story.

And I had told the people they didn't need a middleman.

So they didn't.

They didn't need me.

Which meant I was free.

The next day, I arrived at school and discovered someone had stolen the crutches.

Debbie Randall, I thought. She's exorcising my holy relics--or planning a faith-healing scam at her small but overflowing-with-gullibility church.

Whoever had taken them had left behind an empty tomb-like space in my heart.

That was it.

The moment had passed.

Like all great prophets, I had eliminated myself.

By that afternoon, like all forgotten deities, I retreated to the holy solitude of my bedroom, where I communed with the sacrament of skunky resin and Mint Milanos. There, I contemplated the mysteries of *Who's Next* versus *Dark Side of the Moon*.

Chapter Twenty-Six

The Existential Camper: Reinventing Myself, One Summer at a Time

I don't fully understand existentialism--but then again, neither does anyone else. That's part of its appeal. It's the kind of thing that's both creating and realizing itself as time unrolls. It's existential.

Still, the idea of existence preceding essence--that we define ourselves through our choices--makes sense to me. And nowhere was that truer than at Camp Mi-Te-Na, a boys' summer camp in New Hampshire.

Every year, when my parents dropped me off for two weeks, I had the rarest of opportunities: to choose who I would be. Back home in Durham, I was just another kid--albeit one who set records for classroom disruptions and spontaneous acts of chaos--but at camp, I could reinvent myself.

At home, I was the second-best catcher in my grade. It was a fixed identity, as though it had been handed down by decree:

"Keith Howard has always been the second-best catch-er. Keith Howard is the second-best catcher. Keith Howard will always BE the second-best catcher."

But at Mi-Te-Na? I could arrive with a mitt and declare myself THE catcher. No qualifiers. No competition. Just instant identity, fully accepted.

"Keith's our catcher," I heard my bunkmates say. And that was that.

Camp was the perfect place for the shy, the downtrod-den and the deluded with grandeur. I believe I could have an-nounced myself the bastard king of England and had a handful of kids wanting to buy me Cadbury bars.

For real athletes, Mi-Te-Na was just another playground. The cream always rises. For me--who was barely whole milk, more like 2%--it was a golden opportunity. With only 50 boys in the village, some were bound to be injured, uncoordinated, or simply uninterested in sports. By default, I was in the mix.

Basketball, for instance, was a complete mystery to me. Back home, my basketball career had stalled at the "occasion-ally touching the ball" level. But at Mi-Te-Na? I was on the team.

This had less to do with skill and more to do with every-one making the team by default, but still--there I was, running up and down the court, waving my arms like I had a purpose.

We played exactly one basketball game and one base-ball game per session, which was my ideal level of athletic commitment. The games were against Camp Fatima, a Catholic boys' camp, meaning our opponents played with the confi-dence of kids whose mothers had already signed them up for the priesthood. We, on the other hand, had a team of kids whose athletic abilities were made up of lies and pious hopes.

I don't recall who won any of our battles, but I do remember no one seemed particularly burdened by talent.

Each year, I returned home, lobbying my parents to move to a town half the size of Durham, just so I could hold on to that feeling.

They selfishly ignored my request.

Mi-Te-Na was about showing up. You didn't have to be the best. You just had to not be the worst. And if you were the worst? What the hell--c'mon along.

So I tried everything. Sailing? Sure. Canoeing? Absolutely. Archery? Riflery? Why not?

Even the campfire ghost stories were transformative. By the final campfire, a few lucky campers were inducted into The Tribe, Mi-Te-Na's elite secret society. The Tribe was said to have private meetings, a secret handshake, and even a rumored banquet.

When I was inducted, I discovered that the only real perk was a new form of guilt when I misbehaved.

"Oh, Keith! How could you? You're a member of The Tribe."

As a Tribal Elder, I had two major responsibilities:

1.   Teach new campers the Mi-Te-Na song (most of which I have forgotten).

2.   Shout the final lyric--*"We'll be Mi-Te-Na dead!"*--as we wandered back to our cabins, contemplating mortality.

I embraced my new spiritual duties, fully prepared to haunt the baseball field for eternity, whispering:

"You're the catcher now."

The real transformation, however, happened at the dances with Camp Foss, our sister camp.

In Durham, I was a wind-up monkey--briefly entertaining but not something you bring home. Girls saw me as a disruption, a distraction, a cautionary tale.

At Mi-Te-Na? I was a contender.

It wasn't that I became more attractive--it was just that the competition was minimal, and the expectations were even lower.

Girls were bused in, given Cheetos and Bug Juice, and expected to mingle and dance. The whole system seemed designed to work in my favor.

And then, miraculously, I danced with a girl. I sat with a girl. I talked with a girl.

And . . . a girl kissed me.

She leaned in--Bug Juice on her breath, Cheeto dust on her fingers. Her lips, soft and unfamiliar, pressed against mine for a brief, electrifying second. My brain short-circuited. My knees went liquid. This was real. This was happening. I was officially the king of Mi-Te-Na.

This was not a prank. It was not a dare. It was not a horrible mistake that she would later try to repress.

It was a real, deliberate, no-one-was-laughing kiss from an actual human girl.

For that one moment, I was irresistible.

I returned home each summer with a different swagger, knowing that for two glorious weeks, I had been something more than myself.

Of course, no transformation is permanent. Eventually, the illusion breaks. And if I had to go out, I wasn't going to fade quietly. I would leave Mi-Te-Na the way I arrived--recklessly overestimating my abilities

I would not go gently into any night--I'd shoot out the lights.

At fifteen, I was invited to be a counselor-in-training at my beloved summer camp. An honor. A privilege. A catastrophic miscalculation.

Like all good disasters, this one began with a single bad idea: sneaking into town on our first night off.

The camp directors had warned us about responsibility, setting a good example, all that nonsense. But they had failed to mention the lake police.

I led three other counselors into town, where we convinced some older guys to buy us beer. At the time, this felt like a feat of negotiation worthy of Harvard Business School.

Looking back, I now understand that drunk twenty-year-olds hanging out behind a gas station are always happy to buy beer for fifteen-year-olds.

After drinking six beers at an alarming speed, I determined that the next logical step was to jump off the town pier.

What I had failed to account for--what no one had thought to mention--was that the pier did not have a ladder.

This, it turns out, is an important detail.

In the movies, people jump off piers and then emerge moments later, sleek and refreshed. I, on the other hand, spent several minutes treading water, loudly insisting that I was fine, even as my arms gradually stopped working.

At some point, the lake police arrived.

I don't remember being fished out of the water, arrested, or processed. I do, however, remember waking up the next morning with a pounding headache and a very important question:

"Where is everybody?"

It turned out that while I had been unconscious, my fellow counselors had done the unthinkable: they had apologized.

They had expressed regret and sworn to make better choices. They had even gone full hostage video, claiming that they had been "led astray" by a bad influence.

That bad influence, of course, was me.

By the time I stumbled into the camp office, everyone else had been reinstated.

I, however, was fired.

I don't know what I expected--maybe a second chance, maybe a stern warning, maybe a "boys will be boys" speech followed by a lecture on responsibility.

What I got instead was a ride home.

As we pulled away from camp, I watched the lake disappear in the rearview mirror. Next summer, a new kid would step off the bus and declare himself The Catcher. Another kid would kiss a girl at the dance. And someone else--some other poor idiot--would take my place as the biggest disaster to ever wear a Mi-Te-Na staff shirt.

At least, I hoped so.

Chapter Twenty-Seven

My Life as an Explorer, Playwright, Actor, and Human Kebab

Ever since I was very, very little, I've craved adventure, particularly the brave, foolish and potentially deadly kind. For instance, at 10 I got my first rowboat, a flat-bottomed wooden one perfect for traveling around Beard's Creek, which almost encircled the peninsula on which I grew up.

A fresh-water pond, the creek was separated by a lock under a bridge from the estuarial Oyster River; although I never did so, I pictured myself portaging across the highway, and launching my boat. From there, I would set out downriver, first to Little Bay, then to Great Bay, then to Portsmouth Harbor and finally out into the North Atlantic.

Using no accurate information, I estimated this 15-mile journey, if I traveled with the tide, would take about an hour. From there, I'd row to Greenland, the island, not the town abutting Portsmouth, which I guessed to take a full day. This guess would be accurate if I could row a little over 90 miles per hour.

In the North Atlantic.

I'd spend a few days on Greenland, digging in the snow for the ruins of medieval towns, playing with sheep and penguins, and becoming friends with the Skraelings, whom I pictured as part ghost, part friendly natives.

Holland would be my next stop, where I'd do a little skating, before finally rowing to England. Overall, I figured the journey would take me a week, a shortfall of unknown proportion, which, in my defense, no one had pointed out at the time.

If they had, I would have made the proper adjustments.

This need for adventure, for trying something new--whether I had a knack for it or not--led me to my first theatrical experience, where I was joint writer/director/producer and co-starred in the World Premiere of a romantic comedy adventure.

I was 10 and in fifth grade, and my friend John and I slaved over it, actually rereading it before declaring it finished. It could have been great, given a decent budget, but still was an excellent effort. John and I were not awarded the Tony's we deserved, but such is the life of the thespian artiste and showman.

John and I were both writers, or as writerly as fifth graders can be. While none of our childhood work survives, one of our favorite literary activities was to dramatize literature we'd liked. More honestly, we liked to write plays starring us with plots lifted whole from books, more horse theft than homage. Our tour-de-force came in fifth grade in Mrs. Quackenbush's class, when we wrote our masterpiece.

Helen Mather-Smith Mindlin's *Dangerous Island* features a brother-sister team and their friend, stranded on an island that appears only once every two hundred years. There's gold. There's a helicopter. There's no real explanation for anything.

In short, the entire book is MacGuffins all the way down.

A challenge for staging in a classroom, the story intrigued John and me, and we wrote the play over five feverish days. Our first version was written as a one-hour play. Mrs. Quackenbush gave us a 10-minute window before afternoon recess on Friday. Not a great slot; we'd really need to kill the audience.

That meant cutting the story down to its very bones: sinking island, gold, helicopter rescue and two kisses, one for each male actor. This last bit wasn't in Mindlin's book, but as scriptwriters, John and I felt strongly about its artistic integrity--and its appeal to the female market when we took it on the road. Also, neither of us had ever been kissed, and it would be great to have the first time witnessed by our whole class.

Once we'd identified the necessary plot points, we set to work on characterization of the three characters: the island, the gold and the helicopter. Ingeniously, we handled the sinking island easily. Drawing the island on cardboard, the show would begin with it on a table. Two minutes in, it would be lowered to chair height and two minutes later placed on the stage floor. Genius!

The gold bars were equally a snap: I brought in a sack full of building blocks and a brand-new roll of tin foil. Once we'd wrapped them, we realized they looked *silver*. That problem was solved when I remembered *white gold existed*.

Two challenges down, one helicopter to solve. As producers, John and I agonized over the logistical problems. Neither of us owned a helicopter, and neither did any of our neighbors.

Finally, in a stroke of genius, we realized that if you listened carefully with your eyes squinted just right, a wiffle-ball bat sounds kind of like the *whhhhhooooossshhh* of helicopter blades. John brought in a model helicopter to be hung from the ceiling, completing the visuals. This blockbuster with artistic pretensions--the kisses--was really coming together.

Unfortunately, our roles as producers had taken most of the production time. We spent 20 minutes writing dialog--the least important part of any play--and knew we'd created an important cultural milestone. And a surefire hit. And a way for us to get kissed.

We just needed to find the right actress.

Luckily, the perfect femme fatale was right in our class. As I recall, most girls didn't pay John much attention at that point; I, on the other hand, was positively rank with girl repellent. No fifth-grade girl wanted to be seen with me, much less be recruited into a play, even if I'd tried to convince her this was a great honor and a potential stepping-stone to television, movies or, at least, opportunities in future theatrical productions. It would be up to John to recruit this lucky actress. We both hoped beyond hope she'd be too kind to say no.

Also, we both had crushes on her.

Beth may not have been the prettiest girl in the world,

but she was to me and John.

Beth may not have had the most dynamic stage presence in our grade, but she did to John and me.

Beth may not have been the most adept line-learner in our class, but she was to John and me.

Also, we both had crushes on her.

John approached Beth with the talking points we'd prepared. Out of kindness, she agreed to appear for one performance only, refusing to sign any long-term contract.

Crushingly, she had one other demand: there would be no kissing, no suggestion of romance, no physical contact of any kind. This was on Friday morning, mere hours before showtime. Beth had us over a barrel--she was a master negotiator. Reluctantly, we accepted defeat. Despite our desires to be welcomed into the land of men, John and I would not *beg* for a pity kiss. Especially since our begging would be ignored.

We gave Beth her lines, and she learned all of them quickly. In order, they were:

"Our boat is sinking!"

"It's . . . an island! I don't remember it from before."

"The island is sinking! We're doomed!"

"Look--a helicopter!"

"Please kiss me to celebrate our rescue!

Beth had used a thick black marker to delete that last line.

We'd recruited a crew of three boys to handle the stage-managing duties. Islands don't sink, gold doesn't appear and helicopters don't rescue on their own. Although we couldn't offer the backstage crew a cast party, John and I offered to share our snacks for the next week, a promise we promptly forgot.

Because mere words cannot capture the drama and beauty of such a work of art, I will leave it to the reader to envision the production. It was everything you imagine and more. At least it felt that way to John, Beth and me.

Quite simply and with all modesty, we had created and presented a masterpiece. Being Philistines, Mrs. Quackenbush's fifth grade class merely stared, then went to recess.

Beth moved away that summer. John and I became obsessed with playing baseball. We never wrote together again. A golden age had been wrapped in foil. White gold foil.

Although finished as a writing team, John and I were together in school through junior high. Early in that last year together, I'd revealed to John that Dangerous Island from three years before felt like the pinnacle of my life, and I doubted I'd ever reach such heights again.

John wrote in my yearbook: "To Keith--In hopes that he may peak again!"

So when I was cast in a high school play as an eighth grader, I thought: This is it. My Broadway debut. The comeback tour of John-Keith Productions--minus John. And Beth. And the white gold bars.

My days as a playwright were over, but the stage still called to me. If I couldn't write my own starring role, I'd find one. As a little boy I had wanted to stay little, as little as possible. My dreams of midgethood and jockeydom had been discarded, but I was still among the shortest in my grade, giving me an advantage when I auditioned for "Oliver!" the musical adaptation of Dickens' Oliver Twist. That size and my self-assessed cuteness helped overcome the fact I couldn't sing at all.

Lips could sync, but tall high-school boys couldn't be shortened.

Dancing was another problem. I didn't so much move as spasm, my limbs rebelling against rhythm like an electrocuted frog. The director tucked me in the back for group numbers, my stiff-legged jumps and graceless pivots safely obscured by the taller, more competent cast members. No audience was the wiser.

Rehearsals stretched for weeks, and I fell in love with the world of the Oyster River High School Drama Club. The actors were high schoolers--older, cooler, and mystically sophisticated in ways I didn't fully understand.

The boys had sideburns and deep, practiced voices, already talking about colleges I'd never heard of.

The girls laughed loudly, flipping their hair in ways that felt like a secret language.

I was tolerated, maybe even liked, in the way you might fondly pat a dog that doesn't drool too much.

A few other 8th graders were in Fagin's gang, and a boy named Fred played Oliver. Beautiful voice, talented dancer, but taller than me. I tried to be as helpful as I could, just wanting to bask in the glamor that was the Oyster River Drama Club.

Smoking was part of the mystique. In 1972, anyone could smoke, and the high schoolers disappeared outside during breaks to flick Zippos and suck down Marlboros. I followed them--not to smoke, but just to stand in the fog of adulthood, hoping the scent would cling to my clothes. Maybe my mother would wrinkle her nose when I got home and say, *What have you been up to?* Maybe I'd shrug mysteriously, *Nothing,* and she'd see me as older than I was.

Then, one afternoon, the director needed a microphone.

I don't know why he needed it or how urgent the request was. I only knew this was an errand I was born to complete.

"The music room," he said, waving vaguely toward the long, linoleum-lined halls of the high school. I nodded solemnly, an eighth-grade knight entrusted with a noble quest.

I sprinted, sneakers squeaking on the waxed floor. The air smelled of old textbooks, of pencil shavings and industrial disinfectant. The high school felt huge compared to the middle school--its ceilings too tall, its hallways stretching like caverns leading to unknown worlds.

And I was lost.

I turned one corner, then another. The music room was right there--but cut off.

A security gate, a metal grid with iron spikes on top, had been pulled across the hallway. I could see the music room on the other side, the door slightly ajar, the Holy Grail microphone just beyond reach.

Looking back, that impulse--dream big, worry about the details later--never really went away. Whether it was writing plays, seeking adventure, or later, much later, trying to master the exact right balance between buzzed and obliterated, I was always drawn to the same high-wire act: reckless optimism with a punchline I never saw coming.

I should have gone back. Asked a teacher. Found another route. But I was on a mission, and I had spent too many afternoons climbing trees, fences, and drainage pipes to be defeated by a mere gate.

The metal bars were cool beneath my fingers, smooth but slightly tacky with the grease of a thousand high school hands. I gripped the horizontal bar halfway up, my small hands clenching like a monkey's as I hoisted myself, pressing my sneaker against the metal for leverage.

The hallway behind me hummed with distant chatter, the occasional slam of lockers punctuating the low murmur of after-school noise. My heart pounded in my chest, my breath quick in my throat.

The spikes loomed inches from my ribs, iron teeth glinting in the fluorescent light--an impalement waiting to happen.

Still, I climbed.

I had just gotten my chest over the spikes. I was perched mid-air, holding my upper body up with my arms nearly extended, when it happened.

My sneaker slipped off the crossbeam.

I dropped. Not far, just a few inches.

But enough.

The moment I felt it, I knew. A sharp, sickening punch of pain. A spike pierced my stomach, the metal tip catching just under my ribs, aimed for my lungs.

I was stuck.

For a heartbeat, my brain refused to process it. I hung there, belly speared like a fish on a gaff, my weight pressing downward, metal digging deeper. My ribs ached from the pressure. I imagined what would happen if I let go--saw the spike tearing through my torso like a lobster shell ripped open by hungry hands.

I didn't want to die.

I especially didn't want to die stupid.

I screamed. And screamed. And waited to die.

Footsteps. The slow shuffle of old-man urgency. A janitor appeared at the far end of the hallway, a scowl forming as he took in the scene. He broke into the closest thing to a run a 70-year-old could manage, his heavy keys jangling against his hip.

"Jesus Christ," he muttered, breathless as he reached me. His face was creased with irritation, not concern. He took one look at my ridiculous predicament and sighed like a man who'd seen too much nonsense in his life.

Then, without ceremony, he grabbed me under the armpits and shoved me up.

A blinding flare of pain as the spike slid out of my flesh, followed by a sudden, dizzying relief. My body released.

I fell backward, hitting the tile floor with a bone-rattling smack. I expected agony. Instead, there was a weird numbness, like my stomach had been replaced with a slab of cold meat. Then--heat. Wetness. My own blood seeping under my shirt. And still, more than pain, I felt the mortification of blood pooling, a sign of how foolish I was.

For a moment, I just lay there, breath punched out of

me, my hands pressed against my side. The janitor let out a breath, shook his head, and muttered, "Dumbest damn kid I ever saw."

I didn't argue.

I lay there, feeling the warm trickle of blood seeping beneath my shirt, staring up at the ceiling, grateful to be alive.

The janitor hauled me up like a drunk at closing time, half-carrying, half-dragging me down the hallway. I don't remember who picked me up or how I got there, but somehow, I ended up at the campus infirmary, sitting on an examination table with torn vinyl, trying not to look at the dark red stain spreading across my shirt.

The doctor barely looked up from his clipboard. 'Hmm.' That was it. Just 'hmm.' Like he was inspecting a leaky pipe, not a bleeding eighth grader. I half-expected him to spit in his palm and just rub the wound shut.

Instead, he got to work, and I swear to God, it felt like he was stuffing my insides with sawdust. I could almost hear it--the tamping, the pat-pat of packing it down. I couldn't feel the needle and thread tightening the gash and closing it off.

Finally, he smoothed a bandage over the wound, nodded once like he'd just caulked a bathtub, and said, "That oughta hold."

At rehearsal the next day, I made damn sure everyone saw my bandage.

Every chance I got, I lifted my shirt just enough, revealing the stark white square against my scrawny ribs. The high school girls looked at me with concern. Sympathy.

And--unless I was wildly mistaken--just a hint of lust.

I winced dramatically as I sat down, sighing just loud enough for people to hear.

One girl gasped.

Another whispered, "That looks bad."

I nodded solemnly.

"Yeah," I said, staring into the distance like a war hero.

"But I'll be okay."

And just like that, everything had worked out the way it was supposed to.

Chapter Twenty-Eight

In the Kitchen, Among the Gods

Cast parties were for real high schoolers.

I had spent the last few weeks in strategic concealment. My greatest performance in the play had not been acting but existing unnoticed, my height and placement ensuring I was "well-concealed," as a friend so kindly put it. And yet, despite my invisibility, I had *arrived*.

Not just in the sense that I now knew the names and faces of fifteen high school cast members, but in the grander, more mythic sense of arrival--the kind that mattered to an eighth grader desperate to be seen. Thanks to my nearly fatal skewering by the security fence, and my stoic response to this injury, four or five cast members even knew *my* name. However it was defined, I felt like a *real live boy*.

That realness was confirmed during dress rehearsal when, against all odds, I was invited to the cast party after Saturday night's final performance.

A *party*. A *real live high school party*--with high school girls, high school gods, and, thanks to the drinking age of 18, high school *beer*. This was not a casual event. This required strategy. This required tactical precision. If executed successfully, this party could change my life.

Failure? Inconceivable.

It had been years since I'd attended anything resembling a party--back when they involved birthday cake, paper hats, and balsa wood model airplanes as gifts. There had been a few junior-high boy-girl gatherings, but I had wisely chosen not to be invited to them. What could they possibly have taught me? This, on the other hand, was something else.

A *soiree*. A *fête*. A *bacchanal, a bash, a saturnalia.* And I, against all cosmic logic, had secured an invitation.

The rust on my partying skills was nothing compared to the dust on my beer drinking.

My experience was limited to stolen sips on summer afternoons, sitting on the back porch with Dad as he mowed the last strips of lawn, the air thick with the scent of cut grass and gasoline. He'd open a cold bottle of Miller, take a long, satisfied swallow, then hand it to me. I'd press the cool glass to my lips, bracing for the sharp, bitter taste that always made my tongue curl. I never liked it. It tasted like metal, like something meant for adults who understood things I didn't.

But that had been childhood. I was going to a party now. A *real* party. Yes, I'd drink, but the goal was to solidify my role with high school kids. I'd fit in so well they'd forget I was young. And short. And they wouldn't notice how nervous I was.

They'd see the me I was meant to be.

My parents came to opening night, of course, and told the expected parental lies about how I'd stolen the show and how they could hear my voice loud and clear. Quite good hearing for old people, considering I'd lip-synced the entire time.

On the walk home, I casually mentioned the cast party, scheduled two evenings away, tossing it out like an after-thought, as if I were in the habit of attending glamorous high school soirées. Nothing to worry about, folks. Your son is a man of the world now. Inside, though, my stomach was an over-tightened snare drum, thrumming with a hundred differ-ent anxieties.

What should I wear? Would there be dancing? How could I make the other partiers see *me*--not the awkward eighth grader they thought they knew, but the brand-new, infinitely cooler me--without looking like a poser or a phony?

And, most pressingly: How much beer would I need to drink?

I knew it was the key to transformation. A little was nec-essary--beer was a social lubricant, a ceremonial offering, an unspoken password. But too much, and I'd become a caution-ary tale. I had no experience balancing this equation.

Beer was just for guests. Scotch was Dad's language, poured in two fingers over ice, amber liquid crackling as it kissed the cubes. The few times I'd sniffed it, it smelled like gasoline and firewood, like something a person drank only if they had *seen things*.

I wasn't ready for Scotch. I would never be ready for Scotch.

But beer? That was the lifeblood of every party, every rock concert, every grinning movie star in a backyard barbecue commercial. I could do beer. Probably.

That night, I lay in bed, heart hammering, ears tuned to the slow rise and fall of my parents' snores. When the timing was right, I crept down the stairs in bare feet, feeling each cool wooden slat beneath my soles. The hum of the refrigerator filled the kitchen like a distant generator.

First, I opened a counter drawer and got out a bottle opener. When I opened the refrigerator door, a soft yellow light spilled over my hands. There they were. Four bottles,. Three Budweisers, one Schlitz.. I reached for a Bud;. The glass was slick with sweat, a bead of moisture tracing down the curve of the bottle. My fingers left ghostly prints on its surface.

This was it.

In the bathroom, the light buzzed and flickered for a moment before settling. I opened the bottle. The *whooooossssh* that escaped sounded *too loud*. The bottle sighed, a breath of cold, yeasty air curling up into my nose-- sour, earthy, with an edge of something industrial.

I turned to the mirror, beer in hand.

A man stood there. A handsome, composed, mysterious man. He had a look in his eye--*troubled* but *wise*. I nodded at him. He nodded back.

This was my rehearsal dinner. My pregame for a new life.

I lifted the bottle in silent toast and took a sip.

It was like licking a rusty pipe. Cold, bitter, vaguely rotten--like wet cardboard sealed in a bag of mulch. I swallowed fast. No shudder. No grimace. Just a man. Enjoying a man's drink. As a man should.

While hiding in the bathroom.

I took another sip, slower this time, letting the foam coat my tongue, the carbon dioxide sting my throat. It didn't get any better. But I nodded at the man in the mirror again, and he nodded back.

I was ready for adulthood.

Hell, I was already there.

The final performance of *Oliver!* is lost to me. Maybe my lips moved. Maybe they didn't. It didn't matter. My real debut wasn't on stage--it would happen at The Party.

High school kids had cars, or parents' cars, so there were no limousines waiting to whisk us across town. I rode in the back of a VW Bug, packed in with three others, the vinyl seat sticky against my thighs. The windows were cracked, letting in damp, early-spring air. I breathed deep, willing myself to stay calm.

We pulled up. Two-car garage. Basketball hoop in the driveway. Porch light humming with moths. The living room windows glowed gold from within. It looked like any other house.

Like any other house--hah! *Inside this one lay a portal.* I would walk in as a boy and out as a man.

I hoped.

The door was already open. Laughter spilled out into the night, loose and easy. A faint bassline thumped from somewhere inside, the kind of music that meant something to kids who were older, kids who *knew things.* I hesitated on the walkway, stomach tightening, the porch light on the back of my neck.

Then I stepped through.

The air in the living room was blue with cigarette smoke, turning the overhead light soft and hazy, giving everyone a golden, decadent glow--the decadence of the elect. Someone had set out bowls of chips and pretzels, and kids lounged against the furniture, laughing in that slow, practiced way that suggested they *belonged.*

I moved through the room, trying not to stare. The juniors, the seniors, the ones heading off to college in the fall, all seemed so casual, so at ease, holding their drinks without thinking about it. Meanwhile, I felt like a knock-kneed colt walking into a lion's den, gangly and obvious, too aware of my own hands, too aware of my own heartbeat.

A girl in a faded "Keep On Truckin'" t-shirt flicked ash into an empty Coke can, glanced at me, then looked away.

I swallowed.

Adulthood had begun.

And I needed to keep up.

I looked around the room, hoping no one noticed me. They didn't. I was crushed with disappointment. I became aware I was a phony, a poseur. I didn't belong here, and everyone in the room was avoiding looking at me. Out of pity. Out of contempt.

A tall 18-year-old man with a *beard* addressed the group of us who had just walked in.

"Bathroom's down the hall. Beer's in the kitchen."

I didn't need the bathroom, but I desperately wanted the beer. Not to drink but to hold. I prayed a bottle of Schlitz in my hand would calm my nerves, return my savoir faire. I had entered the Holy of Holies that was a high school party. I needed to act like a man.

The kitchen was even smokier than the living room, but the light from the overhead ring was brighter, illuminating the 10 or so partiers, all male, crammed in there. I saw a few open beer cases on a counter, more piled on the floor. I tried to reattach the cool face I'd shown in my bathroom mirror a few nights before, didn't know if I'd captured it but was happy just to have something covering my insecurity.

"Hey, there, Little Guy," said a man in an Army fatigue shirt. "Aren't you out past your bedtime?"

His tone was amused, not harsh or aggressive. Still, I could feel my cheeks flaming with embarrassment.

I looked the man directly in the face, my heart pounding arrhythmically. I, who was about to be named the funniest kid in eighth grade, needed to find the right words, the coolest words, the hippest words to fire back. My brain and my mouth, which had always worked quickly, seamlessly and wittily together, now seemed like strangers. Strangers on trains moving in different directions. I opened my mouth. Nothing came out. I willed my lips to form words, any words.

The teenage man looked back at me expectantly.

And then he looked away.

It's said that rabbits can die of what's called exertional myopathy, literally scared to death by the appearance of a predator, a very loud noise or--in this case--an inability to find the right words.

I was a bunny and I was a goner.

My life was saved--and lost at the same time. I felt my shame turning me invisible, then incorporeal. Even if I couldn't be the sharp-eyed and quick-mouthed cooligan I'd dreamed of, I couldn't continue living as a dying bunny. I needed to do *something*. Anything.

I took three steps to the beer-covered table, grabbed a room-temperature Schlitz, popped the cap, and took a gulp. It was awful, but I was so ashamed of my silence, I didn't notice. Now, I could sit back, observe and, I hoped, plot my next move into adulthood.

Very quickly, though, the nervousness redoubled, carrying a bag of anxiety, insecurity and a full dose of feeling like a fake. Wanting to stomp these feelings, I needed to do something with my hands.

I lifted my beer to my lips. Again. And again.

And then it was empty.

Plenty more where that came from, I thought. I casually left my empty on the kitchen table and grabbed another beer. This time, the hand holding the bottle opener was a little steadier, more practiced. Maybe even a little cool. I popped the cap off in one fluid motion--no fumbling this time--then tossed it toward the metal trash can without looking.

I heard the *tiiiiiinnggg* of bottle cap on steel and felt pride return. That toss was cool. Very cool. Maybe things were turning around for old Keith. I took a large gulp of the beer. This one tasted a bit better than the first one. It didn't approach *good* or tasty, but it wasn't disgusting. Somehow, the bitterness and mustiness had been turned down.

Still, the kitchen was filled with men--mustached and bearded and muscled and tall. I wanted to leave, look for girls--they were shorter and had friendlier faces--and less hair. First, though, I needed to know I could fit in among men.

I had no idea how to do that.

To fill the void, I took another gulp of beer, then another. I smiled at the comments the men made to each other and laughed when the others did.

They started talking about baseball, the Red Sox in particular. I finished my beer, grabbed another and focused on the conversation. After all, I was a huge and opinionated Sox fan.

"They shouldn't atraded Scott," a Fu-Manchued giant said. "Or even Billy Conigliaro,"

I took a gulp of beer.

"George Scott's over the hill," I said, "and Conigliaro is only in the big leagues because of his brother."

In retrospect neither of these statements were true, but that didn't matter. I was talking baseball. With men.

"And what did they get for them?" Fu Manchu responded.

"Tommy Harper," I said, "a future Hall of Famer. And Marty Pattin, who can win 20 games for this team."

Wrong twice again--but not *terribly* wrong. I finished my beer in a couple gulps and grabbed another. I could talk baseball all night.

The conversation flowed with agreement--the Sox needed more pitching, Carl Yastrzemski was already assured a place in Cooperstown, Carlton Fisk, a New Hampshire boy, had a shot to be one of the greatest catchers ever--and division--over the designated hitter rule, the importance of speed in baseball, whether Hank Aaron could ever match Babe Ruth's 714 home runs.

It didn't matter. I was talking baseball. With men.

And they were talking baseball. With me.

I opened my fifth beer.

It happened.

The nervous tension slipped away, replaced by ease and comfort. My whole life had been a clenched fist. I could let go--finally, I could exhale.

I felt light. I felt golden. I felt... normal.

And I never wanted to not feel this way again.

I'd found the solution to being Keith.

When my arm flew a little too freely and knocked my half-full beer to the floor, I could laugh instead of cringing with embarrassment.

When my mouth stopped producing crisp words and squeezed out sounds like toothpaste from a tube, I knew my boys in the kitchen knew what I meant. We were brothers, after all, they loved me--and I loved them.

I stopped noticing those brothers, didn't see the glances they exchanged as I grew louder. I didn't notice as our select fraternity grew smaller, men peeling off and walking away shaking their heads.

Soon, I didn't notice anything, anything at all. Not when the kitchen stool I was squatting on became unsteady and started tipping. Not even when it threw me to the ground and I struggled to get up.

I did notice my stomach was bothering me. It roiled like the time a few years before when I'd tried to learn how to chew tobacco without knowing tobacco wasn't like gum. The comfort in my soul was overtaken by the pressure in my stomach. Without knowing why, I knew I needed to get outside, breathe some fresh air.

That's the last thing I remember clearly.

● * *

The next morning, I came to in my bed. My eyes burned and my head throbbed as if cancerous chicken yolks had replaced my brain. I felt bruises on my arms and my mouth had something crusted around it. Crusted and awful tasting. Wishing I could die, I needed to pee first, and stumbled to the bathroom. The face that looked at me from the mirror was filthy and bloody and exhausted.

I may have felt like a scared and sore little boy, but the mirror knew better.

It was a man's face looking at me.

I had worried that I wouldn't fit in. That I wouldn't know what to say. But as the beer poured in, those worries poured out. If I could just keep drinking at the right pace, I could finally be what I was always supposed to be.

I got drunk that first night of course. I couldn't wait to do it again.

The hangover sucked.

The missing memories? No big deal.

The feeling? Perfect.

I just had to find the right stopping point. But I loved the way I had felt--the camaraderie with the big kids, the ease and warmth flowing through my body, the silencing of that bastard in my head who never shut up about how I was lacking.

At 13, I had found my escape vehicle.

All I needed to do was find the right balancing point, the perfect dose to achieve that floating, weightless feeling.

Once I figured out when to stop, I could go on drinking forever.

Chapter Twenty-Nine

Handcuffs, Firecrackers, and a Little Bit of Mescaline

I spend a lot of time with people who've spent a lot of time in cages--sorry, 'cells,' if we're being polite--paying for crimes they committed. Since my friends have been real criminals, I don't bother trying to impress them with my record

Still, I was locked in a cell three times before I turned 18

I'll let you decide if I can claim to have done time.

Arrest One

The first time I was thrown into a cell was for a weapons and explosives violation. At least that's my tough-guy, don't take no crap explanation. Another way to look at it is I was arrested for "night wandering" and playing with lady-finger firecrackers. This second explanation is comforting, since it suggests a skylarking approach to life and a simple case of "kids will be kids."

I'll tell you what happened, and you can decide.

Jonas has been my best friend since high school, though technically, we've known each other since kindergarten. (He still has a copy of our second-grade class paper--proof that my literary career peaked early.) We weren't childhood inseparables. Our real bond didn't form over recess or multiplication tables. It formed when weed entered our lives.

By sophomore year, we had perfected the routine: wait for our parents to fall asleep, then sneak out and wander the UNH campus like two very unthreatening ghosts. Jonas lived on Faculty Road, where Baby Boy Newell evolved into whoever I am now. Beards Landing, where I lived, was about equidistant from our usual meeting spot, which happened to be the same path I used to walk with my mom to the library. That felt significant, though I wasn't sure how.

Most nights, we discussed philosophy--by which I mean, we got high and said 'wow and 'whoa' a lot.

On one particular late-May night, we met at midnight. Jonas, always the ideas guy, had a pack of ladyfinger firecrackers--the smallest, most unimpressive fireworks known to man. To prove their explosive potential, he proudly told me that he'd tied three together, lit the fuse, and scared the hell out of some kids camping in a tent near his house. Mission accomplished.

Flush with cash (read: nearly broke), we hitchhiked to Dover for an all-night pizza feast. My financial empire crumbled, leaving me with a single, glorious dollar.

No problem--we tried to hitchhike back. Except... no one picked us up.

So, we walked. Four miles.

Back in Durham, we knew it was time to part ways, sneak

into our beds, and pretend we'd been there all night. But first, we were thirsty. The 24-hour laundromat had a soda machine, and we had just enough for two glorious, thirst-quenching Cokes. The plan was simple: Jonas would walk out the front door, I'd walk out the back, and the night would be behind us.

I pulled out my last remaining dollar, smoothed it lovingly, and fed it into the change machine.

Ker-chunk.

Then... silence.

No change. No bill. Just me, staring at the machine, betrayed.

Clearly, the only logical response to a stolen dollar was small-scale terrorism. I took three ladyfingers from Jonas, twisted their fuses together, and slid them into the electric-eye slot. Then, like any self-respecting teenage genius, I lit the fuse.

BANG! BANG! BANG!

Much louder than expected.

The machine, impressed with my negotiation tactics, exploded in a small but dramatic display of shattered glass and metal.

And that's when we realized we might have overcorrected for the injustice of one missing dollar.

We laughed. What else was there to do?

As it happened, two Durham cops were driving by with their windows down. They didn't hear three ladyfingers; they heard gunfire coming from the laundromat.

Brakes slammed. They surveyed the situation.

Gunfire. Smoke. Shattered metal. Two suspects, possibly

armed. Laughing.

Weapons drawn, they rushed through the front door.

"Don't move!" one shouted.

"Hands up!" said the other.

Stoned, exhausted, and vaguely amused by the contra-dictory orders, I did something that, in retrospect, may not have been the best choice. I bolted out the back door. Jonas followed.

"Stop, or I'll shoot!" one of them yelled.

We didn't stop.

The cops likely realized their quarry was pathetic--just a couple of dumb kids. Still, they couldn't just let us go. Jonas was tackled on Main Street. My capture was far more humiliating.

Employing my elite criminal instincts, I sprinted into a blind alley. Then, doubling down on bad decisions, I started climbing a fire escape.

The pursuing cop didn't even bother running. He just walked over to the bottom of the fire escape and looked up at me.

It was his turn to laugh.

"Where do you think you're going from there, Son?"

We were cuffed and stuffed into the cruiser. Within 15 minutes, Jonas's brother had come down to bail him out. I was read my rights and put into a cell.

But why? Why was I incarcerated?

Being too smart for my own good.

The cops needed to reach my parents and all they could get when they called was a busy signal. I'd taken my parents' phone off the hook before sneaking out of my house--not because I thought I'd be arrested but because I didn't want a wrong number to lead them to look in on me.

After 30 minutes in Durham's Fortress of Justice, I finally broke and told them why they couldn't reach Mom and Dad. They drove me home, and I had to bring Dad down.

"Dad? Dad?" I whispered, shaking him. I didn't want him to wake and prayed the cops would just leave.

I heard a throat clearing downstairs.

"Dad! I'm really sorry but the police are downstairs. They want to talk with you."

Don't forget you love me, I wanted to say.

Instead of going to trial, I was required to go fishing a few times with a member of the force, Ronald "Smiley" McGowen. I don't remember catching anything except for a slight crush on his daughter, Sherry, whom I expect saw me as a notorious and desperate outlaw. Smiley was actually a nice guy who seemed to wish me well, which was kind.

I am no recidivist.

I have never since taken fireworks into a laundromat

Let alone ignited them.

Rehabilitation can work.

Arrest Two

One of the times I was arrested involved an Army buddy of mine, Mike, a 24-year-old who, because of the mathematics of age and authority, was assumed to be my ringleader. That was not accurate.

Mike and I were both studying "military journalism" at the Defense Information School at Fort Benjamin Harrison in

Indianapolis. The course of study to become a DINFOS-Trained Killer involved learning to develop black-and-white film, write inverted-pyramid news stories, and show up for morning formation fully dressed--a requirement I struggled with. Some mornings, I barely managed to make it. But I digress.

The story of the third arrest will come later. Let's talk about the second.

Mike was from Minneapolis, just 500 miles away, so we decided it made sense to hitchhike there for the weekend. We set out Friday after work, knowing that traveling together would hurt our odds--two young, military-aged men with GI haircuts and duffel bags looked more like trouble than one.

We figured we'd split up, meet in the Twin Cities, and somehow--through dumb luck and blind faith--find each other the next day at noon. This was the pre-cell phone era, when "meeting someone" meant setting a time and hoping neither of you got arrested, kidnapped, or run over before then.

My lack of anxiety may have had something to do with the fact that I was spending most of my waking hours in a state of chemical optimism. If I hadn't been eating peyote like Good & Plenty and smoking weed a dozen times a day, my rational side might have won out.

So be it.

2:32 A.M. – Waukesha, WI

I stood beside an on-ramp to I-94, my thumb raised, the highway stretching out like a black ribbon slicked with frost. The occasional rumble of a semi broke the silence, but the road was mostly empty. The streetlights cast long, yellowish beams over the cracked pavement, making everything look paler, colder, lonelier.

I pulled my jacket tighter, but the cold still found ways in--under my sleeves, through the gap in my collar, straight to my bones. My breath came out in small clouds, vanishing almost as soon as they appeared.

Behind me, a gas station sign flickered and buzzed faintly, smelling of diesel, cigarette butts, and old coffee burned down to tar.

I had just settled into my hitchhiker's stance--casual, shoulders loose--when blue lights sprang to life beside me.

At seventeen, I had already been through this routine before. The cop would ask if I was okay. I'd say yes. He'd tell me I couldn't hitchhike on the interstate. I'd say, Why no, officer, I had no idea. He'd instruct me to move to the top of the on-ramp, I'd pretend to leave, and once he drove off, I'd step right back to where I started.

But this cop was different.

His flashlight hit me first, the beam cutting through the dark, landing on my boots, creeping upward like an interrogation lamp.

"ID."

Weird.

I pulled out my driver's license and military ID, the thin plastic cards suddenly feeling fragile in my fingers.

He studied them for a long moment, then:

"So, you're a soldier, huh?"

Even in 1976, that was an unusual tone for a cop to take toward the military. Vietnam had been over a couple of years, and military guys still got some respect--usually.

"Yes, sir. Just trying to get to Minnesota to visit some friends."

He smirked.

"They pay you in the Army, Soldier Boy?"

"Sir?"

"Do they pay you? You got fifty dollars cash on you?"

I had maybe twenty bucks in my pocket. I'd given the rest to Mike so he could buy a half-pound of weed from a guy in the Twin Cities. In retrospect, not the best budgeting decision.

"Sir, I get paid, but I don't carry that kind of money."

The cop's expression didn't change. He was chewing something--gum, tobacco, or just my terrible excuse--jaw working like he was debating which flavor of bullshit I was serving.

"Do you know what vagrancy is, Soldier?"

"It's... like being a bum, isn't it?"

"It's not like anything. In Waukesha, a vagrant is anyone who doesn't have $50 cash on them--especially when they're standing on our interstate."

I briefly considered pointing out that President Eisenhower had built the interstate for national defense, that every five miles of highway contained a mile-long straightaway for emergency plane landings, that I, as a member of the United States military, was technically using the road for its intended purpose.

I opened my mouth.

"Turn around. Hands behind your back."

The squad car smelled like old leather, stale coffee, and something faintly antiseptic. Heat blasted from the vents, thawing my hands. The arresting officer didn't say a word when we got to the station, just walked me inside, saw I was booked and left.

The station itself was all buzzing fluorescent lights and cinderblock walls, cold in a way that felt deliberate. The kind of place where they kept it just uncomfortable enough to make you answer questions faster.

The cop keeping an eye on me sat across the room with one leg crossed over the other, tapping a pen absently against his knee. He was older, maybe late fifties, with a slender frame that seemed more professor than patrolman. His face had a thoughtful, almost mournful quality--delicate around the eyes, as if he might flinch from loud noises or bad news.

He didn't stare, exactly--just watched me in intervals, like he was trying to figure out if I needed help or handcuffs. His uniform was crisp but not showy, the creases in his trousers sharp enough to suggest pride, but not vanity. Every so often, he'd take a sip from a dented metal thermos, wince slightly, then go back to his silent vigil.

After 20 minutes of pacing, I called out:

"Sergeant, can I talk to you for a minute?"

He barely looked up.

"That's what you're doing, isn't it?"

I took my shot.

"I'm supposed to meet someone at noon. In Minneapolis. It's about 350 miles. And, uh, I'm hitchhiking."

"Meeting somebody?"

"A girl," I lied smoothly.

That got his attention.

He squinted at me like a poker player deciding whether to call my bluff.

"What kind of girl?"

I went full Romeo.

"The love of my life. Her parents don't approve of me. I sent her a plane ticket to Minneapolis. She's supposed to meet me at the airport. At 12:15."

The sergeant's mouth twitched. He chewed on the thought.

Then, without a word, he let me out.

Fifteen minutes later, I was in the cab of a heated semi, rubbing my hands together, a crumpled twenty-dollar bill in my back pocket.

As the truck pulled onto the highway, I looked back.

The sergeant was still standing outside the station, watching.

A grin played on his face, but he kept it to himself.

And I couldn't wait to hug my imaginary girlfriend.

Arrest Three

A ways back, I introduced my buddy, Mike, then left him behind like someone you've met at closing time and come to your senses in the bathroom. Mike was 24. I was 17. We both liked drugs. The basic requirement for a strong friendship.

Mike and I hitchhiked from Indianapolis to Minneapolis four or five times in the fall of 1976. Lots of crazy stuff happened on those trips. I bought a 1965 right-hand drive VW Bug from the guy who'd picked us up. He was a sailor who needed to be back in Virginia as soon as possible. We worked out a price. He pulled the VW into the breakdown lane. I got in the driver's seat. Mike climbed in the front seat and we gave the sailor a ride to O'Hare, then drove off in my new old car.

But we didn't get arrested, so I'm not going to present that story.

Another time, in Minneapolis, Mike had bought a half-pound of weed and needed to move it before we hitchhiked out of town. Mike's buddy knew a girl, a bartender, who'd absolutely handle four ounces. We smoked up. I had a super-puffy purple down coat with inside pockets big enough to hold the eight one-ounce bags. We continued to smoke as we rode to the bar.

I was pleasantly wasted, and didn't even notice where we were parking.

Minneapolis-St. Paul International Airport.

This was 1976, 25 years before 2001 and all the subsequent increases in airport security. Still. This was federal property. The bar was past a checkpoint. There was a metal detector at the checkpoint.

Weed makes some people paranoid. I wasn't one of them.

I should have been.

Instead, I just convinced myself I was a clean-cut soldier going to visit a girl in a bar. Stifling a giggle, I thought of the imaginary girlfriend who'd gotten me out of jail in Wisconsin. I had this. Piece of cake.

With a half-pound of weed concealed in my coat, I got in line behind Mike. The young officer smiled at Mike, then moved the wand up one side of Mike and down the other. Silence.

"Have a great rest of your day, Dude," said the officer.

Dude! Nobody in uniform called someone dude in 1976.

I stepped up to the official. The wand went up my left side. Silence. Down my right side. Silence.

I waited to hear the word "dude."

It never came.

Instead, the officer, friendly as you like, said,

"I've just got to look inside that coat."

SCCCCRRRREEEEECCCCHHH. My high was gone, leaving behind all the righteous paranoia I could stand.

"Really?" I said casually, flashing my most endearing smile.

"Yep," he said. "Regulations."

I thought about running. I remembered the last time I'd tun from a cop. I thought about refusing to open my coat. While I was not lawyer, I figured a refusal to open a coat at an airline checkpoint would provide probable cause to tear the thing off.

I thought about crying. I don't think I did.

I unzipped my puffy coat, let the sides drop down and prepared to be arrested on federal charges for possession with intent to distribute. Five years at least. The Army might kind of suck, but not like prison.

I looked at the officer's name tag. Geoff Something. So,

Geoff was going to be the man who helped me destroy my life.

Geoff looked down in the pocket. He could see eight plastic baggies, each with an ounce of weed. He didn't look up right away.

I didn't say anything. Just tried not to shit myself.

Geoff raised his head and looked me in the eye.

"You a good guy or a bad guy?"

I took my own pause. Extended it.

"Mainly I'm I a good guy. But I got a little wickedness I can't seem to shake."

Geoff chuckled appreciatively.

"Me too, Dude."

He pointed to where Mike was waiting.

"Go join your buddy. Have a great rest of your day."

I wanted to hug him. Instead, at the first men's room we got to, I went in, pulled a fistful of paper towels out of the dispenser, shoved in a bag of weed and replaced the towels. We conducted our business with Mike's friend's friend. On the way out, I caught Geoff's eye.

"Men's room towel dispenser's acting up. Might want to check it out."

I wanted to say something profound, but nothing would come.

"Have a good rest of your life, Dude."

Then we left.

But we didn't get arrested, so I'm not going to present that story.

The third time I got arrested was with Mike. We were a couple of weeks away from graduating as DINFOS-Trained Killers and decided to stay closer to home this weekend. Mike had gotten his hands on some reportedly pretty good mescaline, and we decided to take a cab into Downtown Indianapolis. We'd been so busy traveling north we hadn't even been to the local city.

November in Indianapolis feels like a breath held too long--air thick with exhaust and the flat, metallic scent of impending snow. The city, slick with the spit of recent rain, glows beneath the sodium-orange streetlights, everything--sidewalks, parked cars, the stiff fabric of my military-issue coat-- holding the cold like a grudge.

Mike and I push through the revolving doors of JC Penney, stepping into the flat, recycled warmth of the department store. The place smells like winter coats in a high school hallway--wool damp with breath and body heat, the faint ghost of mothballs, a whisper of cheap perfume. Somewhere, Christmas music dribbles from tinny speakers, barely audible beneath the murmur of shoppers.

The mescaline is in us, but we've forgotten. That's always how it goes. You swallow a thing, and then you forget, and then the thing remembers you.

We ride the escalator. Up, down. The rubber handrail is warm and buzzing beneath my fingers. I glance at Mike--his pupils have eaten his irises, black saucers gleaming under the fluorescent hum. He's got that half-smile, the one that says we are about to become astronauts in a very wrong place.

That's when I see her.

A woman steps onto the escalator in front of me, hair the stiff, over-permed variety exclusive to Doloreses and Marges. But it's not her hair I notice--it's the hummingbird. A ruby-throated hummingbird, perched right on the crown of her head, shimmering with impossible life. The green of its wings glows, not from the overhead lights, but from within, like stained glass backlit by morning sun. It bobs once, twice--then, with a flick of iridescent feathers, it turns to look at me and smiles.

The world shivers.

At the bottom, I grab Mike's arm.

"Did you see that?" My voice sounds like it's coming from somewhere behind my head.

Mike just starts laughing. And laughing. His whole body shakes with it, his shoulders rising and falling like he's barely holding himself together. Then his eyes catch something--a display of leather hats, rich and brown, smelling of tanned hide and distant deserts. Mexican hats.

We grab them. Try them on. Start speaking in accents borrowed from old westerns and Taco Bell commercials.

"Ees a fine hat, amigo," Mike says, tipping his brim. The stiff leather creaks as he bends it just so, the scent of tanned hide and department store cologne mingling in the air.

"I must go," I announce, my voice dramatic, my arms sweeping like a silent film actor. "All this buying and selling--it makes me dizzy, makes me sick."

The fluorescent lights above seem to flicker, humming like trapped hornets. Everything in this JC Penney is too bright, too much--aisles of polyester and plastic, shelves stuffed with sweaters folded like artificial landscapes. The white noise of commerce--the beeping registers, the murmured negotiations over discount bins, the rustle of shopping bags--presses against my skull like a migraine in stereo.

Mike's eyes widen, pupils like deep, dark wells. He places a solemn hand on my shoulder, his palm hot through my jacket.

"It's the medicine," he says, voice low and knowing, as if revealing some sacred truth. "It needs sunlight."

We drift toward the revolving door at the front. The brass and glass panels spin in a hypnotic rhythm, each wedge a gleaming little prison cell, cycling endlessly. I stand at the threshold, watching. Five rotations pass. Then five more. Each time, I imagine stepping in, but the thought of getting stuck in that looping carousel of glass and bad decisions makes my stomach turn.

Mike taps my shoulder, breaking the trance.

"Huh? What?" My voice is thick, stuck somewhere between my throat and my brain.

Mike points--off to the side, a regular door. A blessed, boring, conventional door. Its brass handle twitches with movement, pulsing like a heartbeat. I watch its slow, syrupy rotation as someone ahead of us exits, and we make our move.

As soon as my feet slap onto the wet pavement outside, a hand clamps down on my shoulder--hard. Not friendly. Not Mike.

The fingers dig in, stiff and territorial, like a hawk's talons on a bunny.

I turn.

The man in front of me is sharp-edged, narrow, all elbows and angles. A human weasel in his forties, his slicked-back hair the color of stale coffee, his lips constantly working as if tasting the air. His eyes are beady, predatory, fixed on me like I'm something scurrying in the underbrush.

"Forget something?" His voice is nasal, condescending, edged with static like an old radio signal.

His hand snakes over my head and plucks the hat right off me. He flips it over, inspects the tag.

"One hundred twenty-five dollars," he says, drawing out the syllables like they might change reality. "Prepared to pay?"

I can feel the weight of the thirty bucks in my pocket. Paper-thin. Useless.

Beside me, Mike is beginning to drift, his body moving as if he's being carried away by an invisible tide. I can't blame him, but I want to.

Weasel's eyes snap to him, pupils tightening. "Get back here, Hombre, with your expensive sombrero."

A bilingual weasel. Huh.

Mike slinks back, his head low, and removes his hat like a man at a funeral. Weasel squints.

"Money?"

Mike shakes his head.

Weasel clicks his tongue, disappointed but unsurprised. "Follow me."

His hands--one still locked onto my shoulder, the other latched onto Mike's sleeve--steer us back inside. The store's artificial warmth slaps my face, thick with the scent of fabric softener, shoe leather, and stale popcorn from the snack bar by the escalator. The air is too still, too heavy, pressing against my skin like a damp wool blanket.

We retrace our steps, back toward the escalator, Weasel's grip never loosening. The moving stairs stretch upward, an iron river leading to a place I don't want to go.

As I step onto the escalator, my fingers graze my jacket pocket, and my stomach turns to ice. The pipe.

It's still in there.

A tiny, metal betrayer, barely bigger than my thumb, but catastrophic if discovered.

I take a breath. Time is syrup-slow, my fingers moving with what I think is grace, guided by my finely tuned mescaline insights. I slip the pipe from my pocket, its cool weight pressing into my palm. I can't just drop it. Not here. Not now.

Then, an idea.

I extend my hand, deliberate and smooth. The metal chute of the escalator glides alongside us, a perfect delivery system. I visualize it: I'll let go, and the pipe will silently slide away, disappearing into the mechanical veins of JC Penney, never to be seen again.

I let go.

Reality refuses to obey mescaline.

The pipe hits the chute and bounces. Clang.

Then again. CLANG.

It tumbles, ricocheting down the escalator, each impact a metallic gunshot, a cacophony of betrayal.

Weasel stops. Turns. Looks at me.

"Smooth move, Ex-Lax." His grin stretches, gleaming

teeth too white, too even.

At the top, he gestures for us to stop. He takes the down escalator, descending like a vulture spiraling toward roadkill.

I swallow.

Mike sways beside me, eyes fixed on the middle distance, unbothered.

Weasel reaches the bottom, his slick shoes clicking against the tile, his body folding in a practiced bend as he plucks the pipe from the ground with delicate fingers. He holds it up to the buzzing fluorescent lights like a crime scene investigator uncovering a murder weapon, turning it this way and that, his lips pressing together in a smirk of quiet triumph. The tiny bowl gleams, still warm from my pocket, a cursed object now, an artifact of my unraveling.

Then, with slow, deliberate steps, he places one polished shoe onto the rising stair of the escalator, and the machine lurches into motion beneath him, carrying him upward. His smile--sharp, thin, satisfied--remains fixed as he ascends, like some smug deity returning from the underworld with proof of my sins. The distance between us shrinks with agonizing inevitability. My mouth is dry. My hands twitch. The walls of reality waver like heat rising from asphalt.

He takes us to a room the size of a broom closet, stale and airless, the walls painted in the precise shade of institutional hopelessness. A desk, a chair, a buzzing fluorescent bulb overhead that makes the edges of my vision crackle with light halos. The door shuts behind us with a finality that reverberates through my bones.

I try to stop tripping.

It's like trying not to breathe, like trying not to think of white rabbits. Immediately, they appear--multiplying like thoughts themselves, expanding, shifting, standing upright. The rabbits begin talking in clipped British accents, debating the finer points of commercial law. The walls breathe. The floor hums. Time--already a wobbly construct--melts into something thick and honey-like. I have no idea how long we sit there.

Then the door swings open.

Weasel slinks in first, his weasel-smile unchanged, flanked by two cops who carry the unmistakable posture of men who do not want to be here. Their uniforms smell of sweat and fabric starch, their utility belts creak as they shift their weight. They sigh through the processing of us, the way you sigh when your shift is almost over and then someone walks in five minutes before closing.

Handcuffs. The cold bite of metal against my wrists. Mike mutters something about how bad hats always lead to bad luck. We're marched back through JC Penney, past the racks of sweaters and winter coats, past the scent of cheap perfume and broken consumer dreams.

The escalator, again. This time descending. The mirrored walls reflect a dozen fractured versions of ourselves--two young soldiers, two shoplifters, two cosmic clowns caught in a joke that is no longer funny.

Outside, the cruiser waits, red and blue lights throwing erratic colors onto the wet pavement. They shove us in. The seats are hard, molded plastic, unforgiving against my back. The city outside warps and bends through the rain-streaked window, neon signs twisting into unreadable hieroglyphs of the night.

Then I realize something.

The pipe is gone.

Not mentioned. Not produced as evidence. It has vanished into the ether, sucked into some mescaline-induced pocket of reality where all incriminating objects go when they are truly, desperately needed to disappear.

Thank you, Mescaline.

The rest unfolds like a poorly scripted procedural. Booked. Processed. A single bare-bulb cell that smells of piss and industrial cleaner. A phone call. Our commanding officer's voice, flat and unimpressed, delivering the kind of canned speech he's likely given before and will give again.

I won't even try to explain the kaleidoscopic horror show behind my eyes. Tripping in a jail cell is like watching a carnival from inside a locked closet--you can hear the laughter, see the spinning lights through a crack in the door, but all you feel is the cold, hard reality pressing in on you.

A court date, ten days away.

Back to base, under restriction, surrounded by the gray walls of military consequence.

A week and a half later, Mike and I march stiffly into district court, dressed to the regulation nines in our Class A uniforms--creased, pressed, polished. The wool fabric is heavy, scratchy against my skin, the stiff collar biting into my neck. My shoes, buffed to a near-mirror shine, squeak slightly with each step on the scuffed tile floor. The place smells of stale coffee, cheap paper, and something institutional--like old books and bureaucratic despair.

We take our seats on a wooden bench that has been

sanded smooth by the weight of a thousand anxious asses. The room is dim, lit by overhead fluorescents that flicker just enough to make me wonder if it's my imagination. The judge's bench looms ahead, a massive slab of dark wood polished by decades of hands slamming gavels and pointing fingers.

Mike shifts beside me. His mustache, which droops slightly at the corners, does him no favors. He doesn't have the slick, knowing smirk of a guy about to charm his way out of trouble. No, Mike's mustache gives him the air of a guy who stocks the backroom shelves at a 24-hour convenience store-- the one you go to when you need a pack of smokes and a look at a stash of grainy, poorly-lit Polaroids.

The judge--thin, pale, with hair that has lost its war of attrition--squints down at Mike's file. His robe, too big for his bony frame, pools around him like a vulture's wings.

"Case of Michael--" he pauses to adjust his glasses, as if seeing the name clearly for the first time, "--Michael Anthony Fitzgerald."

Mike stands. The wool of his uniform jacket creaks at the seams as he straightens. He clears his throat.

"How do you plead?" the judge asks, voice dry as printer paper.

Mike's mouth twitches. I can see the gears turning, the pre-loaded speech forming behind his eyes, something about extenuating circumstances, misunderstandings, possibly even the tragic death of his childhood dog.

"Well, your Honor, it's like this--"

The judge doesn't even blink. "How do you plead," he repeats, voice clipped, firm. "You've got two choices. Please choose."

Mike sways for half a second, caught mid-thought, his excuses drying up like a puddle in the sun. His shoulders sag slightly.

"Guilty, your Honor," he mutters, suddenly very interested in the floor.

The judge doesn't hesitate. "Three hundred dollars."

More than we expected. More than we have. But still-- payable.

"Next."

I stand. My uniform jacket feels tighter, my breath shallow. I meet the judge's eyes, waiting for the same script to play out. Instead, silence.

His watery gaze studies me, forehead creasing in mild curiosity.

"How old are you, soldier?"

The question throws me. He didn't ask Mike that.

"Seventeen, your Honor."

His mouth quirks at the corner. "Seventeen and in the Army," he muses, as if I'm a curiosity, some rare species found in the wrong habitat. "You needed your parents' signature to join?"

"Yes, your Honor. I'll be eighteen in a few weeks."

He nods. "That's fine," he says, almost offhandedly. "But not pertinent."

I blink. "Your Honor?"

A slow smile creeps across his face, the kind of smile a teacher gives when they realize you haven't studied for the test.

"You, soldier, are a juvenile in the eyes of the law. This court has no jurisdiction over you. We'll transfer your case to juvenile court. They'll be in touch in a few weeks."

My stomach drops. A few weeks? I don't *have* a few weeks.

"Your Honor, I don't mean any disrespect, but I've got orders to leave for Germany next week."

His eyebrows lift. "Germany, huh?" He leans back slightly, steepling his fingers. "I was there right after the war. Beautiful country. Great beer."

Then he looks me dead in the eye, that small smirk deepening.

"But you're not old enough to drink. You are a *juvenile*, a *child* in the eyes of the law."

The words hit like a slap. I want to argue, to insist that I'm a man, that I've earned the right to be treated like one, that I've been trained to hold a rifle, trained to follow orders, trained to--

But that would be stupid.

The judge taps his fingers on the bench, considering. Then he exhales through his nose, his mind made up.

"Under the circumstances," he declares, "since the state misassigned you to my court, and you have military orders to follow, I will dismiss your case. You may go."

Relief crashes over me, so sudden and sharp I almost choke on it.

"Thank you, your Honor," I blurt, louder than I mean to. "Thank you very much!"

He waves me off with a flick of his bony wrist. "And I don't want to see you again," he warns, "not even when you reach the age of majority."

I'd gotten all the luck I could handle. I didn't wait to have it buttered.

I nod. I salute. I get the hell out.

Conclusion

Three arrests. Three cells. No convictions. A fishing trip, a free twenty bucks, and a judge who thought I was too young for crime but old enough for the Army.

So, did I do time?

Or did I just finesse the legal system into a slightly illegal internship?

Chapter Thirty

Collision Course with the Rest of Life

For most people, life is a series of problems to be solved, challenges to be met. But recovery has a truism: emotional growth stops the moment the addict picks up a substance. If that's true, then at 18 I was still 13. At 25? Still 13. At 48--yep, still 13.

Bumper cars are great when you're 13. But eventually, you're supposed to graduate to real ones. I never did.

If my life was a vehicle, it stayed a bumper car--ricocheting through adulthood, colliding with everything and everyone.

By this point, the collisions weren't just coming--they were scheduled. Every exit ramp led to the same intersection. Every escape route was pre-paved with wreckage.

This is where the story slams into the rest of life.

Soon, I discovered an entire fleet of vehicles ready to take me wherever I wanted to go, each promising to leave insecure, awkward Keith behind. Not that anyone else seemed to see *that* Keith. If anything, I had cultivated the opposite persona--class clown, chaos agent, perpetual disturber of peace.

It wasn't until 35 years later, when I got into recovery, that I saw the truth: I was convinced everyone else was effortlessly whole--steak, cooked to perfection. Meanwhile, I only saw myself from the inside out--nothing but raw, bloody meat. But they never saw that.

They saw the charred crust I had seared onto myself.

This is not an addiction memoir. It's not a recovery memoir.

The first two-hundred-and-some pages tell the story of how Baby Boy Newell became Keith Howard and how Keith Howard made himself into a boy, then into a teenager.

But not into a man.

If this were an addiction memoir, it would include a catalog of horrors: the depths to which I sank, the humiliating attempts to stop, the inevitable progression of my addiction.

This book has none of that.

This last part will be a fond farewell to youth, the youth of a boy who found escape vehicles from himself. Over time, those vehicles became his home. When he was 48, living on the streets and stealing mouthwash to drink for the alcohol, the escape vehicle still sheltered him.

But that's for another book--the book of addiction.

And another book--the book of recovery.

Here, we'll take a brief final look at some postcards of madness, have a laugh, maybe shed a tear. I've talked about getting arrested; here are the stories of getting fired from jobs before I was 18.

But first, an exception. I just *have* to tell you about the first time I dropped acid.

February, New Hampshire. Age 15.

I was smoking a lot of weed but not drinking much. Two friends and I managed to score three hits of windowpane acid, rumored to be the strongest and purest to hit the UNH campus in years. None of us had ever tripped before, and I assumed it would be like weed--but with some visuals.

A miscalculation.

Another mistake: We dropped at 8 p.m. I had a midnight curfew.

I'll spare you the poetic descriptions of getting off, how Emerson, Lake & Palmer suddenly made perfect sense and cut straight to me stumbling into my parents' house, struggling to maintain the barest illusion of normality.

The problem? The acid had made one thing perfectly clear: my parents were Nazis.

The proof? I was circumcised. Neither Dad nor Mom was. Connect the dots.

Panicking, I opted for a preemptive strike.

"Mom. Dad. I'm sorry. I had too much to drink. Can you yell at me in the morning?"

Miraculously, it worked.

They told me to go straight to bed. My sister Jennifer had a friend sleeping over, and I was warned not to wake them.

I went upstairs, undressed, and prepared to sleep. Except sleeping on acid? Not a thing.

For hours, my walls shifted and rippled like a flag in the

wind. Then, a light flickered off outside, and it hit me: the world had ended. Even the streetlights looked alive--breathing, pulsing, as if they knew something I didn't.

Still naked, I sprang out of bed and sprinted into Jennifer's room, flipping on the lights.

"The world has ended!" I announced jubilantly.

Next stop: Mom and Dad's room. They needed to hear the news too.

Dad groggily got out of bed, taking in my wide eyes, naked form, and urgent enthusiasm.

He was back to being a Nazi. Damn.

I needed to escape. But where?

Outside, of course. Nazis wouldn't follow me into the cold.

I ran downstairs and bolted out the front door.

Naked.

In February.

In our courtyard, I attempted a heroic high jump over the picket fence, misjudged the distance, and landed directly on the pickets, my back absorbing the full impact.

Bleeding, freezing, and still convinced I was the last man alive, I sprinted to the end of Beards Landing, awaiting further instructions from the universe.

Instead, I heard a familiar voice.

"Keith?"

It was Leigh, one of our over-the-garage tenants--a college student and EMT. My dad, correctly assuming beer alone wouldn't make me this kind of crazy, had enlisted her help.

And suddenly, it all clicked.

The old world was dead. I was the new Adam. Leigh was my Eve. Our first task?

Repopulate the Earth.

(Spoiler: No assault, sexual or otherwise, took place.)

Instead, Leigh calmly led me to her car and drove me to the emergency room, where I was treated for puncture wounds, frostbite, and--oh yeah--acid-induced psychosis.

That night, I got my first injection of Thorazine.

Of course, that wasn't my last brush with professional failure. If anything, it was a warm-up act. By the time I turned 18, I had been fired from more jobs than most people will in a lifetime. I wish I could say I was alarmed, or even mildly concerned. But by then, getting fired was just another punch-line--another story for later. I told myself I was too clever for rules, too restless for clocks. Secretly, though, I was starting to wonder if maybe I was just unemployable.

Let's start with the first one...

Firing #1: The Dishwasher Conspiracy

At 14, too young to legally work, I took a job washing dishes at the Ramada Inn under my friend's name--David Jackson. The kitchen was a cacophony of clattering plates, hissing steam, and the constant bark of the head cook, a chain-smoking man with a voice like gravel in a blender. He insisted on keeping the kitchen radio tuned to a French-Canadian station, staticky and thin. I didn't learn his name or if he even spoke French. The air reeked of scorched butter, dish soap, and something metallic--probably the drain clogged with a week's worth of food scraps. I'd read Sinclair's The Jungle, and wished he'd had time to move on to restaurants. Still, David and I split the shifts and the pay, trading off like a pair of small-time grifters.

The job was perfect until I stumbled upon its hidden treasure: half-finished cocktails sent back from the dining room. I wish I could explain my thinking process, but there was no thinking, just operative conditioning: alcohol within reach, drink immediately.

I swilled from martini glasses still kissed with lipstick, tumblers swimming with the last golden swirls of whiskey, hurricane glasses sticky with rum and melted fruit garnish. It was all there for the taking, glistening under the harsh fluorescent lights, each sip a secret, a thrill, a shortcut to adulthood. I made it my mission: no drink left behind.

At first, it felt like I'd hacked adulthood, like I was in on some grand secret. The kitchen noise blurred into a pleasant hum, my body felt loose and invincible. And then--by my first Friday shift, I was obliterated by 10 p.m., swaying between the industrial sinks, my reflection in the stainless steel warped and wavering like a bad dream.

The floor was slick with grease, and the scent of bleach mixed nauseatingly with the rich, charred aroma of seared steak and garlic butter. My hands, pruned and stinking of dishwater, fumbled with the endless avalanche of plates. Someone--maybe the cook, maybe a hallucination--told me to pull myself together, but the words slurred in my ears like they were coming from underwater. By midnight, I was curled over a mop bucket in the back alley, vomiting up a stomach full of stolen steak and lobster, my body purging the spoils of my ill-gotten feast. The alley smelled like old fryer oil and damp cardboard, and the cool night air did nothing to stop the world from spinning.

Somewhere in the distance, the muffled thump of music from the hotel lounge carried through the heavy night, a cruel reminder that other people were still standing.

By the next morning, I was unemployed. No formal firing, no grand confrontation--just the unmistakable understanding that I wouldn't be coming back. The kitchen door had closed on me, and with it, my short-lived career as David Jackson.

Come to think of it, the real David Jackson may have needed a new name to work again.

I had one to spare: Baby Boy Newell.

Firing #2: The Camp Mi-Te-Na Massacre

I've related the details of this story earlier, so here's a quick recap.

At 15, I was invited to be a counselor-in-training at my beloved summer camp. An honor. A privilege.

A brief tenure.

On our first night off, I led three fellow counselors into town, convinced some older guys to buy us beer, and downed six before jumping off the town pier.

Unfortunately, there was no ladder.

The lake police fished me out, and we were all arrested.

By the time I regained consciousness the next morning, the other counselors had apologized and been reinstated.

I, the ringleader, was fired.

Firing #3, Seeking Revenge for Nothing

The summer I turned sixteen, I landed a job at a local restaurant and ice cream shop--a small-town institution owned by a friend of my parents. Inside, the air was thick with the mingled scents of griddled burgers, fryer grease, and melting waffle cones.

I started as a dishwasher, hunched over steaming sinks, arms slick with soapy water, fingers pruned from scrubbing congealed cheese off ceramic plates and sluicing half-eaten sandwiches into the abyss. But charm--and the rare teenage skill of making change without panicking--soon propelled me to the front counter.

A promotion in my first week!

My replacement in the dish dungeon was Carl, a lumpen proletarian with no political theory at all. Nice kid, but couldn't grasp the basic concept that property is theft--so my habit of grabbing a gallon of ice cream on the way out was liberation, not larceny.

Now the smiling face of the shop, I found ways to "redistribute wealth"--a phrase I much preferred to the pedestrian and judgmental *stealing*. Each night, about fifteen bucks made its way back to "the people," by which I meant me. Think of it as a modest correction to the capitalist model: an untaxed $3-an-hour raise, a direct levy on the exploiters.

The job itself? A dream. $3.35 an hour to scoop towering cones, drizzle hot fudge, and slap burgers onto trays. Best of all, we locked up at 10:30. By 11, I was out the door, pockets lined with my reallocation efforts, headed for a night of cheap beer and questionable decisions.

Until one Friday in late August.

At 10:29 p.m. sharp, a bus the size of a small apartment complex groaned into the lot, brakes hissing like an exasperated sigh from God Himself. The doors opened, and out poured a sea of sweaty, cocksure football players--bruised, loud, and proud--followed by an armada of cheerleaders in high ponytails and higher decibels. Behind them came the swarm: parents, siblings, and locals who had chosen a Catholic high school football game over literally *anything* else, like, say, drinking in a field.

Friday night. Prime party time. In 31 minutes, I was supposed to be shotgunning a beer in someone's barn. Instead, I was about to be shackled to a sticky countertop, slinging sundaes until past midnight. The injustice was staggering. A violation of my inalienable right to debauchery.

But I was no ordinary worker. I had vision. I had strategy. Most of all, I had a deep and abiding commitment to avoiding unnecessary labor.

With no immediate ice cream orders, I slipped through the kitchen like a general retreating from a battle he never believed in. In the clatter and steam of the dish pit, I found Carl. He needed his consciousness raised. As a loyal cog in the capitalist machine, he was the perfect accomplice. Together, we carried a gross--144 eggs--out of the walk-in. The cartons were cool and damp in our hands, ripe for rebellion.

When the moment came, Carl folded. He slunk back to his greasy pans, just another casualty of capitalist cowardice. I had tried.

Under the sodium lights of the parking lot, I set to work. One by one, eggs left my hand, slicing through humid night air and exploding in spectacular splats against the bus's hulking metal hide. Yolk streaked down the windows like war paint, albumen gleaming in grotesque smears. By the time I was done, the bus looked less like a vehicle and more like a crime scene at an industrial bakery.

It was my most revolutionary act yet. My Che Guevara T-shirt would've been proud. I imagined my Abbie Hoffman poster giving a full-fist salute.

Knowing consequences were inevitable, I made a tactical retreat. I summoned my superpower: silencing the voices of contrition and regret. They'd never worked well anyway.

Back inside, I clocked out--because even revolutionaries believe in proper documentation--and headed to the party. It took four beers and some truly excellent Thai stick to rinse off the last traces of guilt.

The phone rang the next morning.

The manager didn't waste time. "You're fired."

I feigned outrage. "On what grounds? What political justification can you offer for this injustice?"

"The bus, Keith."

I sighed and stretched my arm, wincing as if the mere memory of my night's labor caused physical pain. "That's disappointing. Hey, while I've got you--do I qualify for workers' comp? My arm's killing me."

Click.

I like to think that bus still carries faint yolk stains, a relic of one teenager's misguided stand against labor exploitation--or, you know, working late.

Firing #4: The Orange Julius Incident

At seventeen, I made a decision that pulsed with electric anticipation and reckless abandon: I dropped acid thirty minutes before my shift at Orange Julius. Nothing happened at first. Nothing ever happens at first with psychedelics.

At second, though, after 30 minutes, the world responded with loving vengeance. The overhead fluorescents throbbed with unnatural intensity, the tile floor shimmered like a swimming pool, and the sickly-sweet tang of artificial oranges curled in my nostrils, impossibly loud, as if citrus had a volume knob. I was strapped in.

Regret should have followed. Instead, euphoria did.

Apron off. Hands splayed on the sticky counter, fingers stretching, grasping at the air between me and the customers, who walked in looking like melting candles, their faces sagging and reforming with each blink.

Laughter poured out of me, uncontrollable, a bubbling, frothy thing--not unlike the Julius itself, spilling over the rim of my sanity.

If a customer smiled, I laughed.

If she stared, I laughed.

If she grew angry, I laughed.

If she didn't exist, I laughed.

Word spread. It traveled fast, faster than the slow-motion movements of the shoppers, faster than the spinning gears in my warped brain. Mall security materialized, uniforms sharp and ominous, but their heads looked too big for their bodies. My manager arrived next, eyes drilling into me with the heat of a thousand heat-lamp pretzels.

I was fired. Or at least, I think I was. The words left his mouth, but they didn't make it to my ears. They fluttered like startled birds, disappearing into the acid-drenched ether.

And that night, still crackling with neon energy, I slid behind the wheel for the first time on acid.

The first. Not the last.

Never the last.

The world outside the windshield pulsed and breathed, traffic lights stretched into eternity. I was strapped into a bumper car that looked like a life.

By that point, I was finally fully qualified for the career path I was destined for: full-time fuckup.

These stories aren't here for shock value. They're here because even at 17, I had already set the course. At night, I'd lie in bed wondering if I was broken. I couldn't say it out loud--not even to myself--but some part of me had stopped believing I'd ever be okay.

Because I should have seen what was happening--but I didn't. Because if there's one thing addiction makes impossible, it's learning from the past.

For the next 30 years, I kept switching vehicles, each promising a new road. But the destination never changed. It was always the same pile-up, the same wreckage, the same road to nowhere.

I didn't know it then, but I'd already found the solution to everything. I had no idea it would nearly kill me.

Author's Note

This volume ends where the damage begins.

It ends with a boy trying to become someone. Anyone.

A misfit trying to outrun shame, loneliness, and the feeling that he was never quite real.

It ends before the addiction took hold, before the long descent,

before the disappointments and the losses and the almosts.

Before resentment powered, justified, and was only briefly silenced by my drinking.

That boy didn't disappear.

He lived.

Barely.

Volume II
And Then . . . Watching the Wheels Fall Off and Burn

1976–2007

A lot happened.

Some of it was good. Some of it was great.

Some of it was so awful it blurred the line between pain and parody.

Whole stretches were just boring--which, in hindsight, feels like mercy.

But over those thirty-one years, the story kept tilting.

At first, a slow decline. Almost gentle.

There were upticks--brief sunbursts, flickers of hope, moments when it felt like maybe.

Maybe I'd make it.

Maybe I'd found a way forward.

Maybe this time would be different.

But the slope got steeper.

And then, one day, it wasn't a slope anymore.

It was a marble dropped from the edge of a desk.

No more arc. Just freefall.

I was homeless.

Hopeless.

Swallowing stolen mouthwash for the burn, for the booze, for the minty-fresh vomit that followed.

I didn't want to live.

And I don't blame myself.

I had plans.

I had means.

I was ready to snuff out the lamp.

But I didn't.

And that's where Volume III begins.

Volume III

Keith Howard and How He Grew Up

Section 1: The Descent & The Exit

The first part of this book told you how I grew and the beginning of my love affair with getting away from myself.

The second part showed the sad grayness of a life lived in an escape vehicle.

This part is about finding my way out. If you're expecting a tidy, three-step plan to sobriety, I have bad news: I took every wrong exit before stumbling onto the right road. Think of this section as the GPS rerouting after I repeatedly refused to take the obvious turn.

The Upside of Ifs

Rock bottom is a funny thing--mostly because you never realize you've hit it until you start digging. Just when I thought I'd reached the lowest point, life handed me a shovel and said, 'Keep going!' But sometimes, even in the pit, strange little moments throw you a rope.

Let's talk about the 'ifs'--the tiny, ridiculous, unexpected things that kept me from fully self-destructing

On May 21, 2007, I knew exactly what the rest of my life held.

The rest of my life would be over within the week.

I had a three-point plan.

- Take a bus from Manchester to Hanover, New Hampshire, carrying a pack with dried fruit, a sleeping bag, and a pair of sandals. Find the Appalachian Trail--it should be easy, it runs right down Main Street.
- Take on a trail name--Night Train or Easy or Jingles or Soapy--and walk south until my fruit ran out.
- Kill myself.

That was it. That was the plan.

I was drinking stolen mouthwash to keep away the shakes, the horrors, the D.T.'s. Even Dollar Store mouthwash has 25% alcohol--stronger than beer or wine, easier to steal.

Alcohol wasn't my problem. Life was my problem. Alcohol was the temporary solution. Suicide was the permanent one. And I was just a few days away.

My life was at a tipping point. And all the weight leaned toward destruction.

If the nurse at the VA urgent care had told me to go to the fourth floor, Make an appointment, Fill out reams of paperwork at the Eligibility and Benefits Office, I wouldn't be alive today.

Instead, she saw the frightened boy inside the scrawny,

shaggy, smelly, drunken man. The man who said, "My name's Keith Howard. I'm a veteran but I've never been here before . . .And I don't want to be alive anymore."

If the doctor in the loony bin had seen just another bum circling the drain, a middle-aged drunk who only need-ed bottles of pills--for depression, anxiety, insomnia. To make everything better. A homeless vet to be treated and released, I wouldn't be alive today.

Instead, he saw the man behind the shaking body in front of him. A man who wanted to die, yes. But who want-ed--more than anything--a reason to live. A man who needed recovery more than prescriptions.

If the Chemical Dependency unit hadn't invited me in, even though I didn't see the point, if the fellas in that unit hadn't shared their experience, their strength, their hope, if the recovery center at the bottom of the hill hadn't welcomed vets to join their meetings, I wouldn't be alive today.

Because of ifs, I took my first, very tentative steps on this road of happy destiny.

Because of recovery, I'm a man who can be trusted. A man who gives and accepts love. A man for whom the future is a big place.

A man who is alive today--To help the still struggling discover the upside of ifs.

Between Tide and Traffic: The Choice of the Addicted

So, I wasn't completely doomed. Great. But now what? Knowing that you probably shouldn't die isn't quite the same as figuring out how to live. At some point, I had to make a choice: keep going down or take an exit. Unfortunately, the exits weren't well-marked, and I had terrible navigation skills.

My problem has never been drugs or alcohol. In fact, I'd venture the same is true for everyone in recovery or active addiction. For the rest of this piece, I'll be talking about alcohol, but I see no real difference between liquid alcohol (booze), powdered alcohol (cocaine, meth, etc.), plant-based alcohol (peyote, mescaline), or alcohol in pill form. Whatever the delivery method, it all solved and created the same problems for me.

If alcohol had been my problem, I wouldn't have needed to recover. I would have just quit drinking, and my problem would have been put on the shelf. There it could stay forever, never troubling me again--so long as I didn't drink.

My problem was not alcohol. My problem was that my only solution to life was alcohol. It may have been a solution that carried plenty of future complications, but alcohol was the one surefire way I knew to feel significantly better about life.

I know algebra drives some people crazy, but let me try to illustrate this:

If **ALCOHOL = My Problem**

then removing the left side of the equation (ALCOHOL) would balance the right--my problem would disappear.

But if **ALCOHOL = My Only Solution to Life**

then removing alcohol simply leaves me alone, adrift, and answerless.

Without going into great detail, I've attempted suicide twice. Each attempt came at the end of the longest time I'd ever gone without drugs or alcohol.

When I stop drinking--without a program of recovery--I want to kill myself.

Again, if my problem had been alcohol, I wouldn't have needed recovery. I would simply stopped drinking, my problems would dry up, and I'd go about my business. But drinking worked in an immediate way. With alcohol, my life might be unmanageable, but without it, my life was in danger. My experience taught me that avoiding alcohol led to suicide.

Like a man living on credit cards, I might know in one part of my brain that this couldn't continue, while the rest of my being cried out not to stop. I got very good at ignoring that first part of my brain and continued drinking until I was 48--sometimes more, sometimes less, but always climbing.

By the end, I was a man on the Golden Gate Bridge, trying to decide whether to jump left into the bay or right into oncoming traffic.

I'm not a God guy today--whether there's a Big Joker in the Sky or the universe is an unsigned masterpiece makes little difference to me--but I know something happened to me at the jumping-off point. Instead of drowning or stepping into traffic, I sought help.

Instead of jumping, I got off the bridge.

And so can you.

Right now, you might be reading this with a jolt of recognition. Maybe you know the headaches in the morning, the growing dread deep in your gut, the feeling that you *shouldn't* go on but *can't stop now.* Maybe you're contemplating suicide, homicide, uxoricide (a real word--look it up), bossicide (a made-up word--sound it out), or any of the other –cides out there.

Maybe alcohol and drugs have drained the color from your world, and now it's just endless shades of gray, with no excitement at all.

Whether you think you *might* have a problem or you *know* you're an alcoholic, you can get help. Not necessarily from professionals with letters after their name, but from other men and women who have been where you are--where I was-- and where you don't have to stay.

Or you can stay on the bridge, choosing between tide and traffic.

Escape Vehicles: A User's Guide to Running from Yourself

I didn't wake up one day and think, 'You know what would be fun? Destroying my life for sport.' No, addiction wasn't the problem--it was my solution. A faulty, disastrous, definitely-wouldn't-recommend-on-Yelp solution, but a solution nonetheless. And when someone suggests taking away the only thing keeping you afloat, it doesn't feel like salvation--it feels like drowning.

At some point in my life, I realized that every problem has a solution. Unfortunately, my solution was alcohol. And heroin. And meth. And boxed wine, mouthwash, and, for a brief time, conservative Protestantism.

These were not *good* solutions, mind you, but they worked--for a little while. Until they didn't.

I don't think of myself as someone who struggled with alcohol. If alcohol had been my problem, quitting would have solved everything. Just put down the drink, pick up a hobby, get really into model trains or pickleball or birdwatching.

Instead, alcohol was my answer--to every question life

threw at me. Which is why, when I tried to take it away, I lost my goddamn mind.

This was not a new pattern. From the start, I was always looking for the right escape vehicle, something that would let me out of myself. Some people experiment in high school. I went pro.

By the time I hit Germany with the Army in 1977, I was 18 and ready to conduct my own field research into pharmacology--stimulants to keep me awake for days, hash to bring me down, alcohol to smooth the edges. Eventually, speed lost its charm, and I found heroin, which was like crawling into a warm, safe cave where time slowed and the world became distant and unimportant. Perfect, except for the whole addiction and withdrawals thing.

Escape vehicles always end up as uncomfortable as the reality they were meant to avoid.

Speed brought ground teeth, paranoia, and psychosis.

Heroin brought escape from that but its own set of cravings, yearnings, and emptiness.

By April of 1978, I needed escape from escape and sought help for my heroin addiction. My treatment consisted of Scream Therapy (really!!) and the insight it offered. That wisdom? Using heroin would eventually get me kicked out of the service--I needed to replace dope with booze.

It kind of worked.

Johnny Walker held me. Then Alex, the Stroh's dog. Then the joys of stolen generic mouthwash.

Alcohol worked. It was the one true drug: Reliable. Legal. And, if I played my cards right, socially acceptable.

Of course, social acceptance depended on *where* I was drinking. When I became a Baptist minister, I knew that public drunkenness wouldn't play well from the pulpit, so I did what any good man of God would do--I got wasted in secret.

When I wasn't drinking, I was losing my mind--stair-surfing headfirst down flights of stairs, cutting my wrists, wondering why I was so utterly *insane*.

Christianity, it turned out, did not cure me.

Because alcohol wasn't my problem. Alcohol was my answer, and without it, I had nothing.

By the end, when I was drinking mouthwash for the alcohol content and actively planning my own death, my escape vehicle had become the driver. I wasn't running away anymore--I was being taken somewhere, and I didn't have a say in the destination. It was either stop drinking or stop breathing. And, by some ridiculous stroke of luck, I stumbled into a VA hospital and chose recovery.

Here's the thing about recovery: it doesn't give you an escape vehicle. There is no methadone for life. No substitute high to replace the one that used to keep you alive. You have to sit with yourself, sober and feeling everything, and it is *awful* at first. But after a while, you realize that real escape isn't about running--it's about *staying*.

Recovery, for me, has been learning how to be in my own skin without trying to claw my way out.

I got to get off the ride before the final crash.

I still don't know if I believe in God. But I do believe in grace--the kind of ridiculous, undeserved second chances that make no logical sense. And I'll take it.

Because today, I don't need an escape vehicle.

Today, I'm okay just *being here.*

"How Do You Exit Your Escape Vehicle?

So there I was, gripping the steering wheel of my personal escape vehicle, pedal to the floor, headed straight for oblivion. Turns out, hitting the brakes isn't as easy as it sounds--especially when you've removed them entirely. Time to figure out how to get out of this thing without crashing into everything I ever cared about.

In 1978, I was in the Army in Germany, having arrived right after New Year's Day the year before. From the moment I landed, I don't believe a single day passed without my drugging or drinking or both.

While some older alcoholics--or at least folks who have been in recovery longer than I--draw a distinction between drugs and alcohol, that line never existed for me. Simple logic tells us that if two items are equal to a third item, they are also equal to each other. So:

If Alcohol = a way to escape myself, and

Drugs = a way to escape myself, then

Alcohol = Drugs.

Whenever I put any substance into my body, it was simply a **Keith Escape Vehicle (KEV)**. And because I am who I am, I can turn a lot of different things into KEVs--spending, sex, travel, work.

For today, for this minute at least, I'm trying to relax into being Keith instead of grabbing the keys and jumping into a KEV.

At first, I was smoking hash--out of bent beer cans with holes made with the pins on my PFC insignia--smoking opium, and drinking beer and wine.

Within a couple of months, though, I had swum far upstream and was snorting crystal meth to stay up for days, smoking hash during the run to keep from losing control, and drinking to pass out at the end.

That lasted through the summer, until I discovered the efficiency of shooting speed.

Snorting meant having that awful-tasting phlegm always in the back of my throat, knowing I was eating my nasal passages away, and not always getting the KA-BOOM rush. Also, bending over a mirror with a rolled bill in my hand felt so tawdry. Injecting meth solved all three problems--now I had delicious phlegm, a healing nose, and a guaranteed lift-off.

Plus, it was so much more glamorous to use a needle.

Still, even the biggest proponent of better living through chemistry has to admit that being awake while everyone else sleeps gets tiresome.

I once spent an entire night bending and breaking metal coat hangers to fashion a sculptured ashtray holder that would keep my omnipresent cigarette at exactly the right height and distance. I was proud of my creation. My roommates, not so much. They threw it away the next morning.

I knew I needed a break from not ever having to take a break.

Ah-ha, you may be saying, *that's when he quit using drugs.*

Puh-leeze.

There was at least one more KEV in the pharmacological garage, and I knew it was time to take a ride with heroin. My friend Chuck, a corn-fed Indiana farm boy and serious drug experimenter, had already moved on from stimulants to dope, and he set me up the first time. As soon as the needle left my arm--and I was done puking--I knew I'd fallen into the arms of heaven.

Nothing mattered. Everything was perfect. Time flowed as it would--even if I was supposed to be covering a basketball game for the division newspaper. That was okay.

After all, nothing mattered, everything was perfect, and time flowed as it would.

The problem with all these vehicles, for me at least, is that each one quickly became as uncomfortable as the reality I was trying to escape. Speed brought ground teeth, paranoia, and psychosis. Heroin brought escape from that, but its own set of cravings, yearnings, and emptiness.

By April of 1978, I needed escape from escape. I sought help for my heroin addiction and went through "treatment," which consisted of scream therapy and individual counseling. When I completed rehab, I was no longer addicted to heroin, having discovered alcohol as my next successful escape vehicle.

But by then, I'd stopped being the driver of my own vehicle. And I wouldn't understand that for a long, long time.

Section 2: The Fight for Recovery

Fun fact: stopping drinking and actually recovering are two different things. Stopping is like climbing out of a burning car. Recovery is realizing you now have to walk everywhere on foot, uphill, in bad weather, with no map. Buckle up--this next part was somehow harder than the train wreck that got me here.

You know what's fun? Doing something completely impossible. Recovery felt like trying to divide by zero--mathematically unsound, theoretically absurd. The only way to make it work was to believe in something I didn't fully understand. Enter: my highly scientific, entirely ridiculous, and yet strangely effective approach to a higher power.

The Square Root of -1

Some of you know, and those who don't will be shocked to hear, that I attended a conservative Protestant seminary--Gordon-Conwell--and was a minister in a Baptist church, focusing on teenagers. During this time, I believed the Bible was inerrant, down to every last jot and tittle, and that it contained answers to all life's questions.

During this time, also, I didn't drink alcohol in public--although I was an embarrassing drunk when away from the congregation.

If alcohol had been my problem, then becoming a Baptist minister would have been the solution--stay away from alcohol, and stay away from my problem. Unfortunately, alcohol was never my problem. It was my solution--the way I dealt with everything else.

Drastically reducing my alcohol consumption didn't bring balance; it brought dread, foreboding, and suicidality. By the end of my time in the church, I was throwing myself face-first down stairs--stair-surfing, I called it--cutting my wrists, and planning suicide. My wife at the time, who had no idea she'd married a man with a death wish, drove me to a psychiatric hospital. That's where I was treated for depression.

And where I walked away from Christianity.

And where my wife walked away from me.

As she should have.

Having sailed in fairly rarefied waters in the church, I still had some kind of spiritual hunger. But I had no use for a personal God keeping track of my every transgression. Buddhism, with its emphasis on self-awareness rather than sin, seemed like a promising alternative.

I read a few books, started thinking of myself as a secret Buddhist, and, for what it's worth, recorded my first and only CD under the name *Pus Theory*. The album--long since disappeared into some internet black hole--was called *The Sound of One Mind Snapping: Spirituals from the Zen Baptist Tradition*.

But this flirtation with Buddhism, given my unwillingness or inability to sit and meditate, ultimately became the equivalent of a boxed game of Monopoly--kept tucked away on a spare-bedroom shelf and pulled out on a rainy Sunday, only to be shoved back once I realized this activity requires focus, dedication, and a desire to get all the green properties.

But I digress.

By 2007, when I was drinking mouthwash for the alcohol content and back to contemplating suicide, I was lucky enough to be introduced to a group of former drunks who had found a way to treat their alcoholism. Unfortunately, part of their system involved having a higher power (or Higher Power).

Because I am powerless over alcohol--the way I drink when I drink--and because my life is unmanageable--it dissolves into chaos, resentment, and suicidal dreams when I don't drink--I needed a higher power. And I needed one pronto.

People in the rooms told me I could have the group be my higher power--their lives were certainly more manageable than mine. Or I could pick a light bulb--it was brighter than I was. Or a doorknob.

You get the picture.

Having been a Baptist minister, I couldn't exactly worship a doorknob. Or a light bulb. Or even *the group*. I needed something... abstract.

For no earthly reason, I thought back to my junior high algebra class and our introduction to quadratic equations.

Without going into a review of quadratics (says the man who is likely incapable of such a review without sitting down for an afternoon and rediscovering them), let me just say the solution to the equation:

$$X^2 + 1 = 0$$
$$X^2 = -1$$
$$X = \sqrt{-1}$$

requires the use of an imaginary number, represented as *i*, which stands for the square root of -1.

It's imaginary--because negative numbers can't have square roots--but once we've imagined it, *i* becomes indispensable in solving the equation.

And just like that, my higher power became an imaginary number.

Represented by a lowercase *i*.

Referred to as the square root of negative one.

My higher power didn't exist. Couldn't exist.

Yet, once imagined, it became indispensable in solving *my* problem: how to live without alcohol, and how to live a semi-manageable life.

And that's how I stayed sober.

Not through faith.

Not through certainty.

But through an equation that required the impossible.

And so far, that impossible thing has worked just fine.

Early Recovery: The Best, Worst, and Most Necessary Struggle

Okay, so I had an imaginary higher power and the vague sense that I should stop destroying myself. But here's what no one tells you: early recovery is like going through puberty a second time, except now, you're old enough to understand just how much it sucks.

"Any man who finds early recovery easy probably didn't need recovery at all."--Unattributed 19th-Century quotation. *Unattributed because I just made it up.*

When I was using, a lengthy period of abstinence was two or three days--an experience that began with a glorious first day.

"I should have done this a long time ago! Feels so good to not feel bad first thing in the morning. I don't think I'll ever drink again!"

By around two in the afternoon, I was so sure I was done with booze that I realized I didn't need to be fanatical about it.

"I'm not drinking, but I could still have just a couple at the end of the day. The secret to sobriety is learning how to drink responsibly--after all, recovery is a journey, not a destination. I didn't drink last night, so that proves I don't have a real problem. Just need to pace myself."

By five, I was stopping at the drugstore or convenience store or supermarket--never the same place too regularly, lest someone think I have a drinking problem--and buying a 30-rack or box of wine.

"Tonight, I'll just have three or four drinks over the course of the evening. Tonight will be different."

No tonight was ever different.

Recovery is about way more than not drinking. It's about redux--a return to health after a period of sickness. But sometimes, we get so used to being diseased that health feels unhealthy--especially when that disease has been our best friend, our constant companion, our soulmate.

Like a starving man with a meal of diseased meat, we know we must consume--even as that consumption slowly kills us.

Early Recovery is:

- filled with excitement and joy.
- numbness and sorrow.
- a life of freedom.
- a diarrhea downpour with no raincoat.
- peace.
- turmoil, pain, and chaos.

Each of those sentences is true--for me, and for everyone who's ever lived through early recovery. But luckily, millions of us have walked that path.

Early recovery ends.

We have the ability to turn that work into long-term sobriety--or wander into relapse.

Here Are Some Things That Helped Me--They Might Help You Too:

- Go to Meetings--12-Step, SMART, All-Recovery--whatever works. Surrounding yourself with people in recovery is one of the best ways to avoid slipping.

- Celebrate Milestones--I thought chips were hokey... until I got a 30-day one. That recognition felt real.

- Think about attending church or synagogue services--Even if you're not religious, being surrounded by people you haven't used with helps.

- Create (and Maintain) a Schedule--Small routines like making your bed or checking the mail help bring a sense of normality.

- Write a Gratitude List (Daily!)--At first, it felt like trite hokum. Then I did it. Try something simple:

  - *My bed*
  - *My shoes*
  - *The $27 I've got*
  - *My recovery*

- Try to get enough sleep, exercise, and healthy food.

- Avoid major life changes (including relationships!)--*You deserve a better partner than anyone who's attracted to you now.*

- Read Positive Literature--Maybe hold off on

Hunter S. Thompson and Bukowski for now.

- Pick Up a Hobby--Fill dead time with something that makes you feel good about your life.

- Believe, Believe, BELIEVE--Recovery is possible.

These are some of the things that helped me--and may help you. If you've got other ideas, send them my way.

And don't forget:

You matter. I matter. We matter.

And of the Dead, Speak Only Truth--Chuck

*Addiction makes all of us gifted liars. At first, the lying is tactical--I don't want people to know how much I'm spending, how much I'm using, how much I **need** my substance.*

Later, the lying becomes strategic: it doesn't matter whether people believe my lies. What matters is making them go away. Early recovery is a time to embrace honesty--and that can suck. Big time. Some people just can't get over that hump.

People in recovery kept telling me I needed to be honest. 'Rigorous honesty,' they called it. I hated that phrase. It sounded like homework. When I met Chuck, I realized what happens when you refuse to be honest--when you lie to yourself, long enough and hard enough, that it becomes your only truth.

How do you say goodbye to a drunk who never got it? How do you pay respect to a man whose life was built on lies, braced by more lies, stacked up like a house of cards? How do you miss someone whose corpse you found stiff on the floor, the sour stench of vodka and decay filling the air? How do you honor a man whose death was attended by nothing but a half-empty bottle near one hand, an empty just out of reach of the other?

I first met Chuck when I was running a transitional living facility for homeless veterans. He had been in the Army twice--once in the early '60s, stationed in Germany, and again at the tail end of the decade, in Vietnam. I know this because I've seen his DD-214s.

When we met, Chuck had been bouncing between shelters. He told me he'd been sober for sixteen years and had sponsored more men than he could count. The first part was a lie; the second might have been true. But I doubt it.

He told me he had been an infantry scout in Vietnam, slipping behind enemy lines, gathering intelligence to keep his unit safe. His service record says he was a jeep mechanic. I suppose it's possible to do both.

He also claimed to have been a high-end antiques dealer, moving eighteenth-century furniture and making a fortune. That may have been true, but when we visited antique galleries, he knew no more about Chippendale and Queen Anne styles than I did. Still, you don't have to know a market to make a killing in it.

During Chuck's few months at the house, we spent time together--though, really, Chuck spent time with me. I never truly knew him. I knew his routine: coffee scalding hot, black as motor oil. I knew he liked to sit outside at night, cigarette ember glowing in the dark, his hands trembling as he wept. I never knew if he was mourning the people he betrayed or mourning the fact they had caught on.

When Chuck was getting ready to leave the house, he sat me down and made a request.

"Keith, you're my only true friend, the only man I trust in the whole world. I want you to be my next of kin--the person who makes decisions for me if I can't. Will you do that?"

There was no right answer. I liked Chuck, and saw myself in him, or at least a Keith that could have been--if I hadn't gotten it, if I hadn't gotten sober, if I'd stayed on that old original path.

Just as when someone says, "I love you," and you don't know what to say except, "I love you, too," I felt a gun to my head. Anyway, how much trouble could it possibly be?

"Sure," I said.

For three years, I got the calls--from landlords, cops, nursing homes. Chuck had done this or hadn't done that--what was I going to do about it? Usually, I took him out for coffee, helped him come up with a plan, and sent him on his way.

Even when he started pretending to be completely blind--usually so he could grab a woman's breast or butt and then point to his very, very dark glasses--I still answered his calls. I have no doubt his vision was failing.

But he always stepped around dog crap and never stumbled over a curb.

This wasn't Chuck's first fraudulent rodeo. He loved telling stories, always starring himself as the man who got the girl, made the money, saved the day. But the story he never told was why he had spent years in a federal penitentiary.

He liked to brag about his time in a "country-club prison" and the important people he met there. According to Chuck, his crime was internet-related and involved making lots of money. That, of course, was also a lie.

Chuck's crime wasn't glamorous. It didn't make him rich. He had convinced an entire small town that he was dying of cancer. Let them hold fundraisers. Let them cry at his bedside. Let them rally around his wife and kids. Even when the scheme unraveled, he never came clean. Not to his neighbors. Not to his wife. Not to his children. He rode the con to the end of the track.

The real charge? Wire fraud. Scammed his employer out of workers' comp. He faced up to thirty years. He served, I think, five. But that's Chuck's math, and he never was good with numbers.

One day, the VA Homeless Team called me. Chuck was sick and drinking--a lot. Could I check on him? Maybe talk him into a hospital visit?

Every time I saw him, he swore he'd been sober for weeks--even with a tumbler of vodka sweating on the table in front of him.

When I got to his boarding house room that last time, the door was locked. The landlord let me in.

The air inside was thick--stale booze, old sweat, something else. Something deeper, darker, something that curled in the nostrils and wouldn't let go.

Chuck was on the floor. Flat on his back, mouth slack, eyes open and staring at the ceiling. His skin was gray, mottled with the early bloom of death. Rigor had already set in, locking his fingers into brittle curls. The bottle near his right hand was half-full. The empty near his left, just beyond his reach.

Chuck stayed on that ride until it stopped moving. Some of us get off. Some of us can't.

I sat with his body for ten, maybe fifteen minutes.

When the EMTs came, they asked if I was family. I told

them no.

Chuck's ashes sat in my office for months. I never quite knew what to do with them, just like I never quite knew what to do with him. Eventually, we scattered some around house-- the last place I know he was safe, sober, and cared for. A group from the Patriot Guard stood at attention as his remains were interred at a veterans' cemetery. The final salute of men who never knew him.

"And of the dead, speak only good," the old Latin saying goes.

I haven't done that here. Instead, I'll follow another: *De mortuis nil nisi verum.*

"Speak only truth of the dead."

Here are the few truths I know about Chuck:

He was an alcoholic. He was a veteran. I will miss him.

And his last name?

When he died, I tracked down his ex-wife--the woman whose reputation he had helped destroy. After all, who in that small town believed she hadn't been in on his scam?

We talked for ten minutes. I hung up the phone with good feeling for her, their children, and all the others whose trust Chuck had chewed up and spat out.

She has moved on.

She is active in Al-Anon.

She deserves to let the dead bury the dead.

I Couldn't Pick the Winners, But I Could Stick with Them

In early recovery, you spend a lot of time wondering if

you've made a terrible mistake. Everything is uncomfortable. Your emotions are back online, and frankly, they're terrible. The only reason I didn't bolt? Other people who had been through this looked... annoyingly stable. Fine. I'd follow them. Begrudgingly.

I don't know horses.

I mean, I can recognize a horse, distinguish it from a cow or a llama. I have a good picture of "horseness," those descriptors that identify horses from nonequine creatures. Still, I don't know horses the way some who knows horses knows horses. At the racetrack, I'm completely over my head.

I do know people in recovery.

Early on, we've got a lot of commonality. We tend to look like warmed-over garbage. We tend to sit in the backs of rooms. We tend not to make eye contact. We tend to be filled with shame and remorse, not just over the things we did while high or drunk and not just for the things we did to be able to get high or drunk. Most often, we are ashamed of who we are. If you're in early recovery, I probably know you. Still...

If I had to place money on either a horse race or on picking winners from early recovery, I'd be a better bettor at Pimlico or Churchill Downs than at a church basement. At the track, at least I'd have luck on my side--along with a little bit of information about the horses' previous record.

In early recovery, where a few folks look great, but most look like they've fallen way below down on their luck, appearances are deceiving.

When I entered recovery, I had just been discharged from a psychiatric hospital, where I'd been put on antidepressants and introduced to my particular pathway. Going to my first meetings out of the bin, I'm sure I didn't look like a potential winner, someone who'd still be sticking around decades later. If video existed, it would show a scrawny guy with eyes that wouldn't alight on anything for long, looking jampacked with terror and tears.

I can remember being seven or nine days sober and looking at the other newcomers around me. Through my insecure and doubt-filled eyes they all looked better than I did. That lady over in the corner was wearing a dress and the guy beside her had a tan. He looked like a golf-pants model, crisp clothes, white smile and a shirt that cost more than my entire wardrobe put together. My pants were held up by an over-cinched belt and a shirt that was clean but clearly worn past needing replacement.

I just kept coming.

After a month or so, the healthy-looking folks had disappeared. The woman in business attire and the handsome guy were nowhere to be seen. At the time, I assumed they'd only needed a half-cup of recovery and were back to successful lives. Some of the other losers I'd come in with were starting to clean up and look better. I still felt like my sobriety was only as strong as my fingernails and could snap any minute.

I just kept coming.

At six months, a funny/sad/expectable thing happened. I was at the front of a room, being given a plastic token with a 6 on it, and I looked toward the back. The handsome, elegant, tanned guy was sitting in Denial Aisle. He was still nicely dressed, still had a tan, but he also had a hangdog expression and a black eye with regret dripping out of it. Back when we walked in together, I'd assumed he was good to go while I was nearly gone. I know I'll never be anybody's handsome guy. I'll never be the best dressed guy. I'll never be the elegant guy. But I can be the sober guy.

I just keep coming.

If you're in early recovery and your life feels like a dog chewed on your past and peed on your future, keep coming.

If you feel like no one's ever felt as empty and obsessed as you, keep coming.

If you keep on trying to get clean and sober but can't find the way, keep coming.

Things can get better. Things can get better than better. Things can get better enough that you'll laugh about having all those things troubling you.

Just keep coming. Keep coming back. You don't have to be the strongest, the smartest, or the best-dressed--just the one who stays.

Pushing Forward When Every Instinct says Pull Back

I spent more time than I needed in early recovery trying to figure out how things worked rather than letting them work. As a matter of self-respect, I analyzed each suggestion, only to find that some of the most important ones needed to be tried with fear and trembling.

I have a lot of wishes.

I wish I were five inches taller--making me 5'7".

I wish I looked more like John Cusack and less like Jon Cryer (the dorky brother on *Two and a Half Men*).

I wish I were younger, faster, stronger, more dripping with charisma, etc., etc., etc.

But those are just surface-level wishes. The deeper, more important wishes--the ones that have truly changed my life-- came from actions I never would have taken on my own.

It's snowing as I write this at my little cabin, powder hushing all the sound as I sit on the porch, not listening to the flakes. I am a lucky man, and I know it. That luck, though, didn't just happen. It grew directly from actions I took--actions I didn't fully believe in and, in many cases, thought were, to put it mildly, horse manure. But I did them anyway, because people further along the path of recovery told me to.

In the early days of aviation, pilots believed that escaping a tailspin was impossible. Instinct told them to pull back on the stick, to slow the descent. But this only made the spiral worse. Once a plane went into that corkscrew motion toward the earth, there was nothing to do but hope for a quick death--maybe even pray the propeller would dig them a soft grave.

In 1912, RAF Lieutenant Wilfred Parke changed everything.

Flying near Stonehenge, Parke's plane entered a tail- spin at 700 feet. He did what every pilot was trained to do--he pulled back on the stick. It didn't work. His plane kept spiraling toward the ground.

Then, either by sheer instinct or a fatalistic urge to speed things up, he did something completely counterintuitive: he pushed forward on the throttle. Instead of slowing down, he gave the plane more thrust toward the earth.

Fifty feet above the ground, he pulled out of the tailspin.

Wilfred Parke was the first known person to escape one. His method is still the only way to do it.

That story perfectly encapsulates my first months in

recovery, when my mentor/sponsor/call-him-what-you-will suggested I take actions that felt just as reckless--completely counter to everything I believed about myself.

For example: I was not then (nor am I now) an orthodox believer of any kind. I do have a Higher Power, but not a personal God, not a creator of the universe who is outside of time and concerned with my individual struggles. My guide knew this about me, so when I told him about my obsession to drink, his suggestion floored me.

"Get down on your knees and ask a Higher Power to take away the obsession to drink."

"But I don't believe in God," I said. "I thought you wanted me to always be honest."

"I'm not telling you what to believe," he said. "I'm telling you what to do. Get down on your knees and ask."

"Yeah, but..." I trailed off. That was how most of our conversations ended.

That day, I went back to the homeless shelter I called home and did exactly what he said.

I got down on my knees and muttered, "Okay God, you know I don't believe you're there, don't believe this is going to have any effect. Still, I said I'd do it, so... please take away my obsession to drink."

Period.

I can't explain how or why, but from that day in July 2007, I have not felt the overwhelming thirst I thought would haunt me forever. Have I thought about drinking? Of course. But never with the same relentless, all-consuming force. The obsession was lifted--not because I *believed*, but because I *acted*, taking a step that made no sense to me, simply because I trusted someone who had been where I was.

For years, I had tried to pull back on the stick--to regain control my way. But that day in 2007, I finally did the counterintuitive thing. I surrendered.

And just like Wilfred Parke, I came out of the tailspin.

Humanity Replaces Chemistry

One day, I looked around and realized something unsettling: I had accidentally made friends. And worse, I cared about them. Even more disturbing? I had started feeling things without chemical assistance. This was either progress or a terrible prank the universe was playing on me.

Recovery has taught me a lot of things, beginning with how to live life without chemical assistance. When I was using and drinking, chemicals--whether powdered, pilled, herbal, or liquid--solved all kinds of otherwise overwhelming problems. These solutions, of course, came with their own problems, but those challenges could be handled with more and different substances. I was the rootin' tootin' embodiment of Dupont's old slogan: "Better Things for Better Living . . . Through Chemistry."

If recovery had done nothing more than free me from chemistry--opening me up to the joys of biology, poetry, history, and a thousand other interests--it would have been a great move. But there was more. Much more.

For an active user--or at least for this active user--using drugs and alcohol to solve problems meant I never needed to use, or even learn to use, any other tools. From the time I took my first drink at 13 and ended up face down in my own vomit on the lawn outside my first high school party, I had arrived. I had found the tool to meet any need.

When I experienced my first heartbreak, I had alcohol and pills to ease the pain.

When my grades began to slip from their never-very-high peaks, I had acid and weed to convince me I was somehow better than students who wasted their time on homework.

When I was fired from my first five jobs--the last for taking acid at Orange Julius and simply laughing at any customer who came to the counter--I had whatever chemicals were around to support my notion that these jobs were beneath me.

And on and on and on.

For better or worse, I always had a bottle or a bag to change my perspective and help me feel better--and *better than.*

Giving up that solution showed me I had a lot of work to do--a lot of growing up and growing better. Some notions I'd thought were silly or presumptuous really mattered.

- Keeping my word matters.
- Showing up on time--or at least letting folks know I'll be late--matters.
- Not stealing matters.
- Trying (often vainly) to curb my tongue matters.
- Listening to other people matters.

I doubt I'll ever be perfect. I'll never be more than pretty good at these. But the prize is in the attempt.

One thing I have managed to internalize--mainly, and for the most part--is that I don't know what pain and trauma others are carrying as they walk this planet.

When I was using, my needs, my pain, my sorrow were all I cared about. Honestly, they were all I believed in. Those around me were just whining, seeking attention to keep from focusing on the real problems--*mine*.

The moment their lips stopped moving, I took it as my cue to talk about myself.

Today, when someone is short or snappish with me, or seems distracted all the time, my first thought is usually: *I wonder what's going on with them?* I know this sounds like, *"What's their problem?"*--a phrase that used to mean, *"Why aren't they listening to me?"*

But now, it's a sign for me to remember that they might have just lost a loved one, been teased ten minutes ago, have pants they think make them look fat, have a toothache, or simply haven't slept.

When I remember that others have endured pain, sorrow, and loss I can't ever know, I'm a little closer to becoming the man I want to be.

Recovery gave me more than sobriety.

It gave me a chance to be human again.

All because humanity has replaced chemistry.

Undoing the Damage

Like Fitzgerald's rich people, addicts and alcoholics are careless, smashing up things and creatures, then retreating into our booze or our drugs. Let other people clean up the mess we've made. Part of recovery is going back to the damage we've done and trying to make things right. Sometimes all we can offer is acknowledgment and a promise to stay away.

"I never intended this, of course."--first sentence of *What Trouble Looks Like*, my first, unpublished novel.

Years ago, I was special education director at a local high school. My wife and I had split up, so my daughters spent half their time with her and half with me, which gave me two nights a week and every other weekend to begin drinking the way I had apparently always wanted to. The increase in alcohol wasn't immediate, of course, but it was a steady progression with only brief intervals of decline. Seven years later, I'd be homeless, hopeless and suicidal, but that's later. Scott Davis is who I want to write about now.

"Scott Davis" is a pseudonym, of course, the pseudonym he was given in that novel. For what it's worth, I gave myself the name Jonah Moses.

After that, I started an alternative school in the same town where I'd been special ed director, and that's when Scott and I came together. Scott was an elementary-school teacher who'd been toying with leaving education to go into sales. Using a certain pied-piper ability, I convinced him to come work with me instead. In retrospect, I think his choice worked out well for him in the long run. Over the next three years, though, I made it a pretty ~~bad awful~~ horrendous decision.

At first, I was a mentor to Scott, and we did a good job of working with kids for whom public school hadn't worked. Quickly, though, my ego--enhanced by nights of alcohol--left Scott in an uncomfortable spot. While I had and have an ability to think and react creatively in the moment, being outside any structure and drinking steadily at night rendered my judgment and methods erratic, if there was any judgment or method at all. I'd rather not list my behaviors; instead, I'll suffice with the clear-eyed observation that I had stopped being a director or a teacher. I wanted to lead a cult. Scott was there the whole time, watching a man he'd looked up to and respected become, like Colonel Kurtz in *Apocalypse Now,* a man who looked only to the jungle for guidance.

No real crimes were committed--I did allow underage students to smoke on daily walks--but I transformed the school into a dark carnival, and assumed Scott approved and would keep quiet. (And isn't it one of our shining truths that expecting people to keep quiet is a sign you're doing something wrong? It is.) Scott could smell the stale alcohol on my breath, see education fade away and amusement take its place, watch a man he'd loved and respected dissolve into a boozed-up caricature of himself.

After three years, in July of 2004, I was fired. More accurately, after three years, I was given the opportunity to resign in lieu of being fired. My drinking had become noticeable to all, my judgment was unsound, and I needed to be terminated. It was the right thing to do and would have been justifiable a year or more earlier.

Still, I considered Scott an ally, and was surprised he didn't respond to any of my texts, call or emails. In sober retrospect, I had betrayed his trust, complicated his life and gone from being a mentor to an infected albatross.

My recovery pathway/tradition/call-it-what-you-will, suggests that I contact people I've screwed over to take responsibility for my actions, apologize and try to make reparations. After I'd been sober a while, I contacted Scott by phone and asked if I could set up a time for the two of us to get together. Every man has a breaking point, and Scott didn't need me jumping on his long-broken point. His response saddened me, but it's perfectly appropriate:

"Keith, I don't have any need or desire to see you. It's fine you're sober, so say or do whatever you need to, then leave me alone. You've done enough already."

I mentioned a first novel. There is a second. Although I haven't shared it with anyone in the years since I wrote it, it was a rewrite of *What Trouble Looks Like* from Scott Davis' point of view. Here is the opening:

"I am not here to praise Jonah Moses, for he is a wicked, wicked man. Nor am I here to bury him, for he is not dead, but only locked up. Instead, I need to examine him, for his life and mine have been intertwined for two years, during which time I assumed that he was good rather than wicked.

"Note that I said "wicked," not "evil." An evil man looks for that which is good so that he can destroy it. Jonah never wanted to destroy anything except boredom. His wickedness came from the fact that he had no idea nor concern for the consequences of his actions; instead he kept on feeding quarters into the carnival game that he called life, not caring what his actions might lead to. It was all just a game to him. It was not 'good' that Jonah saw as his enemy, but 'boredom,' not that his victims could take much solace in that."

As I've said repeatedly, we all affect everyone with whom we come in contact. I affected Scott deeply. I am sorry for that. But apologies don't fix everything. Some bridges don't just burn; they collapse into the river, unrecoverable.

"Keith, I don't have any need or desire to see you. It's fine you're sober, so say or do whatever you need to, then leave me alone. You've done enough already."

He was right. I had.

Wisdom from the Catacombs

Turns out, people have been doing this recovery thing for a while, and some of them even had great ideas and insights. Unfortunately, they didn't put them in a user manual--just scattered them across coffee-stained basement meetings, where you have to sit still and listen. But some of it stuck.

Church sanctuaries held wisdom for me as a boy. It may have been wisdom I didn't understand, and certainly couldn't apply to my life, but when I went into the sanctuary of the Durham Community Church, I assumed the Reverend Novotny had a pathway to God and therefore some genuine wisdom.

As I grew older, became a Baptist lay person and then a Baptist minister, I found the sanctuary to be more of a stage and less of a font of knowledge. In the words of the non-King Martin Luther, "Sola scriptura" was my watchword--it's all in the Book, Buddy. The Bible held the wisdom.

Later, I left the church, and while I still like the Gospels and the Minor Prophets, the wisdom I find in the Bible is in Ecclesiastes. Short, pithy thoughts that help me understand the human predicament. Life is solitary, poor, nasty, brutish and short, as Hobbes would have it, and that brief essay by Solomon as an old man sums it up pretty well. It does a great job of diagnosing our condition; not so much for *treating* it.

Today, I spend more time in churches than I did as a boy or as a minister, although now I'm in church basements more than sanctuaries. Finally, in those small basement rooms I've found the wisdom I'd suspected the building held. No, I don't hang out with discarded crucifixes, portraits of Protestant bigwigs from long ago or aged Torah scrolls. Instead, like the Christians in the catacombs, I gather with other fallen people who are trying to recover their lives. Luckily, these fellow sufferers are carriers of wisdom, always pithy and sometimes funny. Over the years, I've collected some of that wisdom, and would like to offer it now. I don't remember who said what when or why, but below is some true wisdom, at least as this drunk sees it:

The means aren't justified by the ends. The means *are* the ends.

The idea is always to narrow the gap between what we believe and the way we live.

We can rise above our past and make a difference, or we can allow ourselves to be controlled by the past and make excuses.

Yes, you can change the world. The way you do it is by changing yourself.

If you want to change who you are, change what you do.

If you want to quit drinking, you are going to have to quit drinking. When I was new, I didn't think I had any obsessions until I started thinking about it. Then it was all I could think about. All we ask is that you completely change your attitude as soon as possible.

Quitting was easy. Staying quit was impossible.

I thought you were normal until I got to know you.

Nobody comes here on a winning streak.

Alcohol was my anti-me solution.

If I could drink like a normal person, I'd be drunk all the time.

My basic problem is me.

I'm not responsible for my disease, but I am responsible for my behavior.

I run from those who want me and I pursue the rejecters.

No longer can we be content with "good enough."

What other people think of me is none of my business.

I am one drink away from never being sober again.

Most of my life was a reaction to a reaction.

When things go wrong, I don't have to go with them.

I'm just another Bozo on the bus.

I'm not here because I drank a lot. I'm here because I drank too much.

I kept on "starting over" but I never changed a thing.

When I'm drunk and things go my way, I throw a tantrum.

I violated my standards faster than I could lower them.

Section 3: Meaning & Redemption

Memorial Day

At some point, recovery stops being about not drinking and starts being about living. I didn't just get my life back--I got a purpose.

The microphone crackled.

I stood at the podium in Veterans Park, looking out at a scattered crowd of faces. Some wore hats embroidered with unit insignias, others sported faded jackets that still carried the outline of old patches. Civilians mingled among them, standing respectfully, holding tiny American flags. In the front row, a row of young ROTC cadets sat stiffly, the weight of unearned medals pinned to their chests. I used to be one of them--a kid in uniform, raising my hand, offering to die for my country without truly understanding what that meant.

Now, decades later, I was a different kind of veteran, standing here to speak--not as a war hero, not as a patriot, but as a former homeless drunk, an addict who had barely survived long enough to make it to this podium.

The microphone squawked again as I adjusted it.

I took a deep breath and began.

"Today, we remember our military dead, particularly those who died in battle defending our country. Each of them raised their hand and took an oath--a promise to every citizen in this nation:

I will die for you.

Think about that.

Life is what we live for. Life is all we have. And yet, the fallen warriors we remember today made a promise that, if necessary, they would give it up for you, for me, for people they never even met.

That promise, whether fulfilled or not, is extraordinary. Who offers their death for the sake of strangers?"

I looked up from my notes. A breeze rippled the flags, the soft snap of fabric the only sound for a moment. Some people in the crowd nodded, solemn. Others, like the younger guys in the back, shifted uncomfortably.

I recognized that discomfort.

For years, I had buried myself in that same unease, pushing away any real reflection on what it meant to serve--because if I had to think about service, I had to think about what I had done after I took off my uniform.

"You heard that I am a veteran. That is true.

I was no great patriot--just a dumb kid from Durham, New Hampshire, with a duty to serve my country. So, I joined the Army for four years.

Like every veteran here, I raised my hand and swore the same oath: I will die for you.

But when my enlistment was up, I didn't return home a hero. I did some good things in my life, sure. But I also made large, self-destructive mistakes--mistakes so deep that they led me to living on the streets, drinking mouthwash for the alcohol.

I had nothing.

I had lost everything and everyone, and I was ready to go.

I was no longer offering my death for you--I was ready to die for myself."

The words hung there, heavy in the open air.

This was the part where people leaned in. The veterans who had been in dark places, the ones who knew exactly what I was talking about, their eyes locked onto me. The civilians, the ones who had never felt the particular kind of loneliness that makes a bottle of mouthwash seem like a good idea, their expressions softened into something else--pity? Concern? Confusion?

I kept going.

"But instead of embracing death, I reached out to the Manchester VA medical center.

I was stabilized and introduced to the group that has kept me sober ever since.

I was a suicidal drunk, and I got the help I needed. And now, today, I am the luckiest man on the face of the planet.

Because now, I stand here as the director of a transitional housing program for veterans, where I witness redemption and return to health every single year.

That's the good news.

The bad news is that not every veteran gets that second chance.

I'd like to tell you about three men--three veterans I have known personally--who represent the past, present, and unknown future of recovery."

I shifted my weight, gripping the edges of the podium.

There was no way to soften these stories. They were the truth, and the truth wasn't kind.

"First, there was Ernie.

Ernie served as an infantryman in the 1990s. He was the first veteran I brought into the house, newly clean of heroin. He was a good man--he tried. But the wreckage of his past pulled him back.

He got arrested, went to jail. When he got out, he didn't come back.

Instead, he went back to heroin.

Ernie is dead.

He overdosed in February.

His death was not for you or for me.

His death meant nothing."

A murmur rippled through the crowd.

Ernie was one of them--one of us. And he was gone.

I let that sink in before moving on.

"Second, there is Don.

Don is an Iraq combat veteran. When I met him sixteen months ago, he was finishing treatment for heroin addiction.

He came into the program, got involved in a support group, started rebuilding relationships with his children.

Today, he is working full-time, self-supporting, and completely clean and sober.

His life is filled with meaning, and I am proud to call him my friend."

I scanned the faces. The civilians relaxed slightly. The veterans--especially the ones who had been there--looked at me with the same skepticism I once had.

I knew that look.

That's why I saved Joe for last.

"The third veteran, I'll call Joe.

Joe lived with us for two months. He went to meetings, worked full-time, started regaining his family's trust.

Then, he stopped going to meetings.

He broke the rules.

Now, right this very second, Joe is living on the streets of Manchester, an active heroin addict.

Just Saturday, he stopped by, telling me he was excited about getting clean.

Last night, while I was writing this speech, one of our current residents saw him high on Elm Street.

Joe is still out there, making the same choice every addict has to make--life or death."

I exhaled.

Then, I stepped out from behind the podium, gripping the microphone.

"You have heard of the heroin epidemic in Manchester.

You have seen the overdoses, the wasted promise, the deaths.

I see this every day.

I see the Ernies. The Dons. The Joes.

Joe may be here right now, in this crowd, bumming money or cigarettes off you.

He, like so many others, stands at a crossroads.

He can choose death--by overdose, by neglect, by violent crime.

Or he can choose life.

I am not a praying man, but if you are, pray for Joe.

Pray for all the other Joes and Janes using heroin today--veterans or not.

Pray they are offered the real choice of recovery.

The choice between a life of purpose and a meaningless death."

I stepped back behind the podium, gripping the edges once more.

The crowd was silent.

Then I looked up and said the only thing I could say.

"You matter.

I matter.

We matter."

The microphone clicked off. I stepped back.

And in the quiet of Veterans Park, the wind rippled through the flags again.

Section 4: Larissa: An Introduction to a Fairy Tale of Sorts

I believed, for years, that if I got my life together, I'd be safe. That once you get sober, you stay sober. That's a lie. Addiction doesn't disappear--it waits. Patiently. Larissa is proof of that. She was one of the lucky ones, just like me.

And then she wasn't.

Most of us are familiar with standard plot structure:

Exposition, rising action, climax, falling action, resolution.

Typically, the resolution of the story leaves the protagonist a little bit better off than s/he was during the exposition. In the case of recovery narratives, though, the resolution is an ever-upward line. Almost literally, the sky is the limit.

No matter what kind of recovery meeting you go to, the narratives are likely to follow a predictable path. It's not a bad path--in fact, it's really good--but it is well worn by every other recovery story you've heard before. Briefly, the plot is:

Prologue--The speaker was the child of either very good or very bad parents, or, as in the case of many fairy tales, both. Cinderella's mother, for instance, is dead at the beginning of most versions of that story, and our heroine's father marries a woman who is okay until the father dies, at which point she becomes the Wicked Stepmother. Hansel and Gretel, Snow White and the dozen children in The Wild Swans face a similar fate. In the recovery tale, our speaker's childhood often overflows with feelings of not fitting in, being worthless or having a sense the speaker is different than everyone else. Imagine--being the Other in your own story.

Act I--The speaker discovers alcohol/drugs and from the beginning senses a key has been fit in a heretofore locked door. Finally, freedom. Ease. Comfort. Think Cinderella at the ball. That alienation is gone, at least while the speaker is high or has a buzz of some kind. Our person in recovery has found a way to live that works, has embraced better living through chemistry.

Act II--Devastation. Despair. Destruction. The substance that made life livable has turned its power on the user, leaving her or him worse off than ever before. Like Cinderella at the stroke of midnight, the spell has worn off, the horses have been turned back to mice. This part of the story is usually the longest and most emotional section, likely because it's way easier to describe horror and loss than what is to follow in Act III. There's a reason *Paradise Lost* is way more popular than Milton's preceding work, *Paradise Regained.*

Act III--The resurrection. The homecoming (even to a home you've never been before.) The prince with the lost shoe. Prince Charming's appearance. The recovery from addiction. Strings play, the lights brighten, life has become a glorious phantasmagoria. Typically, the speaker describes her or his pathway--AA, SMART Recovery, NA, etc.--and tells how much better life has gotten now that s/he has removed drugs and alcohol from life. From now on, life is clear sailing!

I'm going to tell you a story about my friend, Larissa beginning in Act II and continuing into a different Act III. Before I begin, though, I should tell you a bit about Larissa, or at least what I think I know.

Larissa was born and raised in Dublin, NH, where her father was an attorney and her mother was a psychiatric social worker. Larissa never complained about her parents, except that they got divorced when she was in fifth grade, and she felt that scarred her. Still, Larissa went to private school where she excelled at drama and softball, the latter earning her a scholarship to Iowa State, where she was named an All American.

After college, she drifted from corporate sales job to corporate sales job until she married at 28 and decided to become a teacher. Except for a year after the birth of each of her two children, Larissa never took time off from teaching. According to her students, peers and supervisors, Larissa was a truly gifted teacher.

Oh, yes. Larissa's drinking. Since high school, Larissa had enjoyed a few (or more) beers on the weekend. As she aged, though, her taste for booze increased, until at 38, she identified herself as an alcoholic. You'll learn a lot more about Larissa, her drinking and her Third Act.

Part I

Too Smart and Charming for Our Own Good

I just got off the phone with a dear, dear friend. Larissa is in her late 30's, holds a graduate degree and works as a teacher, where she is seen by her students and peers as insightful, creative and a dynamite professional. Her classroom is always abuzz with excitement, and her students routinely say she's the best educator they've ever had. Larissa has been married for 15 years, has a couple of great kids, and does volunteer work in her community, focusing on the elderly. In that, she is also highly valued and seen as near-saintly. She is smart and charming and any number of other adjectives.

One word in the previous paragraph is wrong, though, and must be amended. "Works as a teacher" is actually "worked as a teacher."

Friday, Larissa was fired from her teaching job--despite all her gifts--because Larissa is also a drunk, an alcoholic. There had been warning signs and written warnings, hand-wringing and hand-holding, pie-crust promises to change and repeated breakage of those pie crusts.

Larissa has been to rehab three or four times, during the summer and during the school year. She's stopped drinking plenty of times, but hasn't figured out a way to stay stopped. Yesterday, Larissa's students smelled stale alcohol on her breath, reported it to her principal, and she was fired. As she should have been.

At the end, I was allowed to resign from one of the best jobs I've ever had, running an alternative high school program in a dynamic community with engaged kids. I just couldn't control my drinking, couldn't stop drinking, and couldn't stop lying about my drinking. I was where Larissa is today, and it took me another three years of sinking before I finally found myself homeless. Then, I found my solution.

Talking with Larissa was like listening to tapes of me all those years ago.

"I never drank at school."

(Although I drank enough almost every night to still be legally drunk when I drove into work.)

"Some people just metabolize alcohol in a smellier way than most."

(Of course, some people just don't drink, or don't drink on work nights, or don't drink enough to worry about metabolizing times.)

"Who are they to judge what I do on my own time?"

(Even if their concern is the ways what I do on my own time affects students, parents and co-workers.)

"I'm going to see a lawyer, because alcoholism is a disease. They wouldn't fire me for having diabetes."

(Unless I continued to take too much insulin or refused to eat so I was passing out in the classroom, acting shaky or confused or falling asleep regularly.)

"If it weren't for my husband/kids/neighbors/parents/ad nauseum, I wouldn't need to drink."

(Although I would, because I'm an alcoholic, gifted at finding targets to drink at.)

"They're jealous of what a good job I do, and how much the kids like me."

(That may be, but they're also worried about my judgement and decision making, impaired as I am by booze.)

Larissa will find another job. She's insightful and gifted and attractive, and that's what her references will say. They won't say she's a drunk. They won't want to damage her opportunities because "She's so great when she's not drinking. If it weren't for that . . ." Unfortunately, those ellipses never end without change, and that change doesn't seem to come without work on our part.

No one ever passed on that truth about me, either. After all I was creative and energetic, if not attractive. From that lost job of mine, I eventually got a teaching job at a residential school, until I got fired from there, if not for drinking then for behavior brought on by drinking. Then I got a job as a clerk/salesman. Then I got homeless.

Larissa is cursed by good luck and bad genes. She's got everything she needs to be successful--except for the ability to stay away from that first drink.

Larissa and I are both smart and charming, too goddamned smart and charming for our own good when it comes to booze.

There, all the gifts and talents in the world won't keep us sober, although they can keep us from getting sober.

Part II

No More Crises Because That's All Life Is

A little over a week ago, I wrote about my friend, Larissa, who'd just been fired from her teaching job. Larissa is very smart, very creative and very deep into problem-drinking territory. In fact, by her admission, Larissa long ago had her visa stamped at the gates of alcoholism. Regardless, Larissa had called me for help and advice, knowing I'd been in her shoes, and hoping I could help her navigate her way into sobriety.

In a perfect world, I could have driven the four hours

to see her, whispered magic words into an amulet, placed it around her neck, and she'd never drink again.

In a perfect world, Larissa could have met me at her door, asking to go to an AA meeting, where she'd meet a woman who'd offer to walk her through the twelve steps of that organization as Larissa got used to living without booze.

In a perfect world, Larissa could look at the mess she and her drinking had made of her life, put the plug in the jug and move on to a life without alcohol.

This ain't no perfect world, as my friend Tonio K. reminds us.

I sat with Larissa for two or three hours, listening to the same words, phrases and rationalizations I'd told myself for years. It turned out Larissa had already found a new job, beginning in 10 days. Without wanting to betray any confidences (and of course I've changed enough details about Larissa to make her unidentifiable), I can give the gist of our conversation in a few sentences.

"So I just need to figure a way to be perfect for a couple weeks," she said.

"Perfect?" I asked. "That seems like a pretty tall order."

"Not *perfect* perfect," she said. "I just need to not drink at all for a couple weeks, get a few good days in at the new job, then only drink on my way home from work. No more drinking on the way to work."

"So 'perfect' means not drinking until you've had your job for a few days?"

"And not drinking on my way to work after that," she said. "That's an important part. There's just one problem."

One? Oh, yes, the problem of alcoholism's progressive nature and its ability to infect our entire lives and personalities. I wanted to say this, but didn't.

"What's that one problem?" I did say.

"DT's. I get them really bad if I don't drink. Shakes, hallucinations, blood pressure off the charts. Don't worry--I've got a bottle of Benzos. I was hoping I could come and stay with you to help me get through this. You could park my car miles away, and not tell me where the nearest store is."

So Larissa's plan was, in essence, for me to hold her prisoner with no medical support other than her "bottle of benzos" (benzodiazepine, a class of tranquilizers carrying their own addiction risk) and my kind and thoughtful ignorance of all things medical. I may not know how that story ends exactly (death, assault, pathetic lies, fractured relationships?), but I believe it's always tragic. Still, I also know it's the kind of plan I developed for myself, over and over and over, for years, although mine usually included the proviso: "And I'll quit drinking not THIS weekend--I've got too much to do--but next weekend," thus keeping the moment of truth always within sight but never within implementation.

Rather than throw a freezing wet blanket over Larissa's plan, I asked her to call me each day, just to check in, to go to meetings and to try to find a woman locally who might be able to help her during these difficult early days. As I suspected, as I feared, as I goddamned knew when the phone didn't ring it was Larissa. After a few days, I texted her "Daily phone calls?" and got back "oh right sorry my bad," followed by more non-ringing phones.

I don't relate this to embarrass Larissa or anyone else who's struggling to find a way to struggle to quit drinking. I danced that same dance for years, making a decision to quit drinking and believing that decision was the same as accomplishing the goal. Ask anyone who's decided to commit suicide yet is still above ground. "Deciding" is not taking the first step; it's not putting on hiking boots; it's not even getting out of the chair. Deciding is, for many alcoholics, a way to put off doing anything.

For a decade, I firmly intended to quit drinking, and each time a crisis erupted like an infected pimple on a teenager's face, I'd change that intention to a firm decision, iron-clad until the pimple stopped hurting. Then I'd go back to drinking. Of course, one of the nice things about the disease of alcoholism is its progressive nature. The longer I put off doing anything, the more frequent the crises came until eventually my life was the crisis.

Part III

A Free-Association Scream (900 or so Words of Id-Driven Rage at Addiction Poured onto the Page without Editing or Re-Reading)

Larissa's had another red-letter day/week/month with the same red-letteredness I brought on myself near the end of my drinking. Moving from mid- to end-stage alcoholism is distinguished by increasingly common losses (or throw-aways) and satisfaction with less and less and less in life. The border between the stages may come with the recognition that buying Sam Adams is a waste of money. Natty Daddy gives you what you want without all that taste and craftsmanship. (Or, in my case, Chardonnay is for suckers when Lavoris gets me drunk *and* gives me minty-fresh vomit. I quickly slid from brand-name mouthwash to Dollar Store generics, but that was less for aesthetic reasons than for its being easier to steal.)

This week, Larissa, who's just started a new job--she's charming and smart and pretty, in addition to being a nearing-end-stage alcoholic--wrecked two cars in one day, got her first DWI and has been asked to move out of her home. Like a child whistling as she walks past that house with the mean dog, Larissa tells me she's got a plan for pulling things together. As she tells me about it, I taste the same "once-I've-jumped-over-the-canyon-and-swum-the-Pacific" nonsense that had infected all my end-stage dreams, and I'd never faced the public and practical problems of holding down a job with no public trans-portation, no car and, oh yeah, no driver's license.

After losing a second job for drunkenness or its after-math, I quickly went through my tiny savings. (In the previous sentence, "savings" is a euphemism for "what remained in my checking account after I'd paid my rent and bought cigarettes and booze.") When my girls got home from school, they had a chance to see the eviction notice on the door of our s-hole apartment in a section of Nashua just north of Dicey and west of Danger. Ah, memories. Feeling like a victim always, I assumed some deus ex machina would appear to rescue me. Didn't happen. A week later, after the girls had packed up their things and taken them to their mom's, I had a final night alone, alone except for a box of Chardonnay. I laid on the futon in the dark corner of the back room, cradling the wine except for when I lifted the spout up to my mouth. That box made me feel like a wealthy man indeed.

The next morning, homelessness felt like freedom. No more boss telling me what to do! No more wasting money on rent! Finally, I could drink the way I wanted to--desperately and self-destructively, just as God intended.

Larissa today is like a woman in a pool of freshly-poured Plaster of Paris. She can still move, although the cake-batter consistency around her presents a challenge. As time goes on, she'll find life getting slowly but inexorably harder to control as the plaster hardens. The slow-motion thrashing she does will create a space for her inside that solid pool, until she's as snug as a bug in amber, a bug with a taste for booze and little else.

If she's like me (and most of the other drunks I've known), she'll begin to think of suicide, or at least an end to her existence, going to sleep at night praying she won't wake up. Warnings from friends and family will increase.

"If you don't stop drinking," they'll say, "you're going to die."

Promises, promises. Promises that never come true.

Six months after our eviction, when I'd found a series of depths below the deep, I realized there was no "bottom" for this drunk to find until my body thumped onto the bottom of a casket. Luckily, instead of continuing to drop, I reached out for help from the VA and a program of recovery. Many (most?) (nearly all?) aren't that lucky, burrowing deeper and deeper into despair, finding it harder and harder to find lower companions, creating ever-duller red-letter days/weeks/months.

Like Larissa.

Like Larissa, I continued to be charming, if charming means "manipulative and dishonest with no regard for how I affected others."

Like Larissa, I continued to be smart, if smart means "manipulative and dishonest with no regard for how I affected others."

Unlike Larissa, I was never pretty, but I'm afraid alcoholism doesn't leave much beauty inside or out. In women in their forties, booze seems to dissolve their looks, first slowly and then completely.

By the end, I was amazed if not amused that it takes as much energy to be a semi-employable drunk with a taste for mouthwash as it did to direct alternative schools, run an improv theater company and be a homeowner. The energy didn't result in achievement anymore, barely resulted in anything, but I kept on needing it, or at least needed the booze that fueled my energy.

Readers know I'm not a God guy at all, not real interested in whether the Big Joker in the Sky is paying attention. Still, I pray 50 or 75 times a day, saying the same prayer over and over and over: "Thank you, God." For today, I'm going to amend that prayer to "Thank you, God, and please help Larissa find a way to want to find a path to sobriety."

Those of you who have a chattier relationship with a higher power, please feel free to embroider this message, and insert whatever other names are appropriate for you.

Part IV

No Friendly Direction but Down--Six Feet Down: A Larissa Update

Larissa is at the end of her rope--and wishes it were wrapped around her neck.

I had lunch with her a few days ago, then talked with her last night and again this morning. To update you, Larissa will lose her driver's license next Monday--the result of last month's DWI--she's been "asked" to leave her home in Dublin, where her husband and two kids still live. Larry just couldn't take the lying, the not coming home at night, the drunken fights--in short, he can't take Larissa. And neither can her kids, which break's Larissa's heart so badly the only thing she can do is drink.

She's found a room to rent in the Southwestern NH town she's now working in, and is happy it's only five miles from her new school. Of course, the teaching gig she landed is only until the end of the year--precipitated by a maternity leave--and she hasn't told her principal about the DWI or loss of license. She has faith no one in town will Google her name and find out about her arrest, but faith gets shaky in the evening. She worries at night, worries so badly the only thing she can do is drink.

Her parents are both alive, and she feels they're still in her corner. For now. When she asked if she could borrow $20,000 from them to "start over," they turned her down, which gives her premonitions they might turn on her, leaving her alone. That alienation is terrifying, so upsetting the only thing she can do is drink.

Larissa accurately diagnoses her condition.

"I'm an alcoholic".

"I've lied to everyone in my life, and they've all left me. All I've got left is my drinking buddies--and they're all creeps. I guess I'm kind of a creep, too."

"I can't picture a world without drinking."

"Sometimes I feel like the world would be better off without me. At least my kids would have my life insurance money to start them off right."

Suicide. Offing yourself. Doing yourself in. That seemed like the only option to me, and that's where Larissa is now. Each night she passes out with the hope she'll die in her sleep, and when she wakes up in the morning with a foggy and throbbing head, shaky hands and a bellyful of dread, she asks for the courage to kill herself today. So far, thank God, she hasn't found it.

(An aside: when stunning statistics are released about deaths from the opiate epidemic or alcohol poisoning, I assume they're at least 20 percent low, because addicts and alcoholics at the end don't typically leave suicide notes. They've long stopped communicating with anything but their drug of choice and their death of choice. If I'd had a gun for the last six months of my drinking I'd have splattered my brains all over a wall. No note left behind, just a momentary regret I didn't have another couple drinks before pulling the trigger.)

Larissa's world keeps getting smaller. It will shrink and shrink until she can't turn around. That world will be big enough for Larissa and a box of wine. No matter how far apart we are, we breathe the same air. No matter how close we are, there is still air between us. No matter how tiny Larissa's world gets, it will always have room for a box of wine. Or a bottle of mouthwash.

Sometimes sober and more often drunk, she calls me. (By the end stage of alcoholism, "sober" and "drunk" are mere approximations. The dedicated last-gasper has always got enough booze in her blood to blow hot in a breathalyzer. Seeming sober is just one of the gifts of alcoholism.)

Larissa knows I've been within hailing distance of her world, but left that desperate chaos behind. She knows by some completely unmerited act of grace I found a program of recovery still central to my existence. She knows my life today is the best I've ever had. She calls me and seems to want the magic word, the talisman, the secret of sobriety, but I don't have any secret.

I didn't drink. I cleaned house. I had a man I trusted who wouldn't co-sign and notarize my bullshit. I met with other alcoholics every day for a long time, and now do so at least three or four times a week. I worked with newly sober people. I tried to follow a program of recovery

Those aren't secrets, for Christ's sake. They saved my life, but they're not magic words.

Oh, yes, one other thing.

I didn't kill myself.

Please pray Larissa doesn't kill herself, and does find a moment of vulnerability, a second of peace and a glimpse of clarity.

Recovery can work.

But not if you're dead.

Part V

Mortui vero nihil nisi de (Say nothing but truth of the dead)

Larissa is dead.

The circumstances are unclear to me, and matter not one bit. Whether her death was ruled the result of a heart attack, liver failure, overdose or gunshot, Larissa's real cause of death was simple: untreated end-stage alcoholism.

Larissa is dead.

Larissa and I were friends for seven years, a friendship that had its peaks and valleys. At many times, before Larissa's embrace of the chaos that accompanies alcoholism like slaves chained at the ankles, we often talked daily and had lunch once or twice a month. Again, before Larissa's existence started circling the drain like soap suds at the end of a bath, I got to know Larissa's kids some, and her husband a bit better. By the end, her husband called a few times, hoping I had some magical words to get Larissa to go into rehab yet again. I didn't have the incantation, for alcoholism's dark magic is stronger than any mere words.

Larissa is dead.

"Mortuis nil nisi bonum" ("Say nothing but good of the dead.") is of course the more common Latin phrase, but here my aim is truth. I loved Larissa, as did hundreds, even thousands, of other people. She was smart and charming and pretty. And funny, kind and dedicated. Energetic. Sweet. Insert any positive adjective and I'll likely endorse it. She was one of the good ones.

Here, though

Larissa is dead

If you've read this far in the Larissa saga, there's a fairly good chance you're in recovery yourself, this last part is not for you.

If you've read this far, you may have a loved one who's in recovery. This last part is not for you.

If you've read this far, you may just like my writing. Thanks for that, but this last part is not for you.

If you've read this far, you may be worried about your drinking and hoped the Larissa Saga would end happily. You may have wanted Larissa to learn to control her drinking, to drink like a lady, and to return to a normal life. You may have desired that Larissa simply make the decision to stop drinking and then stay stopped. If that's you, welcome! This last part is for you.

Larissa is dead

But you don't have to be. Really.

Recovery is possible and available to anyone. It will take hard work, a desire to change your entire life and a willingness to go to any lengths, but you can get and stay sober, no matter how far down you've driven your life, regardless of the damage you've done to yourself or others, notwithstanding the emotional vacuum you've come to accept as life.

I've stood at the same jumping-off point you are. I was homeless and hopeless and toothless, with no friendly direction available. I entered recovery inside a psychiatric unit, a place I found myself after telling a Veterans Administration nurse, "I don't want to be alive anymore."

Sobriety is available. Recovery is possible. You don't ever have to feel this way again. Really and for true.

Larissa is dead.

I loved her and miss her, but she's dead.

I want you to live. Make that call. Click that link. Reach out for a new, freer and better life.

"In vino veritas" (in wine there is truth) is another Latin aphorism. For folks like me, in vino there is chaos, despair and a death-in-life existence. For folks like Larissa, "in vino mors est" (in wine there is death).

For you, if you are like me, "In vita convaluisset" (in recovery there is life).

Please. Choose life.

Larissa can't.

Larissa is dead.

Requiescat in pace, my dear sweet friend.

Section 5: A Letter from the Future

Larissa is dead. I'm not. If you're reading this, you're not either. You still have time--but so did Larissa--until she didn't. If you grab recovery and hold on to it like a life preserver in the north Atlantic, you can make it.

And if you do, maybe, just maybe, you'll someday get a letter like this one.

At the end of my drinking, I thought I was finished. I had lost everything, and what I hadn't lost, I was in the process of ruining. The best thing I could do, the most logical step left, was to disappear completely. It made sense. It made so much sense that I couldn't believe others hadn't reached the same conclusion. It was obvious that my daughters would be better off without me. That my absence would clear the way for them to have a life unburdened by the shame of my presence. That any love they had for me was misplaced, forced, the kind of affection you offer to a failing relative out of obligation rather than choice. I believed this with the certainty of a mathematician solving for X.

And then I didn't die. I don't know why. Some combination of fear, exhaustion, and the numbing pull of inertia kept me alive one more day, then another, and another, until eventually, the worst of it passed. Until I wasn't actively trying to die anymore. Until I found myself at a desk, skimming through emails and preparing to return to the ordinary rhythms of a life I never expected to have.

That was when I saw Becca's message.

Dear Dad,

Even before I opened it, I braced myself. My daughters love me--I have always known this, even in my worst moments--but there is a part of me that never stops waiting for the catch, for the inevitable "but" that will undo it all. I have spent most of my life convinced that I have harmed them in ways I can never fully grasp, that they will spend decades unpacking my failures in therapy, that when they are older, they will quietly excise me from their lives, not in a dramatic confrontation, but in the slow, quiet way people let go of things that no longer serve them.

I took a breath and began to read.

On the anniversary of your first day of recovery, I want to say thank you.

Thank you for choosing to keep fighting, even though I know how hard it was to do.

It broke my heart to watch your video and hear you describe yourself as a homeless, smelly drunk. In my eyes, you have never been anything but an amazing father and one of the two souls I feel most connected to in the world.

I stopped reading.

I hadn't known how much I needed to hear this until the words were in front of me. Becca didn't say I had been a good father *despite* my past. She didn't say she had forgiven me. She didn't say she had come to terms with who I had been.

She said I had never been anything but a good father to her.

That is a different thing entirely.

I have spent years trying to make peace with what I did during the worst of my drinking. I have made amends. I have tried to rebuild. I have tried to accept that some wounds cannot be healed, only acknowledged. I have told myself that I cannot control how others see me, only how I move forward. And yet, here was my daughter, telling me that all of the self-loathing, all of the certainty that I had permanently damaged my children, might not have been true at all.

You have always made sure to tell me and my sisters how much you love us, and I know this to be true because you chose life on that day, and that choice set off a series of incredible choices (and miracles) that has led our whole family to be safe today.

It is an incredible thing to be proven wrong in the best possible way.

I had spent so much time believing that I had only caused harm, that my presence in my daughters' lives was something they had to endure rather than celebrate. I had never considered that my recovery might have been a gift to them, that my decision to stay alive was not just an absence of pain, but an active good in their lives.

I had never considered that my existence could be a miracle.

Sadly, I do not think this would be the case if you had passed away in 2007, and I don't know if I would have been able to cope with the unbearable sadness of missing you. I hope that day doesn't come for a long time, but as you have always taught me, you must take things one day at a time.

Thank you for giving me this day with you.

That line broke me.

I sat at my desk, staring at the words, feeling their

weight settle over me.

Thank you for giving me this day with you.

All those years ago, when I was at my worst, I had been certain that my death would be a relief to those around me. That it would be painful, yes, but in the way a necessary amputation is painful--a horrible but ultimately freeing act. I had imagined a world where my absence would be a kindness.

Becca imagined a world where I had died, too.

She imagined it as a bleak, unbearable thing, a timeline she was profoundly grateful never came to pass.

She was right.

You have inspired me to embark on my own journey of sobriety. You have showed me no matter how many times you fail, it doesn't matter as long as you get back up and keep going.

If I had died, she never would have written that sentence.

She never would have had a father who made mistakes and survived them.

She never would have had a reason to believe that failure is not final, that broken things can be rebuilt, that love does not disappear when we fall apart.

She would have had a funeral card.

Instead, she wrote me a letter.

I don't know who needs to hear this, but I need to say it.

If you are thinking about killing yourself, **please don't**.

I don't know what your future holds, and neither do you.

But I can tell you that someone is waiting for you on

the other side of this moment, grateful beyond words that you stayed.

Maybe it's your daughter.

Maybe it's someone you haven't even met yet.

Maybe it's you.

All I know is I was certain the world would be better without me.

And then, today, my daughter wrote me a letter.

I love you so much, Dad.

Becca

If you are reading this, there is still time.

Stay.

Please.

Just stay.

Afterword

by Rebecca Howard

When I finished reading my dad's book manuscript, I sat at my office computer blotting a tissue to my weeping eyes, hoping no one would walk by. He had asked my permission to include the letter, but reading it again brought on a wave of emotion as I went back to the day I wrote it—and, more importantly, the day we were celebrating: his 13-year sober anniversary.

Growing up, I only have fond memories with my dad. Adventuring through our neighborhood, taking me and my sisters to Boston on weekends, and summers spent in the white mountains. When my parents divorced, my dad continued these traditions and began new ones in a new city. What I remember most is my dad's unwavering commitment to being there for us. Whether it was showing up as my soccer coach, every school concert or rehearsal, and every after school activity - my dad was there.

Reading my dad's book brought me back to that day in

my mom's kitchen when she took the call on our house phone. On the other line was my dad calling from rehab. He was safe and even at the age of 15 I knew this was a good thing. If he was in rehab, he couldn't get drunk and hurt himself or worse. I had been worrying about him for the past few years as his drinking progressed to the point of passing out on the couch every night. I started to realize this wasn't normal, and as much as I loved my dad, I also worried deeply about him.

My dad chose to get sober at a pivotal time in my life, just as I was entering high school. On weekends, I lived with him at a transitional community for homeless veterans—a unique experience that shaped both my empathy and my personality. He had his own apartment in a building with shared spaces for meals and recovery meetings. As the only teenagers in the building, my sisters and I earned our fair share of noise complaints for fighting. We had to learn to temper our disagreements—not just for peace, but to protect his housing.

Like my grandfather, my dad has always been a calm and even tempered person. When he got sober, he became even more patient with our bickering, our chaos, and especially with my emotional spirals over schoolwork. I remember countless nights where he sat beside me, calm and steady, helping me work through English essays—never writing them for me (no matter how much I begged). Around that time, he taught me how to drive. I'll never forget the night a deer jumped in front of our Jeep—he didn't flinch. He just told me how proud he was of the way I handled it. I can't imagine what my life would've been like if he had kept drinking—or worse, followed through on ending his life. I wouldn't have had him for those moments.

Over the years, I've sat in many church basements, office buildings, and community centers for his meetings. I listened to people stand up, introduce themselves, and share their stories. I remember whispering to myself, "That won't be me." But the truth is, those rituals gave me tools I didn't know I was collecting. They helped me steer clear of alcohol and drugs through most of my teenage and early adult life. It wasn't until after college, when I found myself drawn too deeply into the party scene, chasing a sense of adventure and escape. With my dad's support, therapy, and the lessons I learned in those church basements, I was able to change my path. Today, I'm living in Boston with my partner surrounded by a gaggle of animals (my dream come true).

Reading my dad's book helped me see how deeply our lives are intertwined. I've always been a voracious reader, a runner, and a theatre kid just like him. We both have a sense of mischief and a penchant for questioning authority. Like him, I've wrestled with that sense of emptiness, the restlessness, and the urge to escape. But I've also inherited his resilience, his creativity, and his capacity for hope.

One moment I think about often is my upcoming wedding day and how lucky I feel knowing my dad will be there to walk me down the aisle. That moment, like so many others, almost didn't happen. When someone we love dies, especially by suicide, it's not just their absence that hurts, but all the moments we lose along with them. The milestones. The everyday laughs. The second chances. It's the moments we never get to have that leave the deepest ache.

If you're reading this and you're struggling, please know: there is help. You are not alone. On the next page, you'll find a list of resources—including my dad's personal email —because he knows that connection can save lives. There's always a path forward, and people waiting to walk it with you.

Keith's Email

unclaimedbutloud@gmail.com

I check this daily and promise to respond as soon as I can. Including a phone number can make the response quicker.

📞 National Support Resources for Drug/Alcohol Recovery & Suicide Prevention

SAMHSA's National Helpline

Substance Abuse and Mental Health Services Administration

▦ **1-800-662-HELP (4357)**

🌐 www.samhsa.gov/find-help/national-helpline

🕐 Free and confidential 24/7 treatment referral and information in English and Spanish.

---

988 Suicide & Crisis Lifeline

▦ Dial **988**

🌐 www.988lifeline.org

🕐 24/7 support for suicide, mental health, and substance use crises.

NAMI HelpLine

National Alliance on Mental Illness

▦ **1-800-950-NAMI (6264)**

🌐 www.nami.org/help

🕐 Monday–Friday, 10 a.m.–10 p.m. ET. Emotional support and referrals for mental health.

Alcoholics Anonymous (AA)

🌐 www.aa.org

📍 Find meetings, literature, and support for alcohol recovery.

Narcotics Anonymous (NA)

🌐 www.na.org

📍 Fellowship and recovery resources for those with drug addiction.

www.ingramcontent.com/pod-product-compliance
Lightning Source LLC
Chambersburg PA
CBHW021700120626
46545CB00004B/1328